An Ethnic History of Russia

Recent Titles in
Contributions in Ethnic Studies

Religion, Intergroup Relations, and Social Change in South Africa
Human Sciences Research Council

Latino Empowerment: Progress, Problems, and Prospects
Roberto E. Villarreal, Norma G. Hernandez, and Howard D. Neighbor, editors

Contemporary Federal Policy Toward American Indians
Emma R. Gross

The Governance of Ethnic Communities: Political Structures and Processes in Canada
Raymond Breton

Latinos and Political Coalitions: Political Empowerment for the 1990's
Roberto E. Villarreal and Norma G. Hernandez, editors

Conflict Resolution: Cross-Cultural Perspectives
Kevin Avruch, Peter W. Black, and Joseph A. Scimecca, editors

Ethnic and Racial Minorities in Advanced Industrial Democracies
Anthony M. Messina, Luis R. Fraga, Laurie A. Rhodebeck, and Frederick D. Wright, editors

Asian and Pacific Islander Migration to the United States: A Model of New Global Patterns
Elliott Robert Barkan

Semites and Stereotypes: Characteristics of Jewish Humor
Avner Ziv and Anat Zajdman, editors

Irish Illegals: Transients Between Two Societies
Mary P. Corcoran

The Germanic Mosaic: Cultural and Linguistic Diversity in Society
Carol Aisha Blackshire-Belay, editor

A Legal History of Asian Americans, 1790–1990
Hyung-chan Kim

An Ethnic History of Russia

Pre-Revolutionary Times to the Present

Tatiana Mastyugina and
Lev Perepelkin

Edited by
Vitaly Naumkin and
Irina Zviagelskaia

Prepared under the auspices of the Russian Center
for Strategic Research and International Studies

Contributions in Ethnic Studies, Number 35
Bernard Reich, *Series Adviser*

GREENWOOD PRESS
Westport, Connecticut • London

34319091

Library of Congress Cataloging-in-Publication Data

Mastyugina, Tatiana.
    An ethnic history of Russia : pre-revolutionary times to the
present / Tatiana Mastyugina and Lev Perepelkin ; edited by Vitaly
Naumkin and Irina Zviagelskaia.
        p.   cm.—(Contributions in ethnic studies, ISSN 0196-7088 ;
no. 35)
    "Prepared under the auspices of the Russian Center for Strategic
Research and International Studies."
    Includes bibliographical references and index.
    ISBN 0–313–29315–5 (alk. paper)
    1. Ethnology—Russia.   2. Ethnology—Soviet Union.   3. Ethnology—
Russia (Federation)   4. Russia—Ethnic relations.   5. Soviet Union—
Ethnic relations.   6. Russia (Federation)—Ethnic relations.
    I. Perepelkin, Lev.   II. Naumkin, Vitaliĭ Vĭacheslavovich.
    III. Zvĭagel'skaĭa, I. D. (Irena Donovna)   IV. Title.   V. Series.
    DK33.M28   1996
    305.8'00947—dc20   96–7141

British Library Cataloguing in Publication Data is available.

Copyright © 1996 by the Russian Center for Strategic Research and
International Studies

Library of Congress Catalog Card Number: 96–7141
ISBN: 0–313–29315–5
ISSN: 0196–7088

First published in 1996

Greenwood Press, 88 Post Road West, Westport, CT 06881
An imprint of Greenwood Publishing Group, Inc.

Printed in the United States of America

The paper used in this book complies with the
Permanent Paper Standard issued by the National
Information Standards Organization (Z39.48–1984).

10   9   8   7   6   5   4   3   2   1

Contents

Preface

Russia, being an outgrowth of Slav roots, was gradually transformed into an empire populated by dozens of different ethnic groups in addition to the Russians. She experienced migrations and inroads into her territory by alien ethnoses (the Tatar-Mongols); and in later periods accretion of lands by peaceful settlement, by military seizure, or by means of treaties concluded with neighboring peoples. The "nationalities question" was an area where the finest Russian minds were able to demonstrate their brilliance; but it was undoubtedly also a "raw nerve" of Russian consciousness. Everything pertaining to the domain of the national often had the characteristics of a mystique. It was a battlefield on which the foremost Russian intellectuals clashed in debates, producing new concepts that aspired to explain the destiny of Russia, with all its ups and downs. The crisis of Russia's imperial system was one of the factors that brought about the decline of that system, which ended in the revolution; it helped the Bolsheviks to draw to their side the non-Russian population of the border areas.

In the Soviet period, Russia continued to be a multinational state: the state borders of the Soviet Union were largely the same as those of the Russian Empire despite a few territorial losses. The disintegration of the Soviet Union signified the resurgence of the Russian State, this time within its borders of long ago and without the 25 million ethnic Russians left in the Soviet republics which gained full national sovereignty. Even so, the new Russia, no longer an empire, remains a polyethnic state. Non-Russian ethnic groups account for less than 19 percent of its population—a fairly small proportion; but, by virtue of their historical development, these are

titular ethnoses dwelling in national-territorial entities that are the constituent parts of the Russian Federation. Contrary to the situation in the
United States, most of the ethnoses in Russia, while being an integral part
of Russian society, identify with certain territories, which they see as their
own; hence, cultural autonomy alone will not suffice to meet their national
awareness. What they require is an ethnic-territorial framework.

   Nikolai Berdyaev pointed to the "mysterious contradiction" in the attitude of Russia and the Russian consciousness vis-à-vis "the nationality."
In his opinion, "it is precisely this supra-nationalism that is national in
Russia, precisely her freedom of nationalism"; this he believed to be Russia's unique trait, one that set her apart from the rest of the world. Berdyaev
countered the above thesis with an antithesis, that of Russia being at the
same time "the world's most nationalistic country, as evidenced by the most
ferocious outbursts of nationalism, by the oppression of subjected nationalities via Russianization, and by notorious jingoist swagger."[1] The new
Russian State is still plagued by this poisonous legacy, and Berdyaev's
words still apply, at least in part, to the realities of Russia's present life. It
is for the Russian democracy to do away with this "mysterious contradiction." Yet the new Russian State has retained the principles of the ethnic-
territorial structure whose crisis was a major factor in bringing about the
disintegration of the USSR.

   Throughout the vast post-Soviet space the collapse of the communist
system and the disintegration of the unitary state has given rise to an intense
eruption of nationalism, with ethnic groups and peoples eager to rediscover
their roots and find their true identity. The gradual resurgence of Russian
self-consciousness, which many people in the West have erroneously la-
belled "neo-imperialism," is undoubtedly a stable trend of the country's
development. Not infrequently, this national renascence manifests itself in
ugly forms, with one ethnic group setting itself in opposition to another,
with accompanying tensions and situations of conflict. Another aggravating
factor is the bitter legacy of the past—the lingering aftermath of colonial
wars (e.g., the Thirty Years' War waged by Russia in the Caucasus), Stalin's
deportations involving the total resettlement of large ethnoses (such as the
Ingush, Chechens, Kalmyks, Crimean Tatars, and others), population migrations during the country's massive industrialization, and so on. The differing development level of individual regions, their different resource
potentials, lifestyles and specific features of political and general-cultural
development—all this is conducive to a general mood of opposition to the
federal authority, which wants a strong unitary state and a civic society.
The rivalries among the regional elites, including the national ones, are
bound to thrive on this fertile soil; moreover, the process of the privatization of property and the mounting competition give more edge to these
rivalries. As often as not, the ethnic-regional elites aspiring to stage-manage
political games find themselves to be manipulated by superior forces. Suffice

it to recall how the conservative elements in the Soviet leadership tried to draw on these elites in order to weaken the federal authority of Russia shortly before the disintegration of the Soviet Union.

In the new post-Soviet Russia, the growth of national self-awareness and the striving of ethnic groups for genuine national, religious, and cultural identity is superimposed on the peripheral regions' aspirations toward a greater degree of independence from the central authority, on the desire of the ethnic-regional elites to gain full control of their own resources, as well as on political regionalism, which in some instances develops into separatism. A graphic example is the situation in Chechenia, where the leading political forces have striven for national sovereignty from as early as 1991. Another illustration is the decision adopted on August 18, 1994, by the deputies of the legislative assembly of Perm Region (lying in the Urals) about suspending participation in the Treaty of Public Accord. The deputies believed that the federal administration was unwilling to take any meaningful steps toward equalizing the status of the regions and the republics; as a result, Perm Region allegedly had to contribute to the federal budget more than it can retrieve from funding by the Federal Centre, whereas for Tatarstan and Bashkiria the situation is the reverse. An official of the presidential administration defined this decision as blackmail, adding that the problem of equalizing the status of the "Russian" regions and the titular "national" republics is a matter within the competence of the Russian Federal Assembly.[2]

Daghestan, a multinational republic in the North Caucasus, opted for a course which was different from that taken by its neighbors. Instead of a bicameral parliament, Daghestan has set up a state council, to which all the ethnic groups inhabiting its territory elect their representatives on a quota basis.

Another dimension has been added to the process whereby the model of the new, post-Soviet federalism is designed in Russia: along the counterposition of the Federal Centre and the provinces there has emerged that between the "national" republics (having titular ethnoses) and the "genuinely Russian" territories and regions. The former clamor for a greater share of rights and powers compared to those assigned to the territories and regions, whereas the latter demand equal rights for all the Federation units.

The exacerbation of regionalism and inter-ethnic relations in Russia immediately after the collapse of the USSR actually led some experts in the West to make gloomy prophesies about the inevitable disintegration of Russia as a unitary state. In Russia, too, these problems have become the focus of an intense political struggle. Its outcome is bound to exert a major impact on the country's destiny. The leadership of post-Communist Russia has been confronted with a number of conflictive situations.

These situations of "new-generation" conflicts started to emerge in Rus-

sia even before the disintegration of the USSR—in the years known as
"perestroika," encompassing the principal "ethnic zones" of the Russian
Soviet Federation, namely, the Caucasus, the Volga region, and Siberia,
each of which harbors most of the nationality-based autonomies. Certain
dissident republics, who would not be content with models emanating from
the Federal Centre, came to the forefront. In the Caucasus this was the
selfsame Republic of Chechenia; its president, Jokhar Dudayev, to whom
Moscow denied recognition, put forward the slogan of the Republic's sovereignty. In the Volga region it was Tatarstan, whose leaders demanded
that their relations with the Federal Centre be regulated on a special treaty
basis.

The drawn-out controversy between the Russian federal authority and
Tatarstan, which on several occasions threatened to reach a more critical
stage, ended in a satisfactory solution. Moscow, which for a long time had
tried to steer Tatarstan toward joining the Federation Treaty on the basis
accepted by all the other members, finally made an important concession
by concluding, in February 1994, a special treaty with Kazan, which
provides for delimiting each participant's sphere of competence and for
reciprocal transfer of certain powers. In this way the Tatar leaders ac-
knowledged their republic's status as a federation member, renouncing the
maximalist claims voiced by the die-hard nationalist opposition.

In Chechenia events took a different turn. The dramatic history of that
Caucasian people, who had suffered from extreme forms of national oppression at the hands of Russia, engendered such deep distrust of Moscow
that even the most unrealistic radical calls made by the leaders of the
Chechen national movement elicited supportive response. The complex situation within that republic and its entangled relationship with the Centre
has been further exacerbated by the acute economic crisis which has
gripped it, as well as by the inconsiderate moves of some political figures,
both in Russia and in Chechenia, and by the attempts of certain political
forces to play the Chechenia card in political games. At the end of 1994
Russian troops invaded Chechenia, and a bloody protracted war began.
This war, which was initially waged against Johar Dudaev's armed groups,
later on was inevitably turned into confrontation with a large number of
Chechens, who began to defend their relatives and their homes.

Apart from the above-listed principal counterposition between the Federal Centre and the provinces and the contradictions between the ethnic
and Russian territories, inter-ethnic problems have been manifested in the
sphere of relations between the selfsame ethnic territories. It was in Ossetia
and Ingushetia where the nationality issue claimed its first blood in post-
Communist Russia. This inter-ethnic conflict, which harks back to the period of Stalin's deportations, has not been definitively resolved at this stage,
even though the armed clashes were promptly brought to a halt.

Conflicts in Russia and the other former Soviet republics have given rise to a problem capable of upsetting the situation within the country: the refugee problem. At any moment new refugees may swell the ranks of refugees of various nationalities from all the hot spots, who at present number two million; but their absorption, finding homes and jobs for them in the localities of their own choice, is an impossible task. This is the primary reason for the Russian authorities' extreme sensitivity in the face of the mounting exodus of Russians from the former Soviet republics. The refugee problem has become a major stumbling block to the solution of the Ossetian-Ingush conflict. The stream of non-Russian refugees pouring into the Russian territories has likewise added to inter-ethnic tensions. A case in point is the complex interaction of the local population with the Armenian newcomers in Krasnodar Territory.

The spectre of opinion that exists in Russia's "national" republics concerning the structure of the Russian Federation is extremely wide. Kalmykia, for one, stands in direct opposition to Tatarstan: its elected President Kirsan Ilyumzhinov, a successful young entrepreneur, actually abrogated the republic's constitution, replacing it with the "Steppe Code" and denouncing the declaration of Kalmykia's sovereignty. In a television interview Ilyumzhinov stated that Russia has just one constitution, one sovereignty, and one president.[3]

Kazan's example was promptly emulated by Kabarda-Balkaria in 1994; and Bashkiria became the third member of the Russian Federation to sign an individual treaty with Russia. Valery Kokov, president of Kabarda-Balkaria, was able to do so without damaging his image of a leader fully committed to the principle of Russia's integrity.

"National" republics were followed by "Russian" regions, first by Sverdlovsk oblast, which were striving for an equal status with the republics. The formation of a new federative model of Russian was obviously taking place.

This process arouses mixed feelings in the political circles of Russia. Alexander Solzhenitsyn, during one of his regular TV appearances since his return to Russia, pronounced the signing of such treaties to be an absurdity; he favors a purely territorial approach to the administrative subdivision of Russia by forming "gubernias" which would enjoy the same status irrespective of whether they be Russian-populated areas or areas peopled by other ethnoses. On the opposite side is President Murtaza Rakhimov of Bashkiria, who believes that Russia, if it really wants to be a federal state, must sign bilateral treaties with all the Federation's member republics. "There are some who want to make the republics, regions and territories politically equal," said he, arguing with the champions of the concept of a "symmetrical federation." "This is something that cannot be tolerated. It is on the economic level that everyone must have equal rights."[4]

The treaties concluded between the central authority and the republics provide the legal foundation for their interrelations, but this cannot obviate conflicts connected with the delimitation of spheres of competence and the transfer of powers. Thus, the treaties which both Tatarstan and Bashkiria concluded in August 1994 with Abkhazia, the "Georgian dissident" (they were signed when the Abkhazian leader Vladislav Ardzhinba visited these republics), provoked a protest note from the Russian Ministry of Foreign Affairs, with Vice-Premier Sergei Shakhrai defining them as unconstitutional "in form and content," since they "are formulated in a manner that completely ignores the existence of the Russian Federation."[5] Efforts made by the Russian federal authority toward strengthening the country's unity are likely to run up against attempts by the federated units to exceed their legalized competence in the sphere of economics, politics, and external relations.

The state system of the Russian Federation will probably be subjected to further evolutionary change. That the Russian leadership is aware of this has been demonstrated, among other things, by President Yeltsin's statement in an exclusive interview given to the newspaper *Trud* after a visit to several parts of Russia: "We have to design a fundamentally new model of relations between the Russian federal authority and the territorial units."[6]

In 1995–1996 the development of the Russian federal system was challenged by the Chechen tragedy, which will undoubtedly have long-term consequences and will have a negative impact on inter-ethnic relations in the state.

To gain a better understanding of the political processes currently taking place in Russia, to grasp the full complexity of the problems facing the Russian leadership, and to estimate the potential impact of various development patterns on the international scale, one has to be fully aware of the ethnic component of Russian reality. This book describes the ethnic composition of Russia's population and the country's different "national" territories; the authors, moreover, probe into the ethnic history of the Russian State, revealing the roots of ethnic and inter-regional problems. The old and new ethnic realities of Russia, which are as closely interlinked on the pages of the book as they are in the country's life, are likely to be a source of many unpredictable developments.

Vitaly Naumkin
Irina Zviagelskaia

NOTES

1. Nikolai Berdyaev, *Subda Rossii* (The Destiny of Russia) (Moscow: Sovetskii pisatel, 1990), pp. 14, 16.
2. Cf. *Izvestia* (Moscow), August 24, 1994.

3. *Ostankino* TV channel (Moscow), August 15, 1994.
4. *Segodnya* (newspaper) (Moscow), August 13, 1994, p. 10.
5. *Segodnya*, August 27, 1994, p. 1.
6. *Trud* (Moscow), August 26, 1994.

Acknowledgments

We are most grateful to the Russian Center for Strategic Research and International Studies for the financial support which has enabled us to write this book.

An Ethnic History of Russia

Introduction:
Theoretical Premises of the Work

> The growth of a state means the expansion of the zone of peace, con-
> centration of forces and, consequently, successes of the material culture.
> But the ruin of small or weak peoples absorbed by it kills, often forever,
> the possibility of the flowering of other cultures, at times highly prom-
> ising, perhaps qualitatively higher as compared with their victorious
> rival.
>
> G. Fedotov, *The Fate of Empires*

The view of ethnos as a specific social group based on the community of
culture, understood as a "mode of vital functioning,"[1] and on the unity of
self-consciousness, has taken deep roots in Russian scholarship. According
to several authors, diachronic information links ensure ethnic continuity
(i.e., the existence of the ethnos in time), and synchronous links stabilize
the ethnos in space.[2] The distinguishing of two forms of ethnos: one based
upon diachronic links, and another, ethnosocial organism (ESO), resting
upon synchronous links,[3] seems fruitful.

The ESO or the nucleus of an ethnos, as the main structure unit in the
development of humanity, possesses not only cultural, but also territorial,
political, and economic unity. In the framework of that unity, social links,
in the first place those of production, providing for the "metabolism" between the ESO and its natural environmental locus (niche), continuously
maintain the physical existence, reproduction and development of the ethnic nucleus and, consequently, of the entire ethnos.

The notion of ethnos as a social organism supposes the possibility of
defining stages of its development: conception, development, achievement
of a level of "maturity," and, finally, "aging" and, under certain condi-

tions, even disappearance. It is at the stage of "maturity" that the nucleus of ethnos becomes stabilized and its periphery emerges. It is significant that the main innovation processes take place in ESO, and the ethnic periphery usually is more inert and even archaic. This reflects the gigantic role of the sociopolitical (in the first place the state) structures for the socioeconomic and cultural development of ethnoses.[4] The view of national statehood as an indispensable form of national life was shared, for instance, by Berdyaev, who wrote: "A nation reveals all its potentialities via the state. On the other hand, the state must have a national basis, though the tribal composition of the state may be very complex and varied . . . the state devoid of a national nucleus and national idea cannot lead a creative life."[5]

It is significant that all dynamically developing contemporary states are either mono-national (Japan, for instance), or have at their foundation the ethnic nucleus of a big people (the WASP may be considered to be such a nucleus in the United States). And on the contrary, all empires that had existed in the early 20th century and had several ESOs, disintegrated: the Austro-Hungarian Empire, the British Empire, and so on. Such was the fate of Yugoslavia, the Soviet Union, and Czechoslovakia. There are many historical examples, when peoples lost their national states and restored them again: such was the destiny of Poles, Norwegians, and others. But in certain historical situations, to restore the national statehood proves impossible. In these (frequent) cases, according to our concept, the period of the "aging" of ethnos begins. It still continues to exist, but has already lost its nucleus. Synchronous socioeconomic and political links (and sometimes even the territorial integrity) are pushed to the background, behind the diachronic, "ethnographic" links. Ethnic self-consciousness not supported by real socioeconomic and political unity also gradually gets washed out. The ethnos reaches the brink of disappearance (i.e., assimilation by other ethnoses, transformation, etc.); for example, the Scots in Great Britain, and the Provençals in France.

Ethnic (cultural) diversity is the property of entire mankind, the most important mechanism of its development. The mankind formed by a multitude of peoples seeks to use for its advance thousands of ways simultaneously. Some of them lead nowhere, but others open up the way to everybody. It is clear that under contemporary conditions the preservation of ethnic diversity is, to no small extent, determined by the reproductive policy. We place in the foreground its two most important aspects: (1) organic nature (i.e., absence of pathological shocks, basing on traditions, etc.), and (2) stimulation of the growing diversity of activities and social structures.

A major (and in some aspects the determining) role in the implementation of the principles of organic innovations and growing diversity is played by the political organism: the best is such whose space limits coincide with the ethnic territory. In such cases the reproductive policy is implemented at minimum costs and guarantees the reproduction precisely of the given ethnos. But this means that polyethnic states (and they make up the bulk of the states of the world) are historically stable only if they guarantee sovereign rights to ethnoses, necessary for their reproduction as integral systems, that is, at the stage of "maturity." Successful development of peoples and, consequently, of mankind as a whole may take place only if it has a solid resource base. It is that base that in the first place determines the directions and forms of development, the limits of the given ethnosocial community, with the control over resources being the pillar of its economic sovereignty.

We single out the following types of resources: (1) land, its fertility, the flora and fauna of a given region; (2) mineral resources; (3) solar energy, atmosphere and atmospheric phenomena, world ocean, and other resources which are nonalienable, in principle; (4) information; (5) man himself, his work potential (both as the force of his muscles and the force of his intellect.[6]

It is evident that the first, second, and third types of resources are accessible even to the technologically underdeveloped ethnosocial organisms. Traditional forms of life sustenance of various peoples "demand," for their normal functioning, different amounts of concrete kinds of resources. This means that the structure of ethno-reproducing resources is always individual and specific if the optimum ethnic progress is to be obtained. Therefore, two kinds of problems arise in the multinational societies:

1. struggle for resources particularly important to concrete ESO but becoming deficit at the given level of economic development;
2. contradictions between the ESOs, engendered by radical differences in the hierarchy of needs in the process of utilization of the gamut of resources situated in a concrete territory.

As regards the fourth and, particularly, the fifth types of resources, they possess wonderful common features. First, their consumption does not lead to conflicts, because they are inherent in an ethnos and do not hurt the interests of other ethnoses. Second, they are able to grow in the process of utilization. Therefore, the growth of the creative potential of ethnoses and their transition to the information economy with a corresponding social policy means the removal of many tensions and conflicts of the past and harmonization of international relations as a future prospect.

Speaking of ethnoses, we mainly have in mind the ethnoses of the modern and contemporary periods connected to statehood or some different forms of a political formation. However, ethnos is a historical phenomenon changing in time, with a special type of ethnic community corresponding to each universal socioeconomic stage of development of mankind.

ETHNOSES OF PRE-CLASS SOCIETIES

The following characteristics may be mentioned as fundamental to such societies: appropriating economy (hunting, gathering, fishing), based on "feeding" resources of the territory (i.e., the wealth of flora and fauna); sex and age division of labor; potestary forms of organization of power in relatively small congeneric collectives;[7] distribution as sharing; lack of exchange inside human collectives; underdevelopment of exchange between collectives; personal-nominal type of socio-code (i.e., of the system of signs, ensuring sociocultural continuity in society). This type of socio-code is "a stable in time and finite set of names in which socially necessary forms of activities are distributed in accordance with individuals' possibilities and strength."[8]

Unity of the socium founded on congeneric relations and of the protoeth-nos[9] as a group with common culture and self-consciousness is character-istic of the pre-class societies. This syncretic social organism is placed within territorial and conjugal (endogamic) limits separating it from other similar organisms.

ETHNOSES OF THE EARLY CLASS SOCIETIES

The following traits are characteristic of these societies: productive econ-omy with the soil fertility being the main resource; caste and class division of labor; political form of organization of power; distribution as natural exchange and centralized state redistribution of surplus products; profes-sional nominal scheme of social coding, representing unified sets of roles–skills of various socioprofessional groups (artisans, agricoles, warriors, etc.).[10]

The transformation of the "primitive" socium-protoethnos into the early class society took place independently in many corners of the world, and, in the first place, in the regions most suitable for primitive agriculture. The formation of the early protostate units (city-states) was accompanied and, perhaps, stimulated by the development of a strong political power de-tached from the socium and overriding it. The maintenance of the political and economic unity of the society divided into closed professional groups was a major task of the political power. Special emphasis should be put on the developed economic functions of the state, the leading organizer of the "national economy" and the principal distributor of the surplus products. Formation of polyethnic empires, their permanent growth, alongside the capture of the main economic resource—land, was the leading trend of the development of statehood in the societies of that type.

The emergence of the first forms of the division of labor and, consequently, of social inequality was closely linked up with the development of the individuality, detachment of the individual from the syncretic socium–protoethnos. The detailing of functions led to a more effective organization of human beings. One man was engaged in architecture, another was carving seals, the third was a scribe. Earlier, in a more primitive society, these functions had been sideline occupations; now they were sufficiently important to become professions, and produced an accumulation of talents which previously were maturing unnoticed.[11] Better conditions for the innovation processes than in the pre-class societies developed, being in many cases linked with social mobility. But both the dominant type of the division of labor and the type of socio-code connected with it, and the state power suppressing the elements of civic virtues, put a limit to the manifestations of human individuality. The early class societies saw the prevalence of the corporative spirit: socioprofessional, ethnic ("according to blood"), and so on.

The early class societies demonstrate a different type of ethnicity than the pre-class societies: transition from protoethnos to ethnos had already taken place, and in the process of it, distant ancestors of all contemporary peoples took shape. In our view, consolidation of protoethnoses into ethnoses had been conditioned by the economic utilization by ancient cattle breeders of some natural environmental niches, resulting in the emergence of diverse ethnic cultures. With the appearance of a strong state power the political factor accelerating the unifying consolidation processes became an important mechanism of ethnogenesis.

Ethnoses of the early class societies ensured mainly the functioning of the diachronic (historical) information, while synchronous information (i.e., the actual vital activities of people), was mainly transferred via social (professional groups) and political (state institutions) channels.[12] This type of "channelling" of information streams presupposed the instability of ethnic units and hindered the accumulation of individual achievements in ethnic culture.

Although the state should be recognized as a factor of ethnogenesis, in the early class societies it was chiefly of an extraethnic nature: either a city-state, or (as the main type) a polyethnic empire. The borders of ethnic communities as a rule were either broader or more narrow than political borders of the early class states. This, however, does not mean that the latter were absolutely indifferent to ethnicity: ethnic affiliation ("by blood") was often regarded as a sign of the social status.

State power of the early class type, independent of the civil society,[13] sees external expansion, either in the form of war or diplomatic relations, as its most important task. Mankind as a conglomeration of inimical or allied states was becoming a reality. Trade routes connecting faraway countries were instrumental in the exchange of the results of the creative activities of individuals. Whole ethnic cultures were enriched and received outside stimuli for further development. Peoples (ethnic and tribal groups) lagging behind in their development were rapidly drawn into their orbit.

ETHNOSES OF THE DEVELOPED CLASS SOCIETIES

As many experts point out,[14] the initial prerequisites of the developed class societies had been created in the archaic Greece, but their rise (as a result of social revolutions of the 17th and 18th centuries) was delayed and lasted for several millenia.

Productive industrial economy, developing more and more from the primary utilization of mineral wealth to the resource possibilities of information and human creative potential connected with it, is characteristic of those types of societies. There, division of labor takes the individual professional form. Civil society gradually overrides the state, creating the form of a national state–democratic republic (with all possible variations) adequate to it. Such societies are based on the value (monetary, market) form of distribution. A universal-notional type of socio-code, where social knowledge is both addressless and universal (circuited on the language universalia and meant for "everybody") is adequate to them.[15] A typical figure of such society becomes the intellectual, a man professionally dealing with universal notions (this figure became a feature of social reality relatively late, in the 17th and 18th centuries).[16]

At that stage, the ethnoses of the early class societies transform into nations as the principal ethnic associations of mankind.[17] The new quality appears due to the conjugation of ethnos, state (national state) and socio-professional structure embracing the entire ethnosocial organism.

In our opinion, the formation of a new ethnic reality was due to the basic characteristics of the developed class society. The market form of economic ties, or of distribution, adequate to industrial production and individual-professional division of labor may function regularly only in the homogenous cultural environment. A national market comes into existence covering the territory with ethnically homogenous (or ethnically congeneric) population. Parallel to this, there is the process of consolidation of ethnic groups into nation, reflected in the formation of the literary national language. The literary language serves not only the needs of the national market, but also, through the socio-code, the system of ethnosocial (national) reproduction. The leading role in that process belongs to the national intelligentsia—the principal carrier of the national idea. According to a number of specialists (E. Gellner and others), the latter pursues as its aim the establishment of a national state.

As the civil society (connected with the development of "new" propertied strata of population) gets more mature, the state loses its chief economic functions, but acquires the functions of an arbitrator of the interests of various social groups and individuals (the law-governed state). As now the state's borders coincide with the ethnic borders, general control over the development and reproduction of the ethnic (national) culture also becomes a function of the state:[18] a national state comes into existence, which is not, contrary to what is sometimes maintained in literature, the state of one people. The national state develops on the basis of the dominating national culture and, reciprocally, takes care of its development.

It would seem that the national orientation of the state should lead to the suppression of other ethnic (national) cultures of smaller peoples. But this is characteristic only of the rise of national statehood.[19] History demonstrates a different process: as nations develop, the rights of ethnic minorities become the object of legal protection. This is natural, for a democratic "national state" is equivalent to the "law-governed state," where all citizens, irrespective of their origins, enjoy equal rights. In this sense, of interest is the logic of contemporary international law dispositions envisaging a direct dependence of minorities' rights on the right of peoples to self-determination[20] (i.e., to the creation of a national state).[21] It is important to point out that the evolution of the contemporary international law has been from the condemnation of forced assimilation of minorities to the recognition of the commitment of the national state to facilitate the development of their cultures.[22]

One should stress the unity of the socio-code in all developed class societies, which permits, in principle, the transfer of the achievements of one society to another, the only difficulty being the translation from one national language into another. Thus, the most essential prerequisites have been prepared for the creation of a united mankind, united despite its national cultural diversity. This process is accelerated as a result of the development of economic relations crossing state boundaries; of the improvement of means of communication and information; of the expanded environmental crisis acquiring a global nature; of the development of technology of annihilation, making wars disastrous to everything living; and so on. A political superstructure of the "whole mankind" came into existence, being a common political body of the states of the world (the UN).

Thus, as we have seen, the general development has taken place through the splitting of a syncretically single "individual-socium–protoethnos" organism into its integral elements. By the present time, this process led, on the one hand, to the isolation of the independent individual, and on the other hand, to the formation of mankind. The intermediate element between the individual and mankind, the nation, performs a specific function, accumulating individual achievements and making them significant in the context of mankind.

In light of the above, it should be pointed out that it has become a fashion to speak in a critical vein about the national state. Here is, for

instance, a characteristic proposition: "The national state exhausted its potential and became of no use in the present conditions."[23] But the acquain-
tance with the situations in the developed countries of the world, as well
as the works of the authors of that concept themselves, reveal that what is
meant is not the disappearance of the national state, but the adjustment of
its functions by way of delegation of a number of powers to the world
community, to the common bodies of the developing regional integrated
systems (i.e., "upward"), and also to the local self-government bodies (i.e.,
"downward"). On the contrary, the "basic" functions of the national state
(the stimulation of the cultural development, particularly the encouragement of minorities, as well as the social protection of citizens) gain in importance.[24]

Describing the developed class societies, we centered attention mainly on
those which had registered a natural historical growth from the civilization
of Antiquity, that is, on the societies of Western Europe. But this civilization
and its successors are a unique historical phenomenon, the result of a sociocultural "mutation" that took place in certain early class societies of the
Mediterranean. The bulk of peoples and societies was spurred to modern-
ize, to make transition from the early class to the developed class level by
the influence of European civilization. This influence may be described as
a "cultural synthesis" which rendered the socio-code of the universal-
notional type accessible to the non-European societies. That transition is a
very complex process. We would like to dwell in more detail on its Russian
variant.

ETHNOSES OF ETACRATIC SOCIETIES

From time immemorial, Russia had been developing as a double periphery: on the one hand, of the societies of Europe, and on the other hand, of
the Asian despotic states. European-Russian "cultural synthesis," intensi-
fied in the 18th century, determined the borrowing of the universal-notional
socio-code by the upper social strata (intelligentsia in the broad sense),
while the bulk of Russia's population conserved its traditional mentality,
and the despotic polity of the early class type remained in its place.

By 1917, the growth of industry and other constituents of the developed
class society resulted in a tremendous social explosion bringing about the
predominance of traditional elements which, after more than a decade of
struggle (by the early 1930s), restored precapitalist relations: despotic political power, absence of individual rights vis-à-vis the state, nonmarket type
of distribution. The state operated in all spheres of life (including the economy); civil society was destroyed.

But the new "socialist" (of the early class type) state was forced to develop industrial production, connected with the individual-professional
form of the division of labor and universal-notional socio-code. As a result,

the society faced an inevitable dilemma: either to regress, to reanimate all basic elements of the early class type, or to go ahead, introducing market, restricting the state, and so on. In the ethnocultural sphere, the etacratic[25] societies cannot avoid repetition of such typical traits of the early class societies as the polyethnic empire fixation of the ethnic status (identifying ethnic origins "by blood"). Even the policy of resettling people, existing in ancient Assyria, was repeated in an astonishing way. Nothing new was "invented" in foreign relations, too: xenophobia, external expansion, urge to hegemony (characteristic of the early class state) became prevalent.

After 1922–1924, when the state was formally defined as the union of sovereign republics, reflecting the idea of sovereignty (self-determination) of nations evolved by the Western social thought, centralistic and unitarist tendencies became dominant in the Soviet Union as it developed. The imperial type of state presupposes unification of the ethnic composition of the population for the convenience of administration. From around the late 1930s, characteristic features of the Russifying policy, such as the cutting down of the cultural activity in the languages of the USSR's peoples (particularly small ones, not having even the embryonic forms of statehood); intentional wide spread of the Russian language (including national-Russian bilinguism); and migration policy aimed at the resettlement of large groups of Russian population in the national republics, became more and more evident. The concepts of the "efflorescence and drawing together of nations"; of culture, "national in form, socialist in contents," proper to the USSR's peoples; of "Soviet people as a new historical human community" served as an ideological camouflage. Another characteristic feature of the imperial national state structure also became apparent: its "asymmetry," when the most numerous "state" people (Russians in this case) have not got their "own" national state institutions.

At the same time, elements of the "European way," inevitable in the etacratic societies, also were gradually developing. The formation of the socioprofessional structure, adequate to the industrial production, led to the engendering and development, within all USSR's peoples, of big groups opposing the state omnipotence. Special mention should be made of the development of national intelligentsia, the leading propagator of the "national idea." These ideas were latently, but permanently present in the public mind, such notions as the "people," "self-determination," "peoples' rights," and so on, being parts of the socio-code.

By the middle of the 1980s, this extensive "synthetic" development (transitional state) exhausted itself. Irrespective of the objectives of the authorities announcing the policy of "perestroika," the latter has been, to an ever-growing extent, regarded by public opinion as the final choice in favor of the "European way," as rejection of etacratism. Elements of a civil society took shape in the form of various social movements and political parties, and beginning with 1987–1988 there was the development of an avalanche of national-political movements whose ideas of national cultural revival, of gaining national statehood, and so on, later have been "intercepted" and implemented (often quite primitively or even grotesquely) by the next generation of the former communist nomenclature.

By late 1991, these processes led to the collapse of the Soviet Union and the emergence in its place of independent national states.

The history of the ethnic development of mankind did not stop after the formation of nations and national statehood (though that process, too, is far from being completed). While ethnoses (ESOs) are self-developing units whose growth is based on specific resource foundations, the general progress of mankind depends on the organization of interaction between them. Relations between the national economic complexes obey one common tendency—the ever-expanding specialization and growth of the international (world) division of labor. In essence, that process leads to the creation of a global economic system envisaging the world division of labor as the initial and obligatory prerequisite of production, and no country may profit from the production of the entire assortment of goods, to have everything "its own." Objective economic conditions of contemporary life set a new demand to peoples and national states—that of integration, expansion, and deepening of external relations. Does integration contradict the principle of national statehood? Let us discuss the foundations of the modern integration system.

First, it is the preservation of independence, of the economic sovereignty of peoples and national states, and of their control over resources.

Second, it is voluntary and mutually profitable integration.

Third, it is the precise division of functions (competences) at all levels (beginning with the local authorities and ending with the common integration bodies) and voluntary upward delegation of a part of functions.

Fourth, it is the comparability of potentials and similarity of the levels of the socioeconomic development of states participating in integrational relations.

Fifth, it is a market economy of modern type (with a developed infrastructure and elements of indirect regulation).

Obviously, the maintenance of national statehood is the indispensable condition and prerequisite of developing integration processes.

The above-stated concept of the development of ethnoses justifies several ethnopolitical conclusions:

- inter-ethnic conflicts in industrial societies have two principal causes: The first is the urge of peoples (nations) for independent forms of political life, and as an ideal—the setting up of their own national state (the ideology of nationalism); the second is the deficit of resources for development;

- political structure of a multinational state, insufficiently taking into account the ethnic reality, becomes a permanent generator of inter-ethnic tension and conflicts;

• development of various forms of national-cultural and political self-determination (including national statehood) and the switch-over to integrational relations are necessary for the mitigation of the inter-ethnic conflict situation in the polyethnic societies.

NOTES

1. E.S. Markarian, *Teoriya kultury i sovremennaya nauka: logiko-metodologichesky analiz* (Theory of culture and contemporary science: Logical and methodological analysis) (Moscow: Mysl, 1983).

2. S.A. Arutiunov and N.N. Cheboksarov, "Peredacha informatsii kak mekhanism sushchestvovaniya etnosotsialnykh i biologicheskikh grup chelovechestva," *Rasy i narody* (Transmission of information as a mechanism of the existence of ethno-social and biological groups of mankind, *Races and peoples*) (Moscow: Nauka, 1972).

3. Yu.V. Bromley, *Ocherki teorii etnosa* (Studies in the theory of ethnos) (Moscow: Nauka, 1983), pp. 62–63.

4. One may distinguish several forms of sociopolitical organization of ethnoses: national-political movement, cultural or territorial autonomy, "state" (an element of federal association of different peoples), national-state.

5. N.A. Berdyaev, *Filosofia neravenstva. Pisma k nedrugam po sotsialnoi filosofii* (Philosophy of inequality. Letters to enemies on social philosophy) (Paris: IMKA Press, 1970), p. 83.

6. T. Schultz, the author of the theory of "human capital," proved that the growth of national income in the postindustrial (information) economy depends to the decisive degree on the volume of capital investments into the multiplication of human knowledges and professional abilities.

7. The form of organization of power in the pre-class society, where the inequality of the subject and object of power does not include relations of domination and submission or some privileges for the powerful. See A.I. Pezshits and D. Tzaide, eds., *Sotsialno-ekonomicheskie otnoshenia i socionormativnaya kultura* (Socioeconomic relations and socio-normative culture) (Moscow: Nauka, 1986), pp. 31–34.

8. M.K. Petrov, "Chelovek i kultura v nauchno-tekhnicheskoy revolutsii," *Voprosy filosofii* (Man and culture in the scientific-technological revolution, *Problems of Philosophy*), no. 5 (1990), p. 85.

9. About that notion see: V.A. Shnirelman, "Protoetnos okhotnikov i sobiratelei (po avstraliiskim dannym)," *Etnos v doklassovom i ranneklassovom obshchestve* (Protoethnos of hunters and gatherers [from Australian data], *Ethnos in the pre-class and early class society*) (Moscow: Nauka, 1982).

10. M.K. Petrov, "Chelovek," p. 87.

11. H. Frankfort, H.A. Frankfort, J. Wilson, and T. Yakobsen, *Before Philosophy: The Intellectual Adventure of Ancient Man*, trans. T.N. Tolstaia (Moscow: Nauka, 1984), p. 99.

12. S.A. Arutiunov, *Narody i kultury: razvitie i vzaimodeistvie* (Peoples and cultures: Development and interaction) (Moscow: Nauka, 1989), pp. 17–40.

13. "Civic society is a differentia that appears between the state and the family, though the development of civil society comes later than the development of the state . . . only in the modern world." G.W.F. Hegel, *Philosophy of Law*, trans. B.Y. Stolpnez and M.I. Lievina (Moscow: Mysl, 1990), p. 228 (differentia is an independent category of phenomena).

14. As one of the latest works see: D.V. Dragunski and V.L. Tsymburski, "Genotip evropeiskoi tsivilizatsii" (Genotype of European civilization), *Polis*, no. 1 (1991).

15. M.K. Petrov, "Chelovek," p. 89.

16. G. Pomerantz, "Semero protiv techenia. 'Vekhi' v kontekste sovremennosti" (Seven against the current. "Vekhi" ("Landmarks") in the context of contemporary times), *Oktyabr*, no. 2 (1991).

17. See: A.D. Smith, "The Origins of Nations," *Ethnic and Racial Studies*, vol. 12, no. 3 (1989).

18. It is not accidental that one of the consequences of the Great French Revolution was the introduction of compulsory study of the literary French language.

19. Thus, the development of the Turkish national statehood commenced with the physical annihilation of ethnic minorities (Armenian massacre of 1915, etc.).

20. This is a widespread interpretation of Articles 1 and 27 of the International Covenant on Civil and Political Rights.

21. There are also other forms of self-determination and coexistence of peoples within the framework of one state: cultural autonomy, territorial autonomy, federalism.

22. The Final Document of the Vienna Meeting of representatives of states-members of the Conference on Security and Cooperation in Europe held on the basis of the provisions of the Final Act on the follow-up steps after the Conference, Moscow, 1989, p. 14.

23. O. Lafontaine, *Die Gesellschaft der Zukunft: Reformpolitik in einer verlandertenwelt*. Hoffmann U. Campe, 1988, S. 174.

24. The state retains also some economic functions, for instance, in the regulation of macroeconomic processes at the national level.

25. About that notion and main characteristics of etacratic society see: O.I. Shkaratan and E.N. Gurenko, "Ot etakratizma k stanovleniyu grazhdanskogo obshchestva," *Rabochii class i sovremenny mir* (From etacratism to the development of civic society, *The working class and the contemporary world*), no. 3, 1990; V. Radaev and O. Shkaratan, "Sotsialism ili etakratism?" *Narodny deputat* (Socialism or etacratism? *People's deputy*), no. 10 (1990).

1

Ethnoses of
Pre-Revolutionary Russia

Russia, at least from the early 18th century and up to late 1991, was not a distinct state, but the mother country of a huge multinational empire, a political organism within the broad framework of which all ethnosocial and ethnocultural phenomena—assimilation, migration, ethnolinguistic processes, and so on—took place. The absence of formal political borders in the course of three centuries suggests that the exclusive concentration of attention on Russia's ethnic problems, without consideration of a broader context, hinders the comprehension of the national problems of the Russian Federation proper.

Another consequence of the long existence of the "Great Russia" (empire) is the fact that a considerable part of the special ethnographic and ethnosociological literature deals with the most numerous peoples of the imperial outskirts (later, the Union Republics). From this point of view, Russia proper has been studied much less. The apparent lack of statistical data on Russia's minorities is also felt.

Like the majority of the early feudal states, ancient Rus came into existence on a polyethnic basis: ancient Slav tribes settling in the vast East European plain assimilated the aboriginal Volga and Balto-Finnish tribes, and partly the Baltic peoples (in the northern part of the Kiev state) and Iranian and Turkic tribes (Torks, the "black Klobuks" of chronicles) in the south of their area.

It would be expedient to note that the Kiev Rus had come into existence in the territory practically outside the sphere of influence of ancient civilizations, but at the intersection of several trade routes connecting them. To the west and southwest of Rus lay the world of European Christian culture, to the south (Northern Caucasus) and east (the Volga Bulgaria) lay the northern borders of the Islamic world, to the southeast (Khazar) existed a powerful enclave of the Judaist culture. Thus, at the very moment of its emergence, Ancient Rus had faced the choice of the direction and of the civilization pattern to follow. The preference given to Byzantium (the Ancient Bulgarian Slavic kingdom served as an intermediary between it and Rus) determined in many respects the future of the Russian State.

The Tatar-Mongolian invasion and the Horde yoke were another powerful factor determining the course and content of Russian history.

First, during the conquest ancient centers of the Slavic-Byzantine cultural synthesis were destroyed. The political center of the state moved to the area lying between the Volga and Oka rivers and the lands adjoining the upper Volga tributaries. Large numbers of settlers migrated there from the south, too, strengthening the Slav element in the region and engendering the Great-Russian people proper.

Second, it should be pointed out that land fertility in the new center of Russian statehood was very low. Therefore, "the volume of the aggregate surplus product of the societies of Eastern Europe was considerably smaller and conditions for its creation were worse than in Western Europe."[1] Nature itself favored the emergence and development in that territory of a high rate of exploitation (including also the exploitation by the state) and self-exploitation, provoked by continuous migration and colonizing movements outside the region. These circumstances, the administrative management of the territories newly added to the Russian State, and, later, requirements of the capitalist production, led to a vast settling of the Russian people in the spacious plains of Northern Euro-Asia.

Third, the "surgery" of the Mongolian yoke[2] resulted in the formation in Russia of a despotic state based on the all-embracing subjection of (in contrast to vassalage reposing on a system of rights and guarantees) and denial of any rights to people vis-à-vis the authorities; strict centralization of the state decision making; and concentration in the hands of the state of the bulk of social functions.

Fourth, Mongolian conquest drew Rus inside the orbit of absolutely new international relations, the so-called "Genghisi space." The prominent "Euro-Asianist" N. Trubetskoi wrote that the Kiev Rus

occupied only 1/20 of the present territory of Russia, while the Golden Horde corresponded approximately to that entire territory. Genghis Khan stands at the source of the grandiose idea of unity and sovereignty of Euro-Asia. . . . The enslaved Russian people regarded the Mongolian conquest as a yoke, but could not resist long to the charm of the idea of a world kingdom. This idea was borrowed from the Tatars by the Moscow Great Princedom in the 16th century.[3]

It is interesting to note that the Euro-Asianists, criticizing the despotic essence of the new Soviet state, rejected federalism for Russia, based on the national principle ("in the manner of Austrian projects"): "not nationality, but the real geographic and economic whole in the form of a province or a territory should serve as the principle of federation."[4] In that way it was planned to preserve the traditions of the "Genghisi space" as regards the form of the organization of the national life.

Finally, it was the Mongolian conquest that created conditions under which the "Moscow–Third Rome" idea had been formulated rather early in the 14th and 15th centuries and became the dominant polity idea of Russia. Anti-Horde sentiments, prevailing in that idea at the first stages, acquired a stable imperial-missionary orientation in the process of liberation from the Tatar-Mongolian yoke.

As we see it, by the beginning of the 18th century, these factors led to the formation of the Russian multinational empire.[5] Their inertia was so durable that the Soviet state in the first quarter of the 20th century repeated the typological features of the Russian Empire.

Let us now consider in more detail how the process of "gathering lands" went and how Russia's ethnopolitical map took shape.

The routing of Volga Bulgarians in 1236 by the Tatar-Mongols resulted in the resettlement of a part of the Bulgarian, Bashkir, Mordovian, and Mari population in the Russian lands. Jointly with the resettlers from the southern regions of the Kiev Rus, these "aliens" became part of the composition of the forming Great-Russian nationality. From 1237 to 1240, the Tatar-Mongols devastated the lands between the Volga and the Oka rivers, absorbing them into the Golden Horde. Movement of population from these areas continued farther to the north, but the most intensive settlement of the lands of the Russian North, at that time inhabited by Balto-Finnish, Perm and, more to the east, Ugric tribes, had been started by the Great Novgorod as far back as the 12th century.

It was at the period of the Tatar–Mongolian domination that the nucleus of the Russian centralized state—the Moscow Great Princedom—was formed. The struggle for the *yarlyk* on running the great princedom between the Suzdal, Tver, and Moscow princes had as its aim also the unification of all Russian lands for the fight against the Horde's domination. Gradually, the upper hand was gained by the Moscow Princedom which in the early 14th century was already able to double its territory. The territorial expansion of the Moscow Great Princedom, realized in various forms, did not stop at the boundaries of the Russian lands proper. Thus, as far back as 1472, the territory of the Great Perm (lands along the Upper Kama and Chusovaya rivers) were added to Moscow in the east.

The fall of the Horde's domination from 1380 to 1480 took place in the context of disintegration of the Golden Horde into separate khanates: Kazan, including not only the lands of the Kazan Tatars but also Mari, Chuvash, Udmurt, partly the Mordovian and Bashkir lands; Siberian Khanate (the Irtysh and Tobol basins); Astrakhan Khanate; Nogai and White

Hordes, and so on. The Kazan Khanate, which had a very close political (and dynastic) alliance with the Crimean Khanate in the south and borders with the Moscow Princedom in the east, was the most dangerous enemy of the latter. Constant raids undermined the strength of the Russian centralized state, while political borders put a limit to the growing territorial expansion of Moscow in the east, southeast, and south.

At the same time, the enlargement of the Moscow state's borders in the west was obstructed, because there lay the more developed Christian states: Rzecz Pospolita in the west, Livonian order and Sweden in the northwest. Only in 1514 was Russia able to win back Smolensk and much later to add to her territory the Baltic region, the Ukraine, and Byelorussia. Thus, to move westward, into the territories of the developed European states, Russia had first to increase her might, which was possible only by the expansion of the eastern borders.

After the annexation of the Murom, Meshchera, and Ryazan lands, and particularly in the 1630s, after taking possession of the Moksha and Alatyr areas, the borders of the Russian State came close to the Mordovian, Mari, and other Volga people's lands comprised in the Kazan Khanate. The mid-16th century was a turning point in the formation of the Russian State. It was at that time, after the conquest of the Kazan Khanate in 1552, that lands densely populated by the non-Slav peoples: Kazan Tatars, Mordovians, Mari, Udmurts, and Chuvash became part of Russia. In 1557, Russia also added to her territory the Bashkir lands (with the exception of the Trans-Ural Bashkirs who were ruled by the Siberian Khanate). The year 1552 is also significant due to the fact that Russia for the first time annexed a "foreign" state. The "absorption" of other (ethnically alien) states is characteristic of the imperial territorial expansion.

From 1554 to 1556, the Astrakhan Khanate joined Russia and that completed the inclusion of the entire Volga basin into the Russian State (the attachment of Novgorod in the 15th century meant the submission to Russia of the Northern Volga and Northern Trans-Ural regions together with the peoples of those territories).

Territorial expansion of the Russian State in the second half of the 16th century continued southeastward, eastward, and northeastward. By the beginning of the 17th century the borders in the south and southeast reached the Yaik, Terek, Kuma, Manych, and Don rivers, running close to the Northern Caucasus and the peoples residing there. In the northeast they gradually moved from the Ob basin to the Yenisei River. An important role in the conquest of West Siberia was played by the Solvychegodsk industrialists: Stroganovs who in 1558 received from Ivan IV patent letters for the possession of lands along the Kama and Chusovaya. As a result of the advance of the detachment detailed by industrialists with the approval of the government, from 1585 to 1590 territories of West Siberia with the

Nenets, Khanty, Mansi, Selkup, and Ket, as well as Siberian and Baraba Tatar populations were added to the Russian State.[6]

The first serious successes of Russia's territorial westward expansion were registered in the mid-17th century, when, after the national liberation war of the Ukrainian and Byelorussian peoples and the war with Poland, the eastern Byelorussian and Ukrainian lands became part of Russia. A common boundary existed now along the Dnieper River between the Russian State and the Crimean Khanate, a vassal of Turkey.

In the 17th century, intensive eastward advance to the Siberian lands continued; in the mid-17th century, Russian borders reached the Pacific Ocean, and by the end of that century, Kamchatka. In Siberia, almost fully incorporated into the Russian State by the end of the 17th century, intensive construction of cities as centers of administration and colonization commenced.

The Russian State within the borders established in the 16th and 17th centuries was a complex conglomeration of territories. At that time, many features of the administrative division of Russia reflected the historical and cultural originalities of its lands. As a rule, the local system of administrative management, formed previously, was not radically changed, and the borders of these territories were not substantially altered. In the 17th century, the entire territory of the state was divided into provinces called "cities," *uyezds, volosts,* and camps (*stans*).

In the mid-16th century, because of the expansion of the state borders, the Russian population, concentrated mainly to the north of the Oka River, started to migrate southward and southeastward, colonizing the territories of the Volga region and Dikoye pole (the steppe). In the late 16th century the movement toward Siberia began. The outflow of population from the trans-Moscow area was determined by a number of factors: lack of and low fertility of lands; the policy of introducing serfdom; constant wars waged by the state; and *Oprichnina* (state terrorism).

As during the settlement of the Russian North in the 14th and 15th centuries, peasant colonization of the new territories (the Volga region, in the first place) had been preceded or was accompanied by missionary work and monastic colonization. Thus, the Pechora, Blagoveshchensk, Spasskoye, Arzamas, Troitsk, Alatyr, Makariev, Zholtovodsk, Oransk, and other monasteries were active in the Mordovian, Mari, and Meshchera lands.

It should be mentioned that the peasant colonization of the Volga region was directed by the state power in a planned way. The state also sanctioned the missionary Christian activity, the more so as most peoples in the lands which were included in Russia in the late 17th century (with the exception of Moslems—Tatars, Bashkirs, Kabardians and Kumyks) did not belong to any world religion.

The Russians' settlement southward, southeastward, and eastward led to the formation of various ethnographic groups of the Russian people, Cossacks being the most outstanding among them. At the same time, there was expansion of the Ukrainians' area, principally through the settlement, jointly with the Russians, of the Sloboda Ukraine (to the south of Kursk and Voronezh).

By the end of the 17th century, the Russian State was close to its "natural" borders, by which we mean the scarcely settled lands fit for colonization, which were not parts of other states (the Kazan Khanate was rather an exception). It is interesting that the general outline of Russia's borders by the end of the 17th century coincided with the borders of the present-day Russian Federation. Settling in these territories, Russians chose mainly the no-man's lands: there were still, in the early 20th century, considerable territorial enclaves in the Volga region and Siberia with prevalent non-Russian population. But the territorial expansion of Russia in the 18th and 19th centuries aimed at the annexation of other states located in the centers of ancient civilizations (Central Asia, the Caucasus, Central, Eastern, and Northern Europe) was of a purely imperial nature.

Among territories that became parts of the Russian Empire, in the 18th and 19th centuries, are those now directly connected to the Russian Federation: the Northern Caucasus, Far East, a number of South Siberian regions, as well as the Ingermanland (Izhora land), and Karelia with the town of Vyborg. The latter two became parts of Russia after the Northern War in accordance with the 1721 Nystadt peace. Estland and Lifland—contemporary Estonia and Latvia—joined the Empire at the same time.

In 1722–1723 Peter the Great launched his Persian campaign as a result of which (the Petersburg Treaty) Russia's borders along the Terek River traversing the area of the Terek Cossacks were moved farther to the south along the western and southern coast of the Caspian Sea. At that time, the Caucasus was the arena of clashes between Iran and Turkey. By the 1770s, Kabarda, initially annexed in the 16th century, and Northern Ossetia became irrevocable parts of the Empire. But the final annexation of the Northern Caucasus and Transcaucasia by the Empire took place in the 1870s (San Stefano Peace Treaty with Turkey and the Berlin Congress 1878). It should be pointed out that among the territories and peoples of the contemporary Russian Federation it is the lands and peoples of the Northern Caucasus who were particularly deeply "rooted" in the composition of the Russian State:[7] the annexation of Adygheia was completed in 1864, that of Chechenia and Mountain Daghestan in 1859, after the liquidation of the Imamat (theocratic state established by Mansur and Shamil). The submission of the Northern Caucasus cost both Russia and the local peoples tremendous sacrifices. After the suppression of a number of anti-Russian uprisings, a part of the Mountaineers had to leave their native country and settle in Turkey and other Middle East countries.

The 18th century saw the advance of the Russian territorial expansion into South Siberian lands—the Baraba steppe, Upper Ob, and upward toward the Yenisei. By the 1730s, Chukotka and Kamchatka joined the Empire, followed in 1858–1860 (under treaties with China) by the Amur area and Primorie (Maritime region). In the second half of the 18th century the Northern Kazakhstan lands were incorporated, and in the 1850s Russia took hold of the Southern Kazakhstan, with some *juses* (tribal alliances, or hordes) joining the Empire voluntarily. A springboard was established for the conquest of Central Asia, which took place from the 1860s to 1880s.

Active Russian expansion westward and southwestward was characteristic of the 18th century; it was completed after three partitions of Poland (in 1772, 1793, and 1795) by the incorporation of Western Ukrainian and Byelorussian lands and of a part of the Baltic region (Lifland and Kurland). By 1783 the Crimean Khanate was liquidated. In addition to the Crimea, Russia took possession of the Northern Black Sea area, which received the name of Novorossia (New Russia). From 1809 to 1815, Russia annexed Finland and a part of Poland proper with Warsaw.

Thus, it was the territorial changes of the 18th and 19th centuries that resulted in the Russian Empire being put together and becoming a state comprising not only the lands of the backward peoples not having their own statehood, but also other states or parts of their territories (mainly in the outlying area).

Parallel to the incorporation of new lands, their administrative organization, particularly the centralized administrative territorial division, was undertaken. As far back as 1708, the division of the country into provinces (governments) was introduced for the tasks of military, fiscal, political, and bureaucratic governance.

But the uniformity of the administration of the Empire's lands was not achieved at once. Only after the 1773–1775 peasant war, in which the "alien" populations participated on a mass scale, was the "Establishment for the Administration of the Provinces of All-Russian Empire" adopted, in 1775. With a few changes, its dispositions remained vigorous until 1917.

According to that "Establishment," the entire territory of the Russian Empire was divided into forty provinces with populations of 300 to 400 thousand of "revisional souls" (taxables). Provinces consisted of 12 to 15 *uyezds* with 20 to 30 thousand revisional souls. To render centralization more strict, several provinces were united into *namestnichestvo*, or regions administered by the governor-general (in 1782 their number was 19). They existed until 1796. Provincial division was applied also to areas which previously had had their own peculiarities or autonomy: the Ukraine, the Caucasus, Poland (the autonomy of the Polish Kingdom was gradually abolished after the 1830–1831 and 1863–1864 uprisings). In 1865, the cantonal administrative system introduced in 1798 in connection with the creation of the Bashkir-Meshcheryak force was also liquidated. By the end of the 19th century only Finland (the Great Princehood of Finland), the

Khiva Khanate, and Bukhara Emirate retained autonomy within the Russian Empire. The administrative division of the Empire was highly uniform and gave very little consideration to the ethnic composition of the population.

In the 18th and the first half of the 19th centuries, the above-mentioned colonizing movement of the Russian population into the Southern and Southeastern Steppes, cis-Ural, as well as the Central Black Earth and the Ukrainian Left Bank regions, continued. Russia's northwest adjoining St. Petersburg was also actively settled. The fertile lands of cis-Caucasus and Northern Caucasus were practically deserted until the middle of the 19th century: the indigenes did not exceed half a million.[8] Kazakhstan also was among the scarcely populated areas.

The most impetuous colonizing and resettlement processes began in the second half of the 19th century, due to the development of capitalism. At that time the Southern Steppe and particularly the cis-Caucasus in the European part of Russia, as well as Kazakhstan and the Far East in the Asian part of it became the regions of active settlement. The colonization of Eastern and Western Siberia, of all underdeveloped regions with huge tracts of fertile lands, also continued. At that period, there was another direction of migration, too, into the regions of the growing capitalist industry: the Petersburg Province, the industrial Centre, and Novorossia.

Lack of statistical data prevents the discussion from dwelling in detail on the conditions of the "aliens" in the Russian Empire, particularly in the territory of the present-day Russian Federation. Only the last pre-revolutionary and first Soviet censuses may give an idea of them.

By the end of the pre-revolutionary period, stable enclaves of other nationalities continued to exist within the borders of the present-day Russia: there, indigenous population was prevalent (numbering more than half of the inhabitants), and a stable nucleus of a given ethnic group existed. The regions that joined Russia as far back as the 16th century and experienced mass colonization by the Russians (Tataria and Bashkiria, in the first place) were an exception.

Most of Russia's peoples preserved their native languages and, consequently, other elements of their national cultures. It should be pointed out that although the Russian language had a wide use in Russia (several millions of ethnically non-Russians spoke it), it was not the only "language of international intercourse." That role was played by the languages of many big peoples: Tatars in the Volga region, Lezghins in Daghestan, Yakuts and Nenets in Siberia, and so on.

At the same time, most of Russia's peoples were socioeconomically underdeveloped, as is seen from the percentages of urban population within various peoples, according to the 1897 census. In the Empire as a whole the urbans made up only 12.6 percent of the population, this figure being for Russians, 15.6 percent; Germans, 22.0; Greeks, 17.9; Gypsies, 14.6;

Tatars, 11.1; Jews, 45.8. Among the other peoples of the present-day Russian Federation the percentage of town dwellers was insignificant, and, consequently, the percentage of industrial workers, intelligentsia, and other groups making up the social base of the national liberation movements was also very small. The "alien" population of Russia was chiefly peasant. That is why, as far as these peoples of the present-day Russian Federation are concerned, only Jews and Tatars had their national parties by the early 20th century (Bund, Ittifak, etc.), while the most important national movements developed among the peoples of the outlying regions of the Empire.

Let us now turn to the national policy of the Tzarist government in the territory of Russia proper. In our opinion, this policy had several dominant features which were retained throughout the existence of Russia.

1. The administrative uniformity discussed above. Liquidation of territorial autonomies (usually preserved after various peoples joining Russia at earlier stages) and the division of the compact ethnic nucleus by administrative borders impeded the development of separatist tendencies and the consolidation of peoples into ethnosocial organisms. Thus, the basis for political movements was eliminated, particularly for those peoples who did not have their own statehood. It is significant that many "aliens" of the Volga region participated in the peasant wars of the 18th century, but their movements were rather of social than of national-political nature. Let us also note that during the 1917 revolutions and the consequent civil war, the idea of sociopolitical independence from Russia was not widespread among Russia's national minorities.

2. More "liberal" forms of exploitation as compared with those endured by the Russian people. Most of Russia's minorities did not experience serfdom (perhaps with the exception of the Mordovians in whose lands serfdom was partly known). Usually, the newly annexed peoples either were taxed with *yasak,* or were included in the state-owned peasantry estate. Old forms of exploitation were often maintained in the newly acquired lands. Thus, in Daghestan, only as late as 1913, personal dependence of peasants on the local landlords was abolished by a Tsar's edict.

The "aliens" were partly admitted into the privileged (usually military) Russian estates. Thus, a part of the Buryats was added to the Trans-Baikal Cossack force; Bashkirs and Misharis (an ethnographic group of Tatars) from 1798 to 1865 made up the Bashkir-Meshcheryak force. Their lands were divided into twelve cantons having self-government. A part of the Kalmyks were also attached to the Cossacks.

In 1822, Siberian Governor-General M.M. Speransky and his assistant G.S. Batenkov wrote for the Siberian peoples the "Statutes of the Administration of Aliens." That document postulated the division of the Siberian "aliens" into three groups: vagrants, nomads, and settled. The old system of communication between the administration and the population through the family-tribal upper stratum (the "princelings") was preserved for the "vagrant aliens"—some hunting peoples of Siberia.

The "nomadic aliens" (Buryats, Yakuts, Evenks, Khanty, Mansi, Khakass) were under tribal administration of the *ulus* or encampment (a group of related families) performed by a headman ("starosta") and one or two assistants. Several *uluses* were governed by a "board for aliens" or "steppe duma" (in the case of some peoples). Thus, tribal and feudal upper strata were the main executors of the will of the Tsarist administration. The nomadic peoples retained their lands, the rates of the *yasak* (imposition), and the duties list being established.

The "settled aliens" were conferred the same status as the Russian taxed estates (lower middle classes or state-owned peasants), but they did not have to do military service.

3. The examples given above show that the broad development of the indirect administration, that is, administration through the privileged elites of these peoples, was a major element of the national policy. That system was all the more effective because the ruling estates of the "alien" ethnic groups were usually admitted into Russian ruling classes.

E.P. Karnovich noted the presence among Russian nobility of Ukrainian, Tatar, Polish, Mordovian, Georgian, Moldavian, Baltic German, and other ruling families. "The idea," he wrote, "that all our old nobility is not of Russian, but of foreign origin, has become so common that on the occasion of the publication in 1785 of the general formula for the genealogy lists of the old noble families the decision was taken to formulate the data about the founder of each family in the following way: 'came to Russia from . . . under the rule of Great Prince such and such.' . . . In the middle eastern provinces of Russia a great part of the local nobility consisted of the Christened Tatar Murzas and the so called Mordovian 'Panoks'."[9]

The russification of ruling estates of the "alien" ethnic groups of the Russian Empire deprived the national resistance of head leaders and made the system of indirect administration more flexible.

4. Religious policy should be mentioned as the most important aspect of national policy. It had two main orientations: Christianization (both forced or resulted from missionary activities) and the attempt to find ways of coexisting with the representatives of other big world religions (Islam, in the first place).

"Pagan" peoples not professing any world religion were the first to be Christianized. Frequently, the monastic colonization and the activities of hermits preceded peasant colonization and the incorporation of a territory into the Russian State. Thus, as early as the 14th century Christianization of the Komi was started by Stefan of Perm, while the Komi land itself was added to the Moscow state only in 1478. In the 16th and 17th centuries, intensive Christianization of the Finnish peoples of the Volga region commenced. It is significant that one of the most outstanding figures of the Orthodox church schism, archpriest Avvakum, was a Mordovian.

By 1917, a majority of the "pagan" peoples of the present-day Russia were formally christened, though many of them retained important practices of their pre-Christian creeds. Thus, conversion to Christian orthodoxy of the indigenous peoples of Siberia and the North was mostly nominal. Shamanism, natural, and hunting cults have continued to play no small role in these peoples' lives up to the present time. The state and the Orthodox Church spared no efforts to fight the old religious practices among the "aliens." At times, that fight took the form of political processes with the employment of unscrupulous methods; for example, the "Multan case" (when Udmurts were accused of human sacrifices), which agitated the entire Russian society.

The attempts to Christianize the peoples professing monotheistic religions had never ceased, either. Thus, among the Tatars a substantial stratum of christened people came into existence, forming special ethnographic groups (Kriashens, Nagaibaks). On the whole, however, these attempts were not successful, and the practice of coexistence with Islam, Buddhism, and nonorthodox Christian religions came in their stead. As far back as the 16th century, before the annexation of the Kazan Khanate, there were mosques for the Tatars who became Russian subjects, in the territory of Russia proper. The government abstained from interference in the religious life of these peoples, administrating it only in an indirect way, for instance, through the Religious Board of Russia's Moslems (since 1788 Ufa has become one of its sites).

In this respect, the hardest was the situation of the Jewish (Judaist) population of Russia. There were the Pale for the Jews, a quota for entering higher schools; pogroms for national and religious reasons and forced Christianization of Jewish children (they were called up to military service and christened) became everyday occurrences.

5. Linguistic and cultural policy and practice of Tzarist government did not put obstacles in the way of the use of native languages and national cultures in private life, but prevented their public employment (in schools, public offices, press, etc.). The opportunities for many peoples of Russia to develop their native forms of culture in their own tongues, to form their national intelligentsia, were negligible.

6. Colonization of the newly annexed lands, as mentioned above, was a major aspect of the national policy of the Russian State. Although colonization often did not concern the densely settled regions and the old agricultural centers, it substantially changed the ethnic image of Russia. The practice of inviting foreigners for the industrial and agrarian development of Russian lands should also be regarded as a part of the colonization policy (thus, for instance, in the 18th century a large ethnic stratum of Volga Germans emerged in Russia).

The state frequently took into the colonizing fund large tracts of land which were extensively utilized by the local population. Thus, in the late 19th and early 20th centuries, 53 percent of the Irkutsk and 36 percent of the Trans-Baikal Buryat lands were taken away for the colonization fund. On the whole, the colonization policy resulted in the preservation of the indigenous population in Russia's territory (with the exception of the Northern Caucasus) only in the form of enclaves among the bulk of Russian inhabitants.

Thus, the national policy of the Russian State, though not meant to undermine the national existence of the ethnic minorities, objectively placed obstacles to the further development of Russia's "aliens," to the attainment by them of the highest forms of national life.

The review of the ethnic history of the Russian State in the pre-revolutionary period has shown that already at the period of its rise, it was the carrier of the "gene" of territorial expansion and had an embryonal predisposition to become a multinational empire. Relatively late, only in the 16th century, the state began an intensive expansion into the lands of non-Russian peoples. Since the early 18th century the Russian State had become an empire where the "indigenous" Russian lands, gradually expanding by means of colonization, had been acquiring the functions of a "mother country." Non-Russian peoples of Russia had concentrated in territorial enclaves among the numerically overwhelming Russian population. The national policy of the state ensured a minimum of conditions for the ethnic survival of the non-Russian peoples, but was an obstacle in the way of their consolidation into nations and development of professional forms of ethnic culture.

NOTES

1. L.V. Milov, "Prirodno-klimatichesky faktor i osobennosti Rossiiskogo isto-richeskogo protsessa," *Voprosy istorii* (Natural climatic factors and peculiarities of the Russian historical process, *Problems of history*), no. 4–5 (1992), p. 53.

2. A.L. Yurganov, "U istokov despotizma," *Istoria otechestva: lyudi, idei, re-shenia. Ocherki istorii Rossii IX–nachala XX v.* (At the source of despotism, *History of the fatherland: People, ideas, decisions. Essays on Russia's history of the 19th-early 20th centuries,* (Moscow: Politizdat, 1991), p. 37.

3. L. Lux, "Yevraziistvo," *Strana i mir* (Euro-Asianism, *The country and the world*), vol. 55, no. 1 (1990), p. 118.

4. H. Alexeyev, "Sovetsky federalism," *Obshchestvennye nauki i sovremennost* (Soviet federalism, *Social sciences and the contemporary time*), no. 1 (1992), pp. 121–123.

5. It should be specially stressed that by the imperial type of state structure we understand the unification of several ethnosocial organisms in the framework of one political formation, by the method excluding any independence of individual

ESOs and presupposing the domination of the central political power in all spheres of the life of society. Russian philosopher G. Fedotov defines "empire" in a similar way: "Empire means expansion beyond the limits of long established borders, supergrowth of a mature, historically shaped organism. . . . The advance of a state, even constantly growing, from its habitual geo-political sphere is a moment of transition of quantity into quality: not a new province comes into existence, but an empire with its specific universal political self-consciousness." See: G.P. Fedotov, *Sudba i grekhi Rossii. Izbrannye stati po filosofii russkoi istorii i kultury* (The fate and sins of Russia. Selected papers on the philosophy of Russian history and culture), vol. 2 (St. Petersburg: Sofia, 1992), pp. 305–306.

6. Let us note that Russia's simultaneous westward expansion in the area of the Baltic Sea and the Gulf of Finland suffered a crushing defeat.

7. Tuva, annexed by the Soviet Union in 1944, is an exception.

8. V.Z. Drobizhev, I.D. Kovalchenko, and A.V. Muraviev, *Istoricheskaya geografia SSSR* (Historical geography of the USSR) (Moscow: Vysshaia Shkola, 1973), p. 190.

9. E.P. Karnovich, *Rodovye prozvania i tituly v Rossii i sliyanie inovertsev s russkimi* (Family names and titles in Russia and merger of adherents of other creeds with Russians) (Moscow: BIMPA, 1991), pp. 235–237.

2

Evolution of Russia's Federative Structure

The first ideas of federalization of Russia remount to the early 19th century. They were evolved in the projects of transformation of Russia by the Decembrists. P. Pestel was a consistent advocate of the regional division of Russia, and not the division on the basis of the "national principle." The federalist project worked out by N. Muraviev also proceeded from the purely territorial, and not the national criterion.

Only much later, in the 1870s and 1880s, ideas of cultural autonomy of peoples in the framework of the Russian Empire restructured on federalist principles began to take shape on the Russian soil. It was not accidental that these programs were engendered in the depth of the emerging national-political movements of the bigger peoples of the Empire's outlying regions, for example, the Ukrainians.[1] Autonomist urges originated at the same time in Russia's outlying areas inhabited mainly by Russians, such as Siberia, which subjugated to an overt colonial exploitation. But until its last day, the Tsarist government ignored all demands of national minorities concerning autonomy inside Russia. The only concession to the local self-government was the establishment of *Zemstvo* in the second half of the 19th century, which, however, did not confer the rights of cultural autonomy and self-government to the national (ethnic) groups.

Thus, the problem of the national-political restructuring of Russia became the initial prerogative of political parties and movements of radical tenor (social democrats and, subsequently, the Bolsheviks). As it was the Bolsheviks who, in 1917, had seized the state power in Russia and whose ideas were later implemented in the construction of the multinational state, it would not be remiss to consider the sources and the evolution of their national-political program.

As is known, the project of Austrian Marxists, though critically revised, served as the chief source of the national program of Russian Social Democrats. The projects of Austrian Marxists included cultural autonomy of ethnic groups and concentration in the framework of ethnic organizations of all cultural and educational functions. All other functions of the state should be performed in the framework of purely territorial federative units—lands.

This program, in K. Kautsky's opinion, negated the federalism of national territories because of the multinational nature of the lands of the Austro-Hungarian Empire. (By the way, Kautsky criticized the principle of cultural autonomy, believing that "nations cannot exist without territory.")[2]

Russian Social Democrats introduced into the working out of the national question substantial corrections. First, they came forth with the thesis about "regional (oblast) self-government for the places, where there are special living conditions and composition of the population."[3] Thus, ideas of territorial autonomy of the national (ethnic) groups, absent in the "Austrian drafts," were introduced into the Party program.

Second, planning to create normal conditions for the functioning of national culture (first and foremost, in the field of language and education), Russian Social Democrats regarded in an emphatically negative light the idea of cultural autonomy which, in their opinion, "is no doubt harmful from the point of view of democracy in general and the interests of the class struggle of proletariat in particular."[4] This item of the program contained certain contradictions, as it introduced socio-class parameters into the sphere of national culture.

Third, the item concerning the "right of nations oppressed by the Tsarist monarchy to self-determination (i.e., secession and creation of an independent state)," became the major point of the Russian Social Democratic Labor Party (RSDRP) program. However, the criterion of the expediency of self-determination from "the point of view of the interests of the entire social development and interests of the class struggle of the proletariat for socialism,"[5] was introduced, denouncing, in fact, the right to self-determination.

Evidently, the national program of the Social Democratic Party, despite its many contradictions, was more in line with both the interests of peoples and the prospect of social development. Actually, it contained three leading principles recognized by the contemporary international law regarding national minorities: (1) the right to cultural autonomy, (2) the right to territorial autonomy, (3) the right to creation of their own state (self-determination). Neither during that period nor later (up to the dissolution of the Communist Party of the Soviet Union [CPSU] in 1991) have these theses been officially revised. But what matters is in what measure and in what form they were implemented in practice.

The question of the national-political restructuring of Russia was brought to the practical plane for the first time in February 1917, after the overthrow of the Tsarist government. It should be pointed out that the existence of the Bolshevist constructive program on the reform of the local self-government and the entire national-political structure of the Empire gave the Bolsheviks some political advantages and determined in great measure their victory in October 1917 and afterwards (the so-called "triumphal march of the Soviet power").

Only the establishment of territorial autonomy in July 1917 for Kalmyks—"The Steppe Region of the Kalmyk People"—may, perhaps, go to the credit of the Provisional Government. Otherwise, none of the most burning and topical national conflicts in the territory of the Russian Empire (the Ukrainian, Polish, Finnish issues, etc.) were resolved.

Bolsheviks, on the contrary, at that period paid paramount attention to the national question. Thus, in April (May according to the new calendar), the Seventh All-Russian Conference of the RSDRP(b) was held and repeated, in its resolution "On the National Question," the propositions of the 1913 Poronin meeting.[6] The All-Russian Conference of Front and Rear RSDRP (b) organizations in June 1917 laid a special emphasis on the right of peoples to self-determination. At the same time, the conference stressed that the ideal of the RSDRP (b) "is voluntary and not forced [unification of peoples] in one polity."[7] The enlarged meeting of CC of the RSDRP (b) in August (September) 1917 put into its resolution "On Power," "actual implementation of the right of nations living in Russia to self-determination."[8]

The propaganda force of these resolutions is reflected at least by the fact of a broadscale participation of Russia's national minorities, for instance, the Tatars, in the Civil War on the Bolsheviks' side. The well-known Tatar revolutionary M. Sultan-Galiev wrote: "The number of Tatar Red Armymen reached tremendous figures: at the height of the Civil War at the Eastern and Turkestan fronts Tatar Red Armymen accounted for more than a half of the entire force, reaching sometimes 70 to 75 percent (the 5th army)."[9] But we should remember that Tatars were among the most developed national minorities of pre-revolutionary Russia and therefore their political activity was much higher than that of many other peoples. Nevertheless, other peoples of Russia also were attracted by the Bolsheviks' official attitude toward the national question, which facilitated the establishment of the new state—the Russian Soviet Federative Socialist Republic (RSFSR).

The Constitution of the RSFSR, adopted by the 5th All-Russian Congress of Soviets on July 10, 1918, was very contradictory as regards the national-political structure of the country.

Thus, the Declaration of Rights of the Working and Exploited People, that is, the first chapter of the Constitution, read: "The Russian Soviet

Republic is established on the basis of a free union of free nations as a federation of Soviet national republics." But the second chapter stated:

The Soviets of the regions that are distinguished by their special living conditions and national composition, may form autonomous regional unions headed by regional congresses of Soviets and their executive bodies, like any other regional associations in general, that may be formed. These autonomous regional unions enter, on the federative principles, the Russian Socialist Federative Soviet Republic.[10]

In other words, two lines of the national-political organization of Russia, federalist and autonomist, coexisted in the first constitution of the Russian Federation.

As it follows from the text of the Constitution, the federalist trend was dominant, a considerable competence of the central power which functioned through eighteen ministries (all-Russian People's commissariats). The attributions of the central authority included also "the delimitation of boundaries and competence of the regional Soviet unions," as well as "general administrative division of territory . . . and the confirmation of regional associations."[11] It should be noted that the Russian Federation was seen as a federative association of regional Soviets (and among others, in the territories with a non-Russian population), which exercise full supreme power within the limits of their competence.

The Constitution affirmed the Bolsheviks' earlier formulations on the national question: the right to self-determination (by the way, the right of the national-political associations to secede from the RSFSR was not envisaged), equality of citizens of all nationalities, but at the same time, the division of citizens of each nationality in accordance with social and class criteria (granting "the workers and peasants of every nation the right to adopt at their own plenipotentiary Soviet congress the decision on whether they want, and on what grounds to participate in, the federal government and other federal Soviet institutions."[12]

Such an important state body as the People's Commissariat for Nationalities' Affairs adhered to the autonomist trend, the influence of that body being determined by the weight of its head, I.V. Stalin, member of the CC, Politbureau, and Orgbureau. On the contrary, the federalist orientation was spontaneously supported by the local mass national movements declaring the establishment of Soviet republics.

Most peoples of Russia were content with the federative structure in the framework of which they could obtain real self-dependence. But the Bolshevist leadership, after the seizure of power, strove, on the contrary, to set up a unitary state system, with the party of Bolsheviks as a center, governing nucleus of it. These diverse processes were reflected in the contradictions of the first Constitution of Soviet Russia.

The urge of the party to usurp entire power in the country was demonstrated with a special clarity in its 8th and 12th congresses.

The Programme of the Russian Communist Party (Bolsheviks), adopted by the 8th Congress, stressed the following principles of national policy: (1) recognition of the right to self-determination; (2) the establishment of a united multinational state as the aim of the party; (3) "as one of the forms of transition to full unity, the party proposes the federative association of states organized on the Soviet type;[13] (4) the will of a nation should be determined by the desire of its proletarian and peasant strata. In the resolution "On the Organizational Issue," such an idea was expressed: The state principle of federalism "does not mean that RCP should, in its turn, be organized as a federation of self-dependent Communist parties, in all parts of the RSFSR. All decisions of the RCP and its leadership bodies are obligatory to all units of the party, irrespective of their national composition. Central Committees [of the republican parties] . . . have the rights of the regional party committees and are wholly submitted to the CC of the RCP."[14] This principle was implemented without fail by the party during all the years of its existence.

In the discussion on the program thesis on the right of nations to self-determination, some speakers (especially N.I. Bukharin) spoke against the recognition of the right to self-determination. But V.I. Lenin's point of view prevailed. In his Report on the Party Programme, he said literally the following: "When we win power, and wait a little, then we do it" ("throw away" the right of nations to self-determination).[15] In other words, in fact, already in 1919, Bolsheviks radically revised (without putting it into their party program) a major item of their draft solution of the national question. There was also another important "innovation," that is, drastic centralization of the party, rigorous submission of the republican (national) communist parties to the CC of the RCP (b).[16] After the 12th Congress of the RCP had adopted the thesis on party dictatorship, a supercentralized, powerful organization was set up in the state, which actually functioned outside the framework of the federative structure provided for in the Constitution, and ignored any national autonomy.

Of course, the country achieved full centralization not immediately but, as various studies show, only by the late 1920s or early 1930s. It is of some interest how these processes went on at the lower levels.

Let us turn to A.G. Kushnir's dissertation. According to that author, up to the early 1930s, two confronting trends coexisted in the national-political organization of Russia. The first proceeded from decentralization of power, democratization of administration and allotment of the Soviets with real political force. It was supported by both the local state and central state bodies of power. The second line, advocated by the Central Committee (CC) of the Russian Communist Party (Bolsheviks) (RCP[b]) and, later, of the All-Union Communist Party (Bolsheviks) (VCP[b]) and locally by the

Commisariat of Internal Affairs (NKVD), suggested strict centralism for decision making, the "barrack-socialist method of administration."[17]

It would be interesting to see the change of Lenin's stand, which underwent evolution: in economy, from war communism to the NEP; in the field of state organization, from centralism to moderate decentralization;[18] in the national question, to the recognition of principles of federation and confederation of national states.[19] That evolution, however, occurred in the conditions when processes launched by him became already irreversible.

It was pointed out earlier that, according to the 1918 Constitution, the Russian Federation was seen mainly as a federative association of territories (territorial Soviets). In this connection, an interesting observation was made by A.G. Kushnir: "Parallel to the Centre's struggle against the territorial autonomy, there was going on the process of national-state development, promoted by the Centre itself. It could result in the future transformation of the RSFSR into a purely national federation."[20] In other words, at that stage, the self-dependent activity of Russia's minorities was contraposed to the movement of the bulk of Russian population. A national-state structure took shape, which American Sovietologist F. Silnitski called "asymmetric": the most numerous people of the country, the Russian people, were deprived of their national statehood.

Probably, the greater part of leaders and representatives of Russia's national minorities in the early 1920s did not yet realize that the political line of the Centre in the national question had been drastically changed. The more so as, from 1919, the policy of "indigenousness of Soviet power,"[21] or "translation of it into national languages" (terms heard at the 12th RCP Congress) began rapidly to develop. But some representatives of the national trend in the Communist party proved able to assess the drastic change of the Centre's policy vis-à-vis the national minorities. One of the first was the chairman of the Council of People's Commissars of Tataria, M. Sultan-Galiev, who in a private letter, dated 1923, wrote:

Knowing well the central government, I can categorically assert that the government's policy regarding non-Russian peoples does not in any respect differ from the old great-power line. Promises given in 1917, are not fulfilled. Therefore we must unite with the Kazakhs and Turkestanians at the forthcoming Congress in order to establish a common front and defend our national interests.[22]

Sultan-Galiev's arrest in the same year was the first repressive measure against the "national deviation in the party."

The establishment of the Soviet Union in 1922–1924 drastically changed the configuration of the national question in the country as a whole and in the Russian Federation, in particular. Formally, the USSR initially was formed as a confederation of "independent" (the official term of that time) republics, consisting of two federations—the Russian and the Transcaucasian. But actually, the 1924 Constitution called for a higher degree of centralism and larger powers of the central authority than did the 1918 RSFSR Constitution for the central bodies of the Russian Federation.[23] The exclusive "right to free secession from the Union,"[24] granted to the union republics, deprived once and for all the subjects of federations the right to self-determination ("up to secession"). According to the Constitution, "regional Soviets" (territorial associations) were not among the subjects of federation and the national-political structure finally acquired the multistage (ranged, status-like) form: Union—Union Republic—Autonomous Region. In this way, each people of the country had now a "rank" in the polity.

This situation was confirmed by the subsequent constitutions of the USSR (1936 and 1977), and the degree of centralization of the country envisaged by the Main Law regularly became higher.

Before giving a detailed description of the development of Russia's national-political structure, let us sum up the above.

1. The state structure of Russia developed from federation of territories (including those with a peculiar composition of the population) to territorial autonomy of national quasi-state entities. Thus, the interests of the Russian people were contraposed to those of Russia's minorities. In practice, the establishment of territorial national autonomies which were officially regarded as national-state entities[25] stimulated the becoming (consolidation) of nations in Russia's territory. This positive phenomenon was determined also by the policy of industrialization which led to the formation of modern mass social groups (working class, intelligentsia). The development of Russia's minorities entered a new, national stage.

2. The national-state structure of Russia as a part of the USSR was initially formed as a hierarchical one, depending on the volume of rights of a given state entity. As a result, some peoples were subjugated to others. The Russian people (as well as some minorities for whom no national-territorial or national-political entities were created) found themselves in an uncertain position, the more so as the division of the country into colonies (the outlying territories) and a "mother country" existed no longer. The latter was replaced by a featureless and nonethnic "center," contraposing both the Russian and all other peoples of the country.

3. The name of Federation was retained in Russia from 1924 to 1992 rather as a tribute to the tradition than as a reflection of the real state of things. Thus, the autonomous republics with all their constitutional powers were members of other union republics, too: Uzbekistan (the Kara-Kalpak ASSR), Georgia (the Abkhazian and Adzhar ASSRs), Azerbaijan (the Nakhichevan ASSR); but none of these union republics was considered as federation.

The development of the national-political structure of Russia in the So-viet time proceeded through distinct stages timed to the changes of the constitutional system (Constitutions of 1924 and 1936). The chief feature of the first stage (1917–1924) was the spontaneity of the process, manifes-tations of the initiative of the broad masses of the population. After the establishment of the Peoples' Commissariat for Nationalities' Affairs (Nar-comnatz) the process of setting up autonomies became more regulated. Creation of national states was characteristic of the entire territory of the former Russian empire; but we are going to discuss the development of the national-political structure of Russia proper.

At the beginning of 1918, the Kuban–Black Sea Republic, and the Terek Autonomous Socialist Republic (which comprised the lands of Cossacks and Kabardians), appeared. In July, at the First Congress of the Soviets of Northern Caucasus, both merged into the North-Caucasian Republic. In June 1918, the First All-Russian Congress of Udmurts adopted a decision on voluntarily joining the RSFSR. In the same year, the Commune of the Volga Germans came into existence as one of the first of Russia's auton-omies. On March 20, 1919, the "Agreement of the Russian Workers' and Peasants' Government with the Bashkir Government on the Soviet Auton-omy of Bashkiria" was signed. In 1920, the Tatar Autonomous Republic, the Votsk (Udmurt), Kalmyk, and Mari autonomous regions and also the Karel Labour Commune were established. In 1923, the latter, as well as the Commune of the Volga Germans, were transformed in ASSRs.

After the end of the Civil War in 1921, two autonomous republics: the Mountainous Republic (consisting of seven districts: Karachai, Kabardian, Balkar, North-Ossetian, Chechen, and Sunzhen) and the Daghestan Re-public came into existence. In the same year, the Komi (Zyrian) Autono-mous District, the Yakut Autonomous Republic, and the Buryat-Mongolian Republic were established. At the same time, the former provinces were broken up into smaller units. Intensive national-political development was characteristic of that period, as well as looking for forms which would correspond to the extent of self-determination necessary for this or that people.

After the adoption of the 1924 Constitution and until the middle of the 1930s, the process of national-political development retained elements of spontaneity, but on the whole it remained within the structure fixed by the USSR Constitution. In 1924, the Mountainous Republic was liquidated and North Ossetian and Ingush autonomous regions were set up. In 1928, the Cherkessian Autonomous Region was formed inside the Stavropol Terri-tory for the Adyghei people. The same year saw the establishment of the Mordovian National District within the Middle Volga region. In 1930, the Presidium of the Central Executive Committee of the USSR sanctioned the creation of the Khakass Autonomous Region inside the Krasnoyarsk Territory, and in 1934, of the Jewish Autonomous Region inside the Khabarovsk Territory.

In the late 1920s and early 1930s, national districts inside some regions and territories of the USSR were formed for a number of the socioeconomically underdeveloped peoples, namely: the Nenets district (Arkhangelsk region), Taimyr and Evenk districts (Krasnoyarsk territory), Koryak district (Kamchatka region), Chukchi district (Magadan region), Yamal-Nenets and Khanty-Mansi districts (Tyumen region), Aginsk and Ust-Ordynsk districts (Buryat-Mongolian ASSR), Komi-Permyak district (Perm region). Two hundred and fifty national precincts were established for a number of smaller peoples and ethnic groups.[26]

On the whole, the national-political development at that period involved a broad range of peoples and had sufficiently flexible forms to take into consideration the varied national cultural needs. Although by the end of that period administrative centralization of the country was in essence completed, the national-political development continued under the impact of the inertia of the first post-revolution years.

The middle and late 1930s saw the development of the national-political structure of Russia completed. At that time, a number of autonomies—Mari, Kalmyk, Kabardin-Balkar, Chechen-Ingush, North-Ossetian, Komi—were allotted the status of autonomous republics—parts of the RSFSR. By the end of the 1930s, the fractional forms of territorial autonomy (autonomous precincts and village councils) were liquidated, and Russia's national-political structure acquired the form which existed until 1992.

It should be noted that in the 1940s and 1950s the national-political transformations in Russia were caused, first and foremost, either by external policy (establishment and abolition of the Karel-Finnish SSR) or internal policy (the liquidation, during the Great Patriotic War, of the ASSR of the Volga Germans, the Crimean ASSR, and a number of North-Caucasian autonomies in connection with the deportation of their peoples). In other words, the status of autonomies was purely formal and did not defend their inhabitants from the arbitrary actions of the central authorities.

Mention should be made of difficulties faced by the authors trying to describe the national policy of Soviet Russia. First, literature existing on that issue is devoid of any objectivity: it is dominated by apologetic or similarly uncritical negative attitudes. Second, Soviet national policy underwent great metamorphoses, was highly contradictory, and it was difficult to distinguish any stable trends. Therefore, our considerations are of a rather preliminary nature.

1. The formation of nations deserves on the whole a positive evaluation. Let us remind ourselves that national development has been closely con-

nected with the economic progress (industrialization), and therefore the assessment of national policy cannot avoid the economic aspect.

2. As early as 1923 (the 12th RCP Congress), the central power pursued the policy of rendering economic aid to underdeveloped peoples. The assistance was accorded in the form of redistribution and building of industrial objects in agrarian regions. Often the industrial expansion led also to the migration to new territories of strange (mainly Russian) populations. The ethnodemographic structure of the republics changed, with these processes being ahead as compared with the achievement by the native peoples of a higher level of development. The ineffectiveness of such policy, caused, in the first place, by the dependent nature of the national-political formations, resulted in the considerable economic gap between the majority of Russia's autonomies and the purely Russian territories and regions.

3. The national-cultural policy was dual. On the one hand, a number of smaller peoples were given national written language, schools, opportunities to develop national culture in a professional form. On the other hand, since the late 1930s, the functioning of national languages and national culture institutions has been steadily curtailed. The lack of the notion of extraterritorial cultural autonomy led to the russification of dispersed groups of many peoples, and the same processes developed also in the autonomies. But on the whole, despite all the extremes, it was during the time of the Soviet Union (1922–1991) that many peoples received the opportunity to develop their ethnic culture in professional forms, to get acquainted, through the Russian language, with the achievements of the world civilization.

4. A sharply negative assessment is merited by the religious policy of the state, which had one form—suppression of all kinds of religions. In the 1940s, after the resumption of the functioning of the Moscow Patriarchy, the state left off the exclusively repressive policy and gave the preference to a thorough control and regulation of the religious life. At present it engendered back response—merger of national and religious values, unification of citizens according to confessions. This situation cannot be considered as normal. It is characteristic rather of medieval than modern society. The only possible policy in the field of religion may be the separation of religion from the state and nonintervention of the latter into the religious life.

5. As in the Tsarist time, the principle of indirect administration—through state and party bodies of the autonomies—gained a wide currency. In Soviet Russia, as in the USSR as a whole, it reached perfection (in national republics and autonomies, the post of the second secretary of the Communist party was reserved for a Russian).

6. Colonization policy was continued on a great scale, population migration was encouraged (often it had forced forms like camps and depor-

tation of peoples), policy of "panmixture" was pursued with the aim to create the "new historical community—the Soviet people."

The results of the national policy as well as objective processes going on in the country will be discussed in the subsequent chapters.

Drastic changes of the national-political structure of the Russian Federation have taken place since the dissolution of the USSR and the signing in March 1992, of a number of treaties: "On Delimitation of Competences and Powers between the Federal State Authorities of the Russian Federation and the Authorities of Sovereign Republics as Parts of the Russian Federation"; "On Delimitation of Competences and Powers between the Federal State Authorities of the Russian Federation and the Authorities of the Territories, Regions, Cities of Moscow and St. Petersburg as of the Russian Federation"; "On Delimitation of Competences and Attributions between the Federal Bodies of State Power of the Russian Federation and the Power Bodies of Autonomous Region, Autonomous Districts as Parts of the Russian Federation." These three documents make up the Federative Treaty.

According to that treaty, three types of territorial entities: national republics with the status of sovereign states (former autonomous republics plus some former autonomous regions—Adygheia, Mountain Altai, Karachai-Cherkessia, Khakassia); regions and territories (plus the cities of Moscow and St. Petersburg); and the Jewish Autonomous Region and autonomous districts are subjects of Federation. The last two types of subjects of Federation do not have the state status. In other words, this federal structure of Russia returned close to the model fixed in the 1918 Constitution.

The advance of autonomous republics to sovereignty began in 1990–1991, when the process of signing the Union Treaty within the framework of the USSR was under way. The majority of Russia's autonomies adopted declarations on their sovereignty. But the existing structure of the hierarchic subordination of peoples (national-political entities) did not allow to implement at that time the urge of autonomous republics for independence (in the form envisaged by the treaty relations). Only the disintegration of the USSR in December 1991 opened the way to Russia's federalization.

At the same time, the signing of the Federative Treaty has not solved for good the problem of Russia's national-state structure. It does not even matter that two former autonomies (Tataria and Chechen-Ingushetia) were not parties to the Treaty: there are grounds to believe that they, too, will join it, on certain conditions. Also, the volume of powers retained by the federal bodies or allotted to power and administration bodies of the republics does not matter. In the final account, powers may be redistributed in some other way. The major condition of stability of Russia's federative structure is the existence of smoothly working mechanisms of its functioning and improvement. At present, such mechanisms do not exist in our country.

This is vividly illustrated by the conflict that arose in August 1992 between the federal power bodies and three republics (Tataria, Bashkiria, and Yakutia) on the collection of federal tax. Briefly, the cause of the conflict was the opinion of federal authorities that they should directly, omitting the power bodies of the republics, collect and distribute the federal tax, while the republics believed that to be their prerogative.

Finally, the conflict was resolved by means of talks and mutual concessions, but the mechanism of solving controversies without conflict still does not exist.

In a civilized society, the right to interpret law and resolve this kind of conflict belongs to the sole state instance—the Court. In addition, the judicial precedents show to what extent the existing laws are adequate to the social requirements and, consequently, stimulate the formulation of new laws. But in the discussed and many other similar situations, the Constitutional Court was not addressed and took no part in the settlement of the conflict. In other words, the only possible mechanism of normal functioning of the Federation was not put into action. One conclusion may be made in this case: without a profound and comprehensive judicial reform making courts an equal "third power," the threat of conflictual development of events and, in the final account, of the disintegration of the Russian Federation grows considerably.

The above applies also to the territorial problem: both to the claims of republics to the same territory (conflict between the Ingushetia and North-Ossetia regarding the Suburb district) and to the processes of disintegration of some "double" national republics. These problems may be solved only in court, of course, under the condition that all sides (including the federal authority) would participate in the search for a mutually acceptable compromise.

The search of mechanisms of functioning of the Federation, the working out of the necessary tradition, are, in our opinion, a basis for its firmness and indestructibility. At the same time, it should be pointed out that an important role is played by such changeable factors as the success or failure of the economic reform and the reaction of the central authorities to various national-political precedents. The successful implementation of the economic reform, and here one may agree with the prominent economist G. Yavlinsky, demands the inclusion in that process, as an independent reforming force, of the subjects of Russian Federation: "It is vitally important," writes Yavlinsky, "to seek a new integration as the basis and instrument of economic transformations."[27] In this case the advantages of integration and a united economic, political, and legal space will exceed the stimuli pushing the republics and regions toward separatism, autarchy, and secession from Russia.

The equality of all subjects of federation, territories, regions, and autonomous districts included (which does not preclude in individual cases the transfer to the federal authorities of more important functions as compared to the other subjects of the federation) may be a major condition for the preservation and development of federative relations.

This very principle is incorporated in the Constitution of the Russian Federation adopted on December 12, 1993 by a general vote. (About dramatic events preceding the referendum see Chapter 5.) Paragraph 1, Article 5 of the Constitution states, that all constituent parts of the Russian Federation, i.e., republics, territories, regions, autonomous regions, and districts, etc., are equal members of the Federation. A special mention of their equality in relations with the Federative state powers can be also found in Paragraph 4 of the same article.

The only difference between the republics (or states) and other members seems to be the following: Now the former have constitutions of their own as well as the legislation, while the latter have the Charter and the legislation. Nowhere in the Constitution are these republics-states defined as sovereign and there is no mention of their right to secession. On the contrary, it is clearly stated (Paragraph 3, Article 5) that the federative composition of the Russian Federation is based on its state integrity; on the unitary system of state power with the delimitation of powers between the state authorities of the Russian Federation and the state authorities of its members; that it is also based on the equality and self-determination of the peoples in the Federation. In fact, "in" here means within the Russian Federation. Thus, there is no provision for self-determination up to secession.

The new situation is not devoid of paradoxes. Since the status of a federative republic is defined by the Constitution of the Russian Federation and by its own Constitution, there is a vivid contradiction. The constitutions of many republics-members of the Federation define them as sovereign while this status is denied to them by the Constitution of the Federation.

It is also not yet clear whether all members of the Federation will be ready to accept the supremacy of the federal Constitution. The draft of the Constitution was not supported by the voters in almost half of all republics and autonomies. The referendum in Tataria was brought to naught by the small percentage of voters. This result was mainly attributed to the negative stand of the local authorities. The referendum in the Chechen Republic did not take place at all, as its leaders consider their republic independent from Russia.

It is significant that the republics protested mainly against the equality of all subjects of federation, believing that, in that case, their voices would not be heard in the federal representative bodies. This attitude of the republics was affected also by the previous evolution of Russia's federative structure (from territorial national to purely national) mentioned above. But it should be expected that republics, on the example of concrete precedents (the support given by a number of regions to Tataria, Bashkiria, and Yakutia taking issue on the federal tax), will realize that equality of the subjects of federation will enhance their independence. Thus, in our opinion, the only reasonable prospect for the development of federative relations in Russia is the "horizontal" interaction of its constituents formed according to the territorial or national territorial criteria, under the conditions of: (1) concentration at the "center" of mainly coordinating and strategic functions, and (2) broad development of the extraterritorial cultural autonomy.

As we see it, the evolution of the national-political structure of Russia (1918–1993) manifested the following fundamental tendencies:

1. permanent enhancement of the status of the national-political formations (from an autonomy within Russia to a subject of federation);
2. splitting of some national-political formations into mono-national units (creation of national states);
3. interest of the lands (regions) with Russian population in the federalization of Russia.[28]

These tendencies should be taken into consideration while improving the federative relations in Russia.

In conclusion, we make two remarks concerning the terms. During the Soviet period all national or ethnic territorial entities within the Russian Federation were called "autonomies," while at present they should be called "republics and autonomies." According to the new Constitution, the subjects of the Federation, the former "autonomous republics," have gotten rid of the definition "autonomous." The latter has been retained only by the Jewish Autonomous Region and by the autonomous districts.

Recently, the Russian mass media have begun to use new names for the republics instead of their traditional Russian ones—in fact, a transliteration of their national names. This trend has spread to official documents. So, Tataria has become Tatarstan; Bashkiria, Bashkortostan; Yakutia-Saha; Kalmykia–Khalmg-Tangch. We agree with the majority of linguists who believe that this current has nothing to do with respect for national sentiments of the minorities but rather demonstrates an absolute linguistic ignorance of its inspirers. Disregarding the rules of their own language, they are trying to introduce names that are alien to the Russian, grating on the ears. We do not call Germany Deutschland in respect for the Germans.

Having this in mind, we can't escape the use of the new official Constitutional names of the subjects of the Federation in this book, but out of official context we would adhere to their traditional names.

NOTES

1. See V. Stelmakh, *Sibirskoye oblastnichestvo. Iz istorii dvizhenii za regionalnuyu avtonomiyu v tsarskoi Rossii* (Siberian regionalism. From the history of the regional autonomy movements in Tsarist Russia) (Stolitza, 1992), p. 32.

2. K. Kautsky, *Natsionalizm i internatsionalizm* (Nationalism and internationalism) (Petrograd: Zhizn i znanie, 1918), p. 82.

3. The Programme of the Russian Social-Democratic Workers' Party, adopted at the 2nd Party Congress, 17–30 July through 10–23 August 1903, *Kommunisticheskaya partia Sovetskogo Soyuza v rezoliutsiyakh i resheniyakh s'ezdov, konferentsii i plenumov Ts.K.* (Communist Party of the Soviet Union in the resolutions and decisions of congresses, conferences and CC plenums), vol. 1 (Moscow: Politizdat, 1983), p. 62.

4. Poroninskoye soveshchanie Ts.K. RSDRP s partiinymi rabotnikami. Poronin. 23 sentyabrya—1 oktyabrya (6–14 oktyabrya) 1913 g. Rezoliutsia "Po natsionalnomu voprosu" (CC RSDRP Poronin meeting with party functionaries. Poronin. September 23–October 1 (6–14 October) 1913. Resolution "On the National Question," p. 446.

5. Ibid., p. 447.

6. Ibid., pp. 503–504.

7. Ibid., pp. 567–568.

8. Ibid., pp. 601–602.

9. M. Sultan-Galiev, "Tatary i Oktiabrskaya revoliutsia," *Zhizn natsionalnostei* (Tatars and the October Revolution, *Life of nationalities*) vol. 122, no. 24 (1921), pp. 37–38.

10. See: K.S. Kukushkin, and O.I. Chistyakov, *Ocherk istorii Sovetskoi Konstitutsii* (Essay on the history of the Soviet constitution) (Moscow: Politizdat, 1987), pp. 240–243.

11. Ibid., p. 251.

12. Ibid., p. 242.

13. Vosmoi s'ezd RKP(b). 18–23 March 1919. Programma Rossiiskoi Kommunisticheskoi partii (bolshevikov), KPSS v rezoliutsiyakh . . . (The eighth RCP Congress. 18–23 March 1919. Programme of the Russian Communist Party [bolsheviks], CPSU in Resolutions . . .), Vol. 2 (Moscow, 1983), p. 79.

14. Ibid., p. 105.

15. Ibid., p. 137.

16. The new Party Rules adopted by the 8th All-Russian Conference of the RCP(b) (2–4 December 1919) read: "Party organizations serving the territories of the federative parts of the RSFSR are made equal in all respects to the regional organizations of the party, that is, are fully submitted to the CC of the RCP(b). See: Ibid., p. 204.

17. A.G. Kushnir, *Genezis politiko-administrativnogo ustroistva Sovetskoi Rossii* (Genesis of the politico-administrative structure of Soviet Russia) (Moscow: Institut Istozii SSSR, 1991), p. 35.

18. Ibid., p. 28.

19. See: V.I. Lenin, *K voprosu o natsionalnostiakh ili ob "avtonomizatsii"* ("On the question of nationalities or on the "autonomization"), *Complete Works*, vol. 45 (in Russian) (Moscow: Politizdat, 1977).

20. A.G. Kushnir, "Genezis," p. 23.

21. "Measures to have in all Soviet offices sufficient number of employees knowing Ukrainian and that in future all employees can speak Ukrainian should be undertaken immediately." See: The Eighth All-Russian Conference of the RCP(b), 2–4 December 1919. Rezoliutsiya "O sovetskoi vlasti na Ukraine" (Resolution "On

the Soviet Power in the Ukraine"), CPSU in Resolutions, v. 2, (Moscow: Politizdat, 1983), p. 199.

22. A.V. Sagadeev, *Mirsait Sultan-Galiev i ideologia natsionalno-osvoboditel'-nogo dvizhenia* (Mirsait Sultan-Galiev and the ideology of the national-liberation movement) (Moscow: INION AN SSSR, 1990), p. 76.

23. See: K.S. Kukushkin, and O.I. Chisktyakov, *Ocherk istori*, pp. 266–268.

24. Ibid., p. 268.

25. The Big Soviet Encyclopedia reflecting the official point of view, treated that question in the following way: "Soviet autonomy exists in two forms—political and administrative. Political autonomy embodied in the national autonomous state (autonomous republic) is characterized by a greater volume of rights, existence of own constitution, supreme bodies of state power, legislation, government, supreme judiciary instances, granting the citizenship of the republic. Administrative autonomy . . . applies only to the administration sphere." (Big Soviet Encyclopedia, Moscow, 1970, v. 1, p. 162).

26. See: V.Z. Drobizhev, I.D. Kovalchenko, and A.V. Muraviev, *Istoricheskaya geografiya SSSR* (Historical geography of the USSR) (Moscow: Vysshaia Shkola, 1973), p. 274.

27. See: G. Yavlinsky, "Nizhni Novgorod Prologue," *Moscow News,* no. 37, 1992, p. 11.

28. Mention should be made of the revival in 1990–1993 of autonomist tendencies in Siberia and the Far East.

3

Main Classifications of Russia's Nationalities

In this work we submit four classifications which, on the whole, cover the current ethnocultural and ethnopolitical situation in Russia and help us to tentatively foresee how that situation may develop.

Our basic criterion is language: ethnolinguistic classification. Language reflects kinship ties between different peoples, their common ethnogenetic roots. In our day, common origin is exerting a serious influence on the course of political events. Take, for instance, the upsurge of the ethnocultural and national-political movement of the Finno-Ugric peoples (the creation of a Fund for the Development of the Culture of the Finno-Ugric Peoples, or their congresses and political parties calling for national amalgamation), or the Pan-Turkic political trend. But ethnogenetic differences in many ways explain the efforts of certain "twin" republics inside Russia like Karachai-Cherkessia or Kabarda-Balkaria to split into their constituent parts.

Classification on the basis of religion highlights the "civilizing unity" of peoples, since the world religions have accumulated values common to their believers. For that reason, we can to some extent predict how the followers of a particular creed are likely to behave in a given situation. Furthermore, in the present sociopolitical crisis convulsing all the states of the former USSR, religion emerges as a key political factor.

Our classification of sociopolitical types appraises the specific sociopolitical and cultural aspirations of the different ethnic groups, as well as the potential resources available for their satisfaction. Our final classification concerns the degree to which the diverse nationalities of Russia have moved along the path of modernization—in other words, the road to contemporary society. Their degree of modernization determines what forms inter-ethnic conflicts actually take.

LINGUISTIC CLASSIFICATION

Three large language families are represented in Russia: the Indo-European, Uralic, and Altaic families. Some of its peoples also speak tongues belonging to smaller linguistic divisions such as the Caucasian or Eskimo-Aleutian or Paleo-Asiatic families. As for the Yenisei Kets, they do not come under any known linguistic division.

The Russian, Ukrainian, and Byelorussian languages belong to the Eastern Slavic branch of the Slavonic group of Indo-European languages; Polish to its Western branch.

The Germans represent the Germanic group of Indo-European languages.

The Jews who now live mainly in cities throughout Russia or in the Jewish Autonomous Region formerly spoke Yiddish, a German dialect. Today they speak mostly Russian or the language of the peoples among whom they reside.

The Gypsies' language belongs to the Indian group of the Indo-European family.

The Iranian group of the Indo-European family is represented in Russia by the Ossetians who inhabit North Ossetia as well as some vicinities in Kabarda-Balkaria, Chechenia, Ingushetia, and the Stavropol Territory, but their language, though Iranian in origin, has undergone marked changes under the impact of the other tongues spoken by the Caucasian peoples. For that reason it is considered a language with "double roots."[1] The Tats and Kurds also speak Iranian tongues. Actually, there are very few Kurds in Russia, but there are Iranian-speaking "Tat-Judaists" (or, as they are commonly called, "Mountain Jews") settled in the North Caucasus and Daghestan.

The Armenian language has a place all its own, and actually represents a separate and unique branch of that great Indo-European language family. Its written alphabet is one of the oldest in the world; it was invented by St. Mesrop at the end of the 4th or turn of the 5th century B.C.

The Uralic family includes the Finno-Ugric and Samoyed languages. The peoples speaking these languages are found chiefly in the northern half of the European part of Russia, including the Urals and Western Siberia.

Our north European peoples speak languages belonging to the Finnish branch of the Uralic family. The Komi-Zyrian and Komi-Perm tongues are very similar, and, along with Udmurtan, comprise the Perm subgroup of this Finnish branch.

The languages of the Volga Finns (the Mordovians and the Mari) form a separate subgroup, and each in turn boasts two literary tongues. In the case of the Mordovians, theirs were derived from two basic dialects considered by some scholars to have been distinct though related: Erzyan and Mokshan. The Erzya and Moksha were the two large tribes forming the Mordovian ethnos, which also embraces a distinct group—the Karatai who now inhabit parts of Tataria and have adopted the Tatar language. The Mari likewise boast two literary tongues: "Mountain Mari" and "East Meadow Mari" based on their two separate dialects.

Karelian, Veps, and Izhoran, like Estonian and Finnish, comprise the Baltic-Finnish group, which is associated with the language of the Lopars or Saami. The latter, to be sure, is sometimes classed as a distinct subgroup revealing a marked Samoyed substratum.

Two small northern forest peoples, the Khanty and Mansi, also known in Russia as Ob Ugrians, speak Ugric tongues, which is related to the Hungarian language.

The languages of the Nenets, Yenets, Nganasans, and Selkups, also referred to as the Northern Samoyeds, belong to the Samoyed Uralic group.

The big Altaic family as a rule includes the Turkic, Mongolian, and Tungus-Manchurian languages.

The number of Turkic languages spoken in Russian is quite large. We hear them among the Volga and Urals peoples: Tatar, Bashkir, and Chuvash. The first two are rather closely related; both belong to the Kipchak branch of Turkic languages. Chuvash stands by itself in this Volga group, revealing marked differences from all the other tongues of the Turkic tree; it represents the Bulgar branch. The Tatar language widely spoken today took form as far back as the 15th and 16th centuries, during the reign of the Kazan Khanate. It remains the medium of communication of all the numerous and widely scattered Tatar people. As for their literary tongue, that traces its origin to the second half of the 19th century.

In the North Caucasus, large sections of the population also speak Turkic tongues. The speech of the Kumyks of the Daghestan plateau also pertains to the Kipchak branch, as does that of their close relatives, the Balkars and Karachaians. Other Turkic-speaking peoples include the Nogais, dispersed about the steppelands of North Daghestan, the Stavropol Territory, and elsewhere; and also a small group of Turkmenians who migrated from Central Asia to the North Caucasus in comparatively recent times and settled largely in the Stavropol Territory. Some Azerbaijanians living in Daghestan speak a tongue related to the Oghuz branch of the Turkic family.

The languages of the Turkic-speaking peoples of Siberia form a separate group. Foremost among them are those who have written languages of their own: the Yakut, Tuvan, Altai, and Khakass peoples. Then come those without written tongues: the Shorians and Chulyms and, related to them, the small Altai peoples called Karagases, or Tophalars, Kamasins, as well as the northern Dolgans who reflect a strong Yakut strain. Then there are the varied Siberian Tatar communities of Tobolsk, Tara, Baraba, Tomsk, and so on, likewise Turkic in origin.

In Russia there are eight small Northern and Far Eastern peoples who speak Tungus-Manchurian tongues: Evenki, Eveni, Nani, Negidas, Ulchi, Orochi, Oroki, and Udeghei. Only the first three have written languages, devised for them in the Soviet period.

The languages spoken by the Kalmyks and Buryats belong to the Mongolian branch of the Altai family.

The Caucasian languages are represented in Russia by the Northwestern, or Abkhazian-Adygei, and Northeastern, or Nakh-Daghestan groups. To the first belong the Abkhazians, some of whom dwell in the Krasnodar Territory, and also their linguistic relatives, the Abazinians of Karachai-Cherkesia, and parts of the Stavropol Territory. The Kabardinian, Cherkes, and Adyghei peoples all speak practically the same version of Adygheian. The Adygheis themselves reside mostly in the Adyghei Republic proper or nearby Krasnodar Territory. Aside from Kabarda-Balkaria and Karachai-Cherkessia, there are also Kabardinian and Cherkessian communities in the North Ossetian town of Mozdok or scattered about the Stavropol countryside.

Chechen and Ingush belong to what is known as the Nakh group. These two languages have preserved common roots to such an extent that they are mutually intelligible to their speakers. At the same time there are important enough differences between them to warrant their being considered independent tongues, not simply dialects. The Chechens inhabit mostly the eastern and central parts of what used to be the Chechen-Ingush Republic and also adjacent Daghestan areas. Ingush is spoken largely in the western part of the republic and somewhat in North Ossetia (the environs of Vladikavkaz).

The Daghestan group of languages common to the many nationalities abounding in the mountainous part of this republic are usually divided into two large subgroups: Avar-Ando-Tsez (or Avar-Ando-Didoyan) and Lezghin. Neither of the two includes Lak and Darghinian. As for the Ando-Tsezsk peoples (Andians, Botlikhs, Didoyans, etc.), Avaran actually serves as their second tongue. Lezghins and Tabasarans comprise six-sevenths of those who discourse in the tongues of the Lezghin subgroup. Related to the latter are still smaller nationalities (Aguls, Rutuls, Tsakhurs, and others). The Kubachin and Kaitak people speak tongues resembling Darghinian. Five of Daghestan's largest languages: Avaran, Lezghin, Darghinian, Lak, and Tabasaran first acquired written Russian alphabets only in Soviet times.

Many peoples not related to the language families heretofore mentioned have been classified, in accordance with an accepted scientific tradition, as Paleoasiatic peoples, thus implying common descent from the aboriginal inhabitants of Siberia. Thus, Chukchi, Koryaks, Itelmens, Yukaghirs, Eskimos, Aleutians, and often the Nivkhi and Kets were originally called Paleoasiatic peoples. Their designation as one group was based on the negative principles that they could not be assigned to any other big language family or group. In actual fact, no such single "Paleoasiatic Ethno-Language Family" ever existed to our knowledge.[2] Further research has revealed genetic relationships enabling us to distinguish the Chukot-Kamchatka and the Eskimo-Aleutian language groups. The first embraces the Chukchi, Koryak, and Itelmen (Kamchadal) tongues all native to Chukotia and Kamchatka; the second, the languages spoken by the Asian Eskimos who inhabit Chukotia and Wrangel Island and also by the Aleutians of the Commander Islands. The languages of the Yukaghirs and their close kin the Chuvans, the Nivkhs (formerly known as Gilyaks) of the lower Amur and Sakhalin, and also the Yenisei Kets, form an isolated group. The Ket speech, used by more or less one thousand persons in recent decades, is marked by such peculiarities that it is often viewed as belonging in a class by itself.[3]

RELIGIOUS CLASSIFICATION

Most religious Russians, and with them many Ukrainians and Byelorussians residing in Russia, belong to the Russian Orthodox (Pravoslavni) Church which prevailed for many centuries as the official state religion of the Russian Empire.

In some parts of Russia (Altai, the Trans-Baikal, etc.) there are congregations that broke away from the Orthodox Church in the 17th century, and called themselves *Staro-Obriadtsy* or "Old Believers."

Among the diverse Protestant denominations in this country, the most numerous are the Baptist-Evangelical, Pentecostal, and Seventh-Day Adventist congregations. Some Russians, Byelorussians, and Ukrainians, largely in the cities, as well as Poles and Lithuanians resident in Russia, adhere to the Catholic faith.

Russia's German population is of either Lutheran, Catholic, or Mennonite persuasion. The Mennonites represent a distinct ethnoconfessional group.

The traditional Jewish religion is Judaism, but there are many Jews here who have converted to Orthodoxy or other Christian faiths. In Daghestan and some towns in the North Caucasus live the Tats, followers of Judaism.

The Volga-Kama peoples are devotees of either Christianity or Islam. Islamism appeared in the Volga area long ago and by the 10th century it emerged as the official state religion of the Volga Bulgars. The Tatars and Bashkirs have always been Moslems and remain so to this day. The Mari, Mordovians, Chuvash, and Udmurts were converted to Christianity following the annexation of the Volga area by Russia in the 16th century. Nevertheless, pre-Christian beliefs and practices still survive among them and are particularly evident in their agrarian and ancestor cults, intermingling with their Christian tenets and persisting as throwbacks in their spiritual life. Much the same is true of the Finnish-language groups inhabiting the northern part of European Russia: the Karelian, Veps, Izhora, Komi, Komi-Permyak, and Lopar peoples. Pre-Christian religious rites have been widespread among the Lopar (Saami) reindeer breeders with their worship of a "Reindeer Mistress" and other supernatural patrons of their sundry occupational activities, their belief in Sacred Stones, and their Shamanistic hangovers.

Certain Tatar groups, such as the Kriashens and Nagaibaks, were forcibly converted to the Russian Orthodox Church, as were various native groups in Siberia and the Far North—but among the latter, Christianity never went far beneath the surface. Shamanism, hunting, and other nature cults persisted and continue to play the same role in their lives to this day. Most of the republics of the North Caucasus, Daghestan, the Tatar and Bashkir republics are predominantly Islamic. The Russian Orthodox Church has followers among the North Ossetians.

The traditional religion of the Buryats and Kalmyks has always been Lamaism, a variation of Buddhism. The western Buryats of the cis-Baikal area practiced Shamanism until the Russians arrived with their missionaries, who succeeded in converting some of them to Christianity. Others resisted this pressure, however, and chose Lamaism. But echoes of Shamanism still persist here and there among the western Buryats. From the 17th century on, Lamaism began to spread among the Sayany-Altai peoples, as in Tuva. Some of the Khakass and Altaians became Christians. It was during this process of conversion to the new and, to them, alien world religions that there sprang up a number of new religions, one of which worships the god Burkhan and so is called Burkhanism.

In olden times the West Siberian Tatars, like the native people around them, also practiced Shamanism. But that period ended when they were converted to Islam in the 16th century.

Shamanism, the belief in man's ability to communicate with the spirits above and utilize their supernatural powers to effect cures and achieve other practical results, was a most widespread ritualistic practice among the Northern and Siberian peoples. It assumed a variety of forms in one or another ethnic group. In the most archaic societies and cultures, as among the Itelmens, all the aged, and especially the old women, usually performed as Shamans. Survivals of the same traditions prevailed among the Chukchi and a number of other groups where all senior heads of families were expected to participate in Shamanistic rites; the Yukaghirs, Khanty, Mansi, and Nganasans regarded their Shamans as professionals whose duty was to serve the clan cult in which all adults took part ("Clan Shamanism"). The highest form of professional Shamanism, in which the Shaman is invested with a special status in the clan, is remunerated for his services and his role made hereditary, was recorded not long ago among many of Siberia's Yakuts, Evenks, Nenets, and Selkups as well as the Tungus-speaking peoples of the Amur. Shamanism and other related religious beliefs and practices, whether occupational, ancestral, familial, or clan cults, existed side-by-side among the peoples of Siberia and the North. By the end of the 19th century most of the native Siberian population had been formally converted to Christianity, but their archaic beliefs never disappeared and continued to exert a marked influence on their conduct and outlook on life.

PRINCIPAL SOCIOPOLITICAL NATIONALITY (MINORITY) TYPES IN RUSSIA

The minorities of the Russian Federation include not only non-Russian ethnic groups, most of which have their own republics or autonomies, but also the Russians who have made their homes within these national entities.

A distinction must also be drawn between the status of the minorities who have their own republics or autonomous territories, and those without such. Then there is the difference between national statehoods outside Russia but within the confines of the former USSR, and those beyond its borders.

We must also recognize the fact that although political and juridical status is important, it is not the only criterion in classifying the minorities. Societies which adhere to highly traditional patterns of life constitute a distinct category. And then there are some minorities which do not fit into any of the classified types, thanks to their unique historical backgrounds and destinies.

Therefore, the types of minorities listed in the following are based not only upon logical but also upon empirical criteria.

RUSSIANS (INCLUDING RESIDENTS IN THE NATIONAL REPUBLICS AND AUTONOMIES)

According to the 1989 census followed throughout here, there were 119.9 million Russians (81.5 percent of the total population) living in the Russian Federation, which may accordingly be termed a mono-national country. Of the republics which constituted the erstwhile USSR, only Armenia and Lithuania could boast of a higher percentage of the basic nationality.

Nevertheless, even within the territory of the Russian Federation, Russians find themselves in the position of a national minority within different republics and autonomies. The term "national minority" is used here in its political and juridical context, seeing that in many of these entities the proportion of Russians is more than half the total population.[4] Then there are also republics and autonomies in which Russians form less than half the total population while at the same time constituting the largest national group there numerically.

The status of the Russian residents in the republics and autonomies is poorly defined at the present time. It depends upon the balance achieved between two contradictory tendencies: the consolidation of Russia's sovereignty as the sole authority on the one hand, and the trend among its national constituents toward greater sovereignty for themselves, on the other hand. Obvious examples of that confrontation are apparent in the North Caucasus, particularly in Chechenia, but also in Tataria, Bashkiria, Tuva, and Yakutia. It is highly probable that the near future will see the problem of protecting the rights of the Russians as a national minority come acutely to the fore in these former autonomous republics.

MAIN PEOPLES OF THE NATIONAL REPUBLICS AND AUTONOMIES

The distinguishing feature of these peoples (minorities within the Federation as a whole) is that they are invested with varying degrees of national statehood (circumscribed by definite limits).

Concentrated in the republics or autonomies there exists a compact nucleus (usually more than one-half of the particular people or peoples who gave it its name). But there are some exceptions, such as the Nogai groups dispersed about the republics and territories of the North Caucasus (Daghestan, Stavropol, Karachai-Cherkessia, Chechen, and Ingush republics); the Mordovians, resident largely in Russia and interspersed with its population; the Tatars, many of whom live in the Bashkiria and other republics, the Volga area and elsewhere in Russia; and the Jews. Although in most of the republics and autonomies the indigenous population does not account for even half the total, they may rightly be recognized as national-state or national-territorial formations of corresponding peoples.

A widespread striving for ethnic rebirth has gripped the main peoples of Russia's republics. Politically, this drive was expressed in the fact that in 1990 the overwhelming majority of them declared their sovereignty and erased the word "autonomous" from their official names. It remains, however, that this drive of the republics for sovereignty has come up against a number of objective obstacles. These are:

1. Most of the peoples in this category have no tradition of national statehood. There are exceptions: the Tatars, whose Kazan Khanate was subjugated by Ivan the Terrible in 1552; or the Tuvans, whose independent People's Republic of Tannu-Tuva, proclaimed in June 1918 (before it had been the Uryankhai Territory under Russia's protectorate), was annexed by the USSR in 1944 and given the name of Tuvan Autonomous Soviet Socialist Republic. As for the Karelians,

their position is unique in that they have enjoyed a higher status throughout the Soviet period thanks to the existence of the Karelian-Finnish S.S.R.

2. The bulk of these peoples do not constitute a majority in their own republics.[5]

3. Some nationalities (the Tatar, Nogai, Mordovian, and to a lesser extent the Udmurt, Mari, Karelian, Chuvash, Bashkir, and Komi-Permyak peoples) have spread out beyond the confines of their own national administrative boundaries.

4. Attainment of sovereignty has been obstructed by such factors as the lack of integrated economic structures within the republics, their objective geopolitical dependence on the Russian Federation, and the arbitrary boundaries set for them under Soviet rule.

Mention must also be made of certain specific problems facing the inhabitants of the national republics.

1. Some of Russia's republics are characterized by unusual ethnic combinations. The Chechen-Ingush Republic was composed of two culturally related groups, the Chechens and Ingush, and it still did not survive as a single republic. The Kabardians and Balkars who are the principal inhabitants of the republic that bears both their names speak tongues belonging to different linguistic families. A similar situation prevails in Karachai-Cherkessia. Entirely unique is that which is encountered in Daghestan, inhabited by one kinship group of ethnic relatives (Avars, Lezghins, Darghinians, Laks, etc.) and at the same time by two peoples—the Kumyks and Nogaian—who belong to a quite different culture. That is why we are witnessing divisive processes today in the like national-state formations. In the case of Chechen-Ingushetia, the actual completion of this divisive process has taken place.

The same tendency is reflected in the efforts of certain other peoples living within common borders to make known their territorial claims. A plan has been suggested to partition Karachai-Cherkessia into five ethnic enclaves: Karachaian, Cherkes, Russian, Abazinian, and Nogain.

In principle these processes, provided they assume democratic forms, as by means of plebiscites, need not be regarded as negative. But in Daghestan, one of the most ethnically diversified regions of the world, it is difficult to foresee what practical forms that kind of ethnopolitical division may take. There, as in other territories with mixed populations, it would be better for an extraterritorial principle to be followed in furthering cultural autonomy and for them to develop a system that would represent different communities and smaller, self-governing provinces.

At the same time, integrational tendencies persist in the national-state formations of the North Caucasus and the idea is heard of restoring it to what it was like in the 1920s Mountainous Republic, uniting most of its peoples. Such integration could potentially be combined with the development of a national autonomy of each people. At the present stage what is being suggested is not the creation of one state in the North Caucasus, but the political coordination of its peoples or, to be more precise, of their leaders.

2. The dissimilarity between the ethnic geography of the country and its ethnopolitical structure is reflected in the fact that several peoples have attained more than one autonomous status, sometimes in different republics. Such is the position of the Ossetians living in the North Ossetian Republic, which enters into the composition of the Russian Federation, and also in the South Ossetian Autonomous Region, which is part of Georgia; or of the Buryats, who have a Buryat Republic plus the Ust-Orda and the Aginsk Buryat Autonomous Districts, all three formations within the Russian Federation. The striving of such peoples for unification is perfectly understandable.

Although the Buryat formations are separate from one another, their political unification, if not just coordination, presents no fundamental problem, since they are all three situated within Russia. Whereas the Ossetian formations adjoin each other closely via a Caucasian mountain ridge, the border that separates them happens to be the border between two sovereign states: the Russian Federation on one side and the Republic of Georgia on the other. That's why obstacles stand in the way of cultural, economic, and political ties between these two Ossetian states, now greatly aggravated by the inter-ethnic conflict in South Ossetia and the Ossetian-Ingush conflict in the North. A somewhat similar problem confronts the Lezghins, most of whom reside in neighboring Azerbaijan areas not invested with either territorial or cultural autonomy.

Thus, on analysis, we find that the situation which has developed in the diverse Russia's republics and autonomies differs greatly from case to case. No one universal approach is possible.

THE SMALL PEOPLES OF THE NORTH

Of all the ethnic minorities, the peoples whose traditional way of life is, by the accepted international terminology, known as "tribal" have a place all their own. Designated in Russia as "the small peoples of the North," they number: Nenets (35,000), Evenks (30,000), Khanty (25,000), Evens (17,000), Chukchi (15,000), Nanis (12,000), Koryaks (9,200), Mansi (8,500), Dolgans (6,900), Nivkhs (4,700), Selkups (3,600), Ulchi (3,200), Itelmens (2,500), Udegheis (2,000), Saami (1,900), Eskimos (1,700), Chuvans (1,500), Nganasans (1,300), Yukaghirs (1,100), Kets (1,100), Orochi (900), Tophalars (700), Aleutians (700), Negidals (600), Yenets (200), and Oroks (200). Aside from their distinctive social and cultural features, their main characteristic is that they have retained their traditional mode of survival by means of such occupations as hunting (on land and sea), fishing, reindeer breeding, and plant gathering. These are not class societies; the stage of development they have reached is reflected in such aspects of their social and cultural life as the existence of tribal clans, fraternal associations, and aboriginal religions like Shamanism.

These peoples pose a serious problem for many civilized states. There are very few examples of their having been absorbed as equals in the cultural, economic, and political life of the countries where they live. National legislation and international law recognize the special status of these "tribes"; the maintenance of said status entails considerable government support and expense.

In Russia, only some of the small peoples of the North were granted special status, realized by creating autonomous districts for the Dolgans, Koryaks, Chukchi, Khanty, Mansi, Nenets, and Evenks. It follows that most of the small peoples of the North and Far East lack their own national territories.

The autonomous districts, even when they accommodate the bulk of a native population, cannot ensure the preservation and development of the traditional economy and culture of these small peoples. That is chiefly because the name "autonomous district" does not imply that it is a zone protected by the state against the colonizing and economic encroachments of the surrounding (usually Russian) population. Today Russians make up the majority in these territories. Over the years of Soviet rule the peoples who pursued their traditional way of life have as a result undergone noticeable degradation. That should not be attributed to the evil machinations of the authorities; rather, it is due to the fragility of the traditional culture and its deformation at even the slightest contact with industrial civilization.

The present dramatic plight of the peoples of the North has led to extremely short life spans, widespread alcohol addiction and other illnesses, and frequent suicides. These ills are obviously reducing its numbers.

At the same time, there are signs of national resurgence among the small peoples, a trend inspired by their national intelligentsia. The recently established Association of Northern Peoples has made the welfare and rights of these peoples its special concern.

A Convention (No. 169) adopted by the International Labour Organization in 1989 is devoted to the "native" and "tribal" inhabitants of the independent states with an eye above all to the preservation and development of their unique cultures. International Law proclaims the following fundamental rights of the peoples who have retained their native traditions:

1. Maximum possible control over their own economic, social and cultural development.

2. An equal share in the overall life of the state via their own institutions.

3. Recognition of the traditional rights of these peoples to their lands in perpetuity.

4. Economic and cultural self-determination.

5. Encouragement by the state of their traditional occupations and crafts so as to preserve their cultural heritage.

6. Education in their own language as transcribed by their own scholarly authorities.

7. The opportunity to observe their traditional religious rites and beliefs; to preserve, protect, and have access to their own religious centers.

8. First rights to the objects of their material culture, including sites of archaeological digs within their territory, their paintings and other art objects, as well as the technologies involved in creating them.

9. Recognition by the state and respect for their traditions and customs as the basis of their legal rights.

MINORITIES (SMALL PEOPLES) OCCUPYING HEREDITARY SITES NOT GIVEN TERRITORIAL AUTONOMY

In Russia these minorities include, in addition to most of the Northern small peoples mentioned above, 73,700 Nogais and 33,000 Abazinians in Karachai-Cherkesia; 19,400 Tats in Daghestan; 85,700 Shorians in the Altai Territory; 12,100 Veps in the Leningrad Region; 11,300 Mountain Judaists in Daghestan; and 800 Izhorians in the Leningrad Region. They are highly diversified in character. The lack of territorial autonomy and, consequently, of their national and cultural institutions places them all in a most disadvantaged position.

These peoples live compactly as one or several ethnic communities intermingling with the other nationalities around them. Some of them have succeeded in preserving their autochthonous features thanks alone to their comparative geographical isolation, as the Shoria mountain dwellers. On the other hand, the ethnic survival of the Veps and Izhorians of Leningrad Region may be judged to be endangered; they have reached the critical stage of assimilation and are beginning to forget their native tongues; their ethnic self-awareness is dwindling; they are abandoning their original dwelling places and resettling in the cities. In a word, their native culture has lost its inherent quality and is disappearing under the impact of their new surroundings. Perhaps the only way to put a stop to such cultural extermination is to create cultural-territorial autonomies, at least in the form of national areas.

Administrative demarcations which originally intersected the native lands of some of these peoples now became, following the dissolution of the USSR, political frontiers. For example, the Nogais are dispersed today throughout Daghestan to the number of 28,300, thus forming one of its principal constituents; at the same time they total 28,600 in Stavropol Territory, another 13,000 in Karachai-Cherkessia, and still another 6,900 in

Chechenia and in Ingushetia. Tats and Mountain Judaists to the number of 12,000 live in Russia and another 5,500 in Azerbaijan, hence the difficulty of creating ethnic autonomies for these peoples. Waiting to be solved is the problem of creating extraterritorial forms of cultural autonomy overlapping definite administrative and state borders.

DIASPORA IN RUSSIA OF PEOPLES OF FORMER UNION REPUBLICS

This minority category embraces the following, numerically large groups: 4,362,900 Ukrainians; 1,206,200 Byelorussians; 635,900 Kazakhs; 532,400 Armenians; 335,900 Azerbaijanians; 172,700 Moldavians; 130,700 Georgians; 126,900 Uzbeks; 70,400 Lithuanians; 46,800 Latvians; 46,400 Estonians; 41,700 Kirghiz; 39,700 Turkmenians; 38,200 Tajiks, and also 21,300 Crimeans Tatars; 10,100 Gagauz; 7,200 Abkhazians. We might note that in those parts of the Russian Federation that border on the Baltic republics, Byelorussia, the Ukraine, the Trans-Caucasian republics, and Kazakhstan, similar minority groups may prove to be indigenous.

The largest of the above minorities, the Ukrainians and Byelorussians, have much in common in the way they are dispersed. They are concentrated largely along the borders between Russia and their particular republics, or throughout the so-called main belt of the Russian people's settlement, which stretches latitudinally from the center of European Russia along Southern Siberia and the Far East to the Pacific Coast. Most of Russia's Ukrainians and Byelorussians live in the cities, but there are some relatively compact rural settlements.

On the whole, these peoples have become highly assimilated as to language and culture, although many Ukrainians and Byelorussians have retained, if not their own language, certainly a sense of their ethnic identity. With the attainment of political independence by the Ukraine and Byelorussia, we may predict that the national pride of these two peoples will grow.

The Kazakh minority is living mainly along Russia's borders with Kazakhstan. There are 111,500 Kazakhs concentrated in the Orenburg Region; the Omsk Region, 75,000; the Altai Territory, 21,700. Along the lower Volga they number: about 126,500 in the Astrakhan, 41,500 in the Volgograd, and 73,400 in the Saratov regions.

The Armenians, that classical example of urban diaspora, have made their homes in the North Caucasia since olden times: 182,200 in the Krasnodar, 72,500 in the Stavropol Territory, and 62,600 in the Rostov Region. They are also found in the large cities, including Moscow, 44,000 and St. Petersburg, 12,100. Since the 1989 census the size of the Armenia diaspora in Russia has been augmented by the increase of refugees from Azerbaijan.

The Azerbaijanians are dispersed throughout Russia in smaller urban groups with the exception of neighboring Daghestan, where they live to the impressive number of 75,500. Wide dispersion also characterizes other such minorities.

The special political and juridical status of this group of minorities hinges upon the important role it has begun to play in Russia's relations with the other republics of the Commonwealth of Independent States (CIS), as well as the Baltic States. Obviously, protection of the rights of the minorities inside the CIS calls for mutual bilateral and multilateral guarantees backed by the other former Soviet republics. In this connection we might note that the creation of an effective mechanism for the protection of Russia's minorities' formal status is not only an essential element of it becoming a law-based state and its integration with the civilized international community, but also a good means of support for the Russian minorities.

It goes without saying that all the minorities in this category must be allowed to enjoy cultural and national autonomy as concerns the right to use their own language in their press, educational establishments, and cultural centers, and to establish associations, clubs, and fraternal societies. Increasing exercise of these rights might be encouraged by their respective governments. Everywhere that these minorities have formed compact settlements they may be allowed to create their own, even small national precincts.

Guaranteeing the rights of the minorities requires as a preliminary condition that all disputes concerning citizenship that arise in the newly independent states be properly adjudicated. In that connection the advantages of the institution of double citizenship are obvious, promoting as it does family, kinship, ethnic, and cultural ties between Russia's such-and-such minority and the related people or state. The institution of double citizenship is thus an additional guarantee of minority rights. It is to be expected that some members of a minority group may prefer citizenship of "their own" sovereign state (former Union republic) to Russian citizenship; naturally, they too must enjoy all the fruits of the right to cultural autonomy.

DISPERSAL OF PEOPLES FROM RUSSIA'S NATIONAL REPUBLICS

As a result of the migrational process that started centuries ago and then became pronounced in the Soviet period, Russia's many peoples were widely dispersed, spreading beyond the confines of their own territories and forming what are called "minorities of the second order." A particularly large diaspora is characteristic of numerous peoples of the Volga Belt once involved in the Russian colonization of vast expanses of the Urals, Siberia, and the Far East. This state of affairs is also explained by the fact that in the Volga Belt administrative and political frontiers do not coincide with ethnic demarcations—an inevitable disparity considering the interlacing of local peoples' enclaves.

Today, Tatars live in many diverse parts of Russia, forming especially massive groups in Bashkiria (1,120,700 persons), in and around the Tyumen (227,400), the Cheliabinsk (224,600), the Ekaterenburg (183,800), the Ulyanovsk (159,600), the Orenburg (158,600), the Perm (150,500) and the Samara regions (115,300), as well as a population of 110,500 Tatars in the Udmurt Republic. Tatar communities are also found in Moscow (157,400) and St. Petersburg (44,000).

The Bashkirs account for sizeable minority groups in the Chelyabinsk (161,200), the Orenburg (53,400), and the Perm regions (52,300).

The Chuvash have spread beyond their own borders, chiefly around Samara (117,900) and Ulyanovsk (116,500), and also to the republics of Tataria and Bashkiria where they number 134,200 and 118,500, respectively.

A great many Mordovians have settled around Samara (116,500), Penza (86,300), Orenburg (68,900), and Ulyanovsk (61,100).

Mention must also be made of the Mari minority of Bashkiria (105,800), as well as the Karelian settlers of the Tver regions (23,200). The precursors of the present Tver Karelians arrived in the vicinities they now inhabit as early as the 17th century. This category of minorities has on the whole identified itself culturally with the surrounding population (largely Russian) and has not made it a point to disassociate itself from its neighbors. That state of affairs may change in the present upsurge of ethnic awareness, as the former autonomies achieve more sovereign rights.

Until recently, even the large minority groups had only a slim chance of preserving their identities or maintaining cultural ties with their mother republics. It goes without saying that such a state of affairs needed to be changed. It is already changing. And while we stand for the strengthening of cultural ties between the republics and their diaspora, we cannot view with anything but alarm the noticeable trend toward the politicization of their relations. For instance, we regard as legally untenable the demand of Tatar nationalistic movements that all ethnic Tatars living in Russia must be made citizens of the Tatar Republic (Tatarstan), should such a law be passed there.

Protection of the rights of these and many other minorities must be implemented by means of extraterritorial cultural autonomy. Given the approval of the proper regional or republican authorities, autonomous precincts should be established for such minorities.

The most aggravating situation affecting this category of minorities concerns the Tatar population of Bashkiria. The census figures for that republic (21.9% Bashkirs, 28.4% Tatars, and 39.3% Russians) show that there are more Tatars than Bashkirs living there. Until recently, these Tatars did not enjoy any intrinsic rights as an ethnic group and faced the danger of enforced assimilation. The problem of Bashkiria's Tatars is being debated at the present time by the two republics.

MINORITIES WITH NATIONAL STATES OUTSIDE THE FORMER USSR

This minority group includes 842,300 Germans,[6] 536,800 Jews,[7] 107,100 Koreans, 94,600 Poles, 91,700 Greeks,[8] 47,100 Finns, 32,800 Bulgarians, and 9,900 Turks.[9]

Special interest attaches to this category in the light of the role our country has assumed in the international setup for the protection of the rights of the minorities. Many countries throughout the world are expressing a growing interest in the position of their "compatriots" in Russia and the other newly independent countries of the CIS, and have demonstrated their readiness to ensure the necessary bilateral cooperation. Germany has voiced its willingness to help solve the problem of Russia's Germans. The like prospects are praiseworthy.

We must admit that in respect to this minority group it behooves us to face up to the grim heritage which the Stalin period of Soviet history bequeathed to us. It was inevitable that these peoples were destined to suffer the harshest treatment as a result of the xenophobia characteristic of the Communist regime from the 1930s. Many were forcibly deported, including entire national groups: Germans, Koreans, Turks; others endured partial deportation: Poles, Bulgarians, Greeks, and Finns.

Formally, the Jews can point to their own autonomous territory in the Russian Federation: the Jewish Autonomous Region. But this artificial structure does not play a significant role in the cultural life of Russian Jewry, concentrated as it is mostly in the large cities of European Russia, especially Moscow (with 174,700) and St. Petersburg (106,100 Jews), forming the third largest constituency there next to Russians and Ukrainians. Contemporary Jewish culture, its development obstructed for years by the government's anti-Semitism, now finds itself in considerable straits. Inasmuch as the majority of the Jews who inhabited the western parts of our country were massacred by the Nazis during World War II, the advancement of Jewish culture has a reduced basis in dispersed urban communities, and linguistic assimilation of the Jewish population has already made deep inroads while at the same time being offset by a notable rise in national feeling. As contacts between Israel and the Jews of Russia continue to grow, more interest is being expressed in Hebrew historic, cultural, and religious values. Continuing maintenance of contacts with Jewry in other countries is a requisite of development of Jewish culture in Russia.

The Jews, like the Germans and Greeks, have been actively involved in the wave of mass emigration. It has been sparked not only by the country's grave economic plight, but also by the specific problems of the Jewish minority. Although state anti-Semitism has become much less pronounced in recent years (without having entirely disappeared), the Jewish population still encounters a growing threat of "unofficial" anti-Semitism emanating from and disseminated by certain politically oriented civic organizations. The problem of anti-Semitism in Russia is viewed with anxiety by the international community; it is to be regretted that Russia's leadership has given this acute problem so little attention.

Russia's German minority, as a group descended from previous 18th-century colonists, had its own large Volga German Autonomous Republic until 1941. The Law on the Rehabilitation of the Repressed Peoples adopted in Russia applies fully to the Germans here. But the restoration of German autonomy has come up against no few stumbling blocks and has been complicated by the underestimation of the importance of the problem by Russia's leadership.

Restoration of German autonomy on the Volga is the only way to prevent or substantially reduce the mass exodus of Russia's German population, which threatens the actual disappearance of this national group from Russia. The attempts to improve the conditions of the Germans now settled in the Altai Territory and the Omsk Region by offering them national precincts in these lands are no more than palliatives.

We must not forget that the problem of the German minority concerns not only Russia and Germany. It also affects the other states of the CIS, such as Kazakhsktan, where the 1989 census reveals a German population of 957,500; or Kyrghyzia, with its 101,300 Germans, besides similar communities in the other Central Asian republics. As for the Ukraine, the number of Germans there is not very large—37,800. But the statement of Ukraine president L. Kravchuk that his republic is willing to accept the Germans living in the other countries of the CIS and resettle them in the Ukraine's southern areas including the Crimea has aroused wide interest.

Like the Germans, Russia's Greek minority can also point to a long history of acclimatization on Russian soil. It differs generally from its surrounding ethnic environment in respect to cultural traits and, to an extent, language. This Greek minority is concentrated largely in the Krasnodar (29,900) and Stavropol (20,500) territories. It was never granted such territorial autonomy as the Germans had. But the task of restoring even the degree of cultural autonomy it was allowed prior to 1937 now stands again on the agenda.

DISPERSED GROUPS LACKING THEIR OWN ETHNIC TERRITORY

This distinct Russian minority group consists of 152,900 Gypsies and 9,600 Assyrians.

Russia's Gypsies, like those in other countries, are poorly integrated with their surrounding ethnosocial environment, chiefly because of their traditional, unusual way of life. It is true that professional forms of Gypsy culture were developed over the years in the USSR, but these raised social and cultural barriers between the Gypsy urban intelligentsia of Moscow and other cities and the ordinary Gypsy vagrant groups. Attempts at forming simple Gypsy ethnic associations in our opinion do not offer much hope for the attainment of real cultural autonomy by the Gypsy people. They will evidently choose to cling to their habitual pattern of life, due mainly to its singularity.

Gypsy integration into Russian society may be possible in certain forms suited to their seminomadic habits, their occupational inclinations, and their traditions. Efforts aimed at such integration must be cautious and tactful. Manifestations of anti-Gypsy attitudes in Russia, up to the pogroms in some towns, were provoked by a widely accepted, hostile view of the Gypsies as an antisocial element. Such attitudes are not only unjust—they are impermissible. A special effort must be made, especially by the mass media, to correct these ugly prejudices against the Gypsies.

IMMIGRANT GROUPS ("GASTARBEITER")

This category was not common in Russia until recently. It refers chiefly to the temporary Vietnamese workers in some of our large, urban industrial enterprises, to the North Koreans employed here chiefly as loggers, and to the Chinese engaged in farming in a number of Far Eastern and Siberian areas. Not much is known or publicized about the conditions afforded to these unusual categories of workers. There are grounds for postulating that some of them may have met with discrimination or suffered indignities, and therefore their lawful rights must be upheld in case of arbitrary or ill treatment by the administrators of their enterprises or even by their own countrymen.

SUBETHNIC LINGUISTIC AND CONFESSIONAL GROUPS

These groups are usually not considered national minorities. But the Final Document of the Vienna Meeting of the CSCE, adopted in 1989, requires the member states (therefore Russia as well) to protect the cultural rights of those who are related to such small ethnic groups or, as they are called, "regional cultures."

Our census figures do not provide information on the names, numbers, or distribution of these small minorities of highly diversified origin. To mention just a few, they are the Don, Kuban, Terek-Greben, Ural, and Ussuri Cossacks; the "Old Believers" and other confessional communities in Siberia; the Molokans and Nekrassovans—all Russians in origin. Then there are the Mountain and Meadow Mari; the Erzya and Moksha Mordovian ethnolinguistic groups; the Orthodox Christians of Tatar origin; the tribal and subethnic groups of Altaians and Khakass; the Saami, Veps, and Karelian dialectical divisions; the coastal and reindeer-breeding Chukchi; and so on. The problems of these groups call for more study and analysis. It is clear that the problems have already come to the fore. That is illustrated by the rebirth of the Cossacks' traditional institutions, as one example, or, again, recognition of the Mari Mountain and Meadow dialects as equal tongues, or the demand of the Shapsugs, a subethnic Adyghei group, for a national district (such as they had prior to 1945) to be reestablished for them in the Krasnodar Territory.

The complexity of the present situation springs from the fact that processes of consolidating nations often relegate to a back place the great ethnic diversity of Russia. The nationalities policy of any civilized state must be based on the premise that every element of a cultural and historical heritage is equally important, whether it pertains to a people as a whole or to their fractions. The experience of other countries tells us that cultural self-determination thrives on both a national and regional basis, thus permitting us to preserve and to develop all the aspects and manifestations of the peoples' cultures.

The case of the Shapsugs raises the wider problem of whether every and any society has the right to ethnic self-identification. That right is often ignored for political reasons, as when, between 1944 and 1987, the Crimean Tatars were arbitrarily included by Soviet statisticians in the overall total for Tatars. Or that right may be overlooked when different peoples, each of whom wishes to retain its traditional territorial and tribal identity (as in the case of the Altaians or Khakass), are artificially classed together in order to lend support to the idea of ethnic amalgamation. A population census must at least contain the names by which all the ethnic groups call and know themselves, regardless of their size.

TYPES OF MODERNIZATION PROCESSES AMONG RUSSIA'S PEOPLES

Various empirical facts bearing on this complicated and many-sided process as reflected in its indirect manifestations are usually called upon to evaluate one or another ethnic or national degree of modernization. Such analyses of the facts naturally suffer in the direction of oversimplification, which, however, is quite permissible in deciding administrative matters. For our purposes in evaluating the degree of modernization of Russia's peoples, we have selected two indices: (1) degree of urbanization and (2) educational level.

The degree of urbanization may be defined in terms of the percentage of city dwellers to the total population of the given national group. In 1989, 73.4 percent of Russia's population lived in its cities. In accordance with the world standard, the average of about 70 percent is pretty high and warrants our considering such a society urbanized. Urbanization and modernization are related phenomena, contemporary society having developed primarily in the cities. Urbanization figures may therefore be taken as a basis in assessing degree of modernization.

We have defined the educational level as the number of persons with higher or incomplete higher educations per every 1,000 of the population of the given nationality. Educational level is not so decisively linked to the process of modernization as urbanization, yet also pertains indirectly to the same category of phenomena.

Let us compare the two indices.

In both cases, the peoples of Russia are divided into five groups. With respect to the names printed in italics in Table 3.1, we shall return to them later. Meanwhile, we can conclude that, on the whole, levels of urbanization and education coincide. Let us disregard some cases where the indices for a given people vary slightly, for example, Ukrainians, who come under Group 2 for urbanization, but Group 1 for education.

Comparison of the groups differentiated according to degree of urbanization and educational level reveals four types of Russia's peoples different in the way they are undergoing the modernization process.

Type I (groups 1 and 2). The peoples listed here (Jews, Russians, Ukrainians, Byelorussians, and Armenians), who basically comprise the majority of Russia's population, reveal high urbanization and educational levels, and may be judged to be completely modernized.

Type 2 (group 3). These peoples (Tatar, Komi, Kabardian, Kumyk, and Karelian) are characterized by somewhat lower but sufficiently high levels of urbanization to be classed as nearing the final stage of modernization.

Type 3 (groups 4 and 5). This type is represented by the Chuvash, Bashkir, Avar, Darghinian, Tuvan, Mordovian, Mari, Udmurt. These are Komi-Permyak and Chechen peoples who have attained only low levels of urbanization and education and are still in the midst of an ongoing process of modernization which is relatively far from accomplished.

Type 4. The peoples whose names are printed in italics (Ossetian, Buryat, Lezghin, Yakut, Kalmyk, Karachaian, Cherkessian, Adyghei, Balkar, Khakass, Ingush, and Altai peoples) all stand at diverse levels generally remote from the ultimate stages of the modernization process. Basically, they might have been listed with Type 3 (except for the Ossetians, related to Type 2). But it was deemed necessary to list them as a separate group because in urbanization and education they stand at very different levels; in other words, these two aspects of the modernization process are found to be proceeding for them at different paces, their degree of urbanization obviously lagging behind their educational level.

The gap between these two aspects of the modernization process, their incoordination as reflected in Type 4, confronts the given peoples with such

Table 3.1
Modernization Indices for Some Peoples of Russia, 1989

Groups	Degree of Urbanization	Educational Level
1.	Jews (98.4)	Ukrainians (168), *Ossetians* (185), Armenians (194), Jews (542), *Buryats* (205)
2.	Russians (76.7), Ukrainians (78.0), Byelorussians (79.9), Armenians (70.7)	Russians (132), Byelorussians (146), *Kalmyks* (145), *Karachaians* (135), *Cherkessians* (128), *Adygheis* (149), *Balkars* (138), *Lezghins* (120), *Yakuts* (143), *Khakass* (118)
3.	Tatars (65.7), Karelians (61.2), *Ossetians* (66.2)	Tatars (92), Komi (89), *Ingush* (84), Kabardians (109), Kumyks (97), *Altaians* (96)
4.	Chuvash (49.8), Bashkirs (49.2), *Kalmyks* (49.7), Mordovians (52.2), Udmurts (48.1), Komi (48.7), *Balkars* (59.9), Mari (40.7), *Adyghei* (41.5), Kabardians (44.3), Kumyks (45.4), Lezghins (44), *Buryats* (42), *Khakass* (42.5)	Chuvash (74), *Bashkirs* (81), Karelians (71), Avars (87), Darghinians (77), Tuvans (79)
5.	Komi-Permyaks (39.8), *Ingush* (37.6), *Cherkessians* (36.1), Chechens (26.8), *Karachaians* (32.6), Avars (32.3), Darghinians (29.2), *Yakuts* (27.7), Tuvans (30.5), *Altaians* (18)	Mordovians (61), Mari (61), Udmurts (66), Komi-Permyaks (57), Chechens (61)

difficulties as the distancing of the intelligentsia from the masses, the menace of sociopsychological frustrations, and so on. This particular level of modernization is fraught with all kinds of social unrest and inter-ethnic confrontation.

Among the peoples listed in Type I and to an extent Type 2, urban population growth has not been very marked in the past two decades. The principal change they show in the realm of education is the increasing proportion of those with higher or incomplete higher education as against the numbers with only secondary or lower schooling. On the other hand, certain peoples in Type 3 and 4 achieved a considerable increase between 1970 and 1989 in both urban population size and simultaneously in educational level, thanks to an increase in the number of secondary schools, or—in Type 4—also higher school graduates. In a word, the pace of modernization achieved by these peoples over the past decade has really been high. At the same time (as so often proves the case) these formal sociological indices progress much more rapidly than new social and psychological orientations actually do. Such in particular is the prospect for Type 4.

We have thus established that the majority of the peoples of this country, its largest ethnic exponents, have completed the process of modernization or reached stages close to its culmination. At the same time, a good many smaller groups are still going through various stages of modernization. For them the process is still far from finished.

NOTES

1. V.I. Abayev, *Osetinski yazyk i folklor* (The Ossetian language and folklore) (Moscow-Leningrad: Izdatelstvo AN SSR, 1949), vol. 1, p. 75.

2. *Etnographiya. Uchebnik* (Textbook on Ethnography), edited by Yu.V. Bromley and G.E. Markov (Moscow: Vysshaia Shkola, 1982), p. 290.

3. Ibid., p. 289.

4. Buryatia, Karelia, Komi, Mordovia, Udmurtia, Yakutia, Adygheia, Mountain Altai, Jewish Autonomous Region; the Khakass, Koryak, Nenets, Taimyr, Ust-Orda, Khanty-Mansi, Chukchi, Yamal-Nenets Autonomous Districts.

5. Bashkiria, Mari, Karachai-Cherkessia.

6. Not counting emigration during the past three years.

7. See note 6 above.

8. See note 6 above.

9. Except the Turkic Meskhetian refugees from Uzbekistan following the Ferghana 1989 clashes.

4

The Main Demographic, Ethnocultural, and Ethnosocial Processes in Russia in the Years of Soviet Power

THE NUMBERS AND DISTRIBUTION OF THE PEOPLES

Statistically estimated dynamics of the numerical strength of the peoples living on a definite territory depend on a number of factors. Of these, the following can be named as the principal ones.

1. The rate of natural (demographic) growth of the given national group. It depends on the birth and death rate. Mention should be made of the action of the historical law which experts call "demographic transition": the transition from traditional society to industrial is connected with a change in the type of demographic behavior. The traditional demographic behavior is expressed in a high birth and death rate; if "traditional" peoples are included in an industrial society with its medical care system, a "demographic explosion" takes place, that is, a rapid growth of the population. The demographic structure of the given people sharply changes in favor of the young (unworkable) ages, reaching, together with the pensioners, 60 or more percent of the population. With a low labor productivity, this results in a growing pauperization, and the population becomes unable to maintain itself and dependent on external resources. The peoples of Central Asia, and also a number of peoples of the Northern Caucasus and Siberia, found themselves in such a situation.

The process of modernization, however, gradually leads to a lower birth rate and makes life longer. The demographic structure of the people changes in favor of the mature (working) and older (pensionable) ages. At this stage there arises another danger—that of a negative growth of the population and an increasing proportion of people no longer able to work (which is not disastrous with a high labor productivity). It should be stressed once again that the type of demographic behavior is the most important factor regulating the population.

2. Migration processes, which often determine the proportion of members of one nationality or another on the given territory. There are migrations of two types: compulsory and unavoidable (forced) and natural (voluntary). Both types of migrations were widespread within the former Soviet Union and Russia.

3. Assimilation processes implying that part of one people acquires the ethnic self-consciousness of another people. The people that is being assimilated is becoming smaller in number. Assimilation processes take the form of intermarriages, especially when the descendants acquire the self-consciousness of one—dominating—people.

4. Consolidation processes in which a number of related ethnic groups acquire a common self-consciousness, transforming into a nation. Among a number of peoples of Russia this process was widely developed.

5. The changing of territorial borders, administrative or political, connected with the changed numerical strength of the people within the bounds of the given territory. The more intensive processes of formation of Russia's internal (administrative) structure were taking place until the end of the 1930s. Mention should also be made of the incessant territorial expansion of the Soviet Union, especially in the 1940s, with the resulting inclusion of new peoples or parts of them into the sphere of our internal ethnosocial and ethnocultural processes.

6. Losses among the population (including decline in the number of births) owing to various kinds of sociopolitical disasters (war casualties, reprisals, famine, deportation of whole peoples, etc.).

Naturally, the above six factors acted differently upon different peoples of Russia making up its *ethnic structure,* as on the dynamics of that structure. The poor statistical base, moreover, makes it very difficult to distinguish the action of individual factors and to indicate which factors prevailed in some period of time or other.

Between 1937 and 1989 the population of the USSR increased by 76.7 percent, with the annual rate of growth being 1.5 percent. During the same period, the population of Russia grew by 41.5 percent, showing an increase of 0.8 percent per year. The greatest difference in the rate of growth of the population of the USSR and Russia within the given period falls between 1937 and 1959, when the population of the country as a whole grew by 29.1 percent (the annual rate of growth being 1.3 percent), and the population of Russia by a mere 13.1 percent (an increase of 0.6 percent per year).

Russia's lagging so much behind the USSR in population growth was due to a number of factors such as a higher rate of natural growth in the republics of the Central Asian and Caucasian regions of the USSR and intensive out-migration from Russia. The main reason, however, was undoubtedly the territorial changes—the inclusion in the USSR of the Baltic republics, the western areas of the Ukraine and Byelorussia and of Bessarabia, and the transfer of the Crimea from the Russian Federation to the Ukraine in 1954. Russia (although Tuva was joined to it in 1944) even lost a noticeable part of its population, whereas the population of the USSR greatly increased. Unfortunately, the influence of sociopolitical disasters on population growth in Russia and the USSR is hard to appraise, but it can be supposed that the war, and especially the political reprisals (just as the deportation of whole peoples), hit the Russian population above all.

Subsequently, the territorial changes factor lost, in effect, its significance with the resulting substantial approach in the rate of growth of the population of Russia and the USSR as a whole. Thus, during the 20 years from 1959 to 1979, the population of the USSR went up by 25.5 percent, with the annual increase of 1.3 percent, while Russia's population increased by 17.2 percent, growing by 0.9 percent a year. During the decade from 1979 to 1989, the population of the USSR grew by 9.0 percent (0.9 percent annual growth), whereas for Russia the figures were respectively 7.0 percent and 0.7 percent. In other words, population growth in the USSR and Russia since the end of the 1950s was most appreciably influenced by such stable factors as different rate of natural growth for different peoples, and migration processes.

The above causes brought about an incessant decline in the proportion of the Russian Federation in the population of the USSR. In 1937, 64.2 percent of the country's population lived in Russia; in 1959, 56.3 percent; in 1979, 52.4 percent; and in 1989, 51.5 percent. The decline of Russia's share in the population of the country amounted in 52 years to 12.7 percentage points. Mention should again be made of the leading role in this process of the "mechanical" factors—territorial changes and migrations. Russia is probably the only republic in the former USSR whose relative population has in the years of Soviet power so much decreased.

Recent years have seen a reverse process gathering momentum: the mechanical rise of Russia's population owing to the refugees and migrants from other republics. The absence of reliable statistics does not allow us to appraise the scale of the process, but clearly hundreds of thousands of people are coming to reside in the Russian Federation from the various hot spots in the former USSR.[1] There can be no doubt that this trend in migration will in the coming few years be developing, even if it does not assume the nature of an exodus triggered off by the growing ethnic and social tensions in the "outlying" republics of the former USSR.

Let us now analyze the growth of numbers of the individual peoples of Russia. For convenience the reader should remember the following figures: the population of the USSR increased from 1937 to 1989 by 76.7 percent, while the population of Russia during the same period rose by 41.5 percent. From 1979 to 1989, the population of the USSR and the Russian Federation grew respectively by 9.0 percent and 7.0 percent. We shall need these figures when comparing the growth of a particular nationality with the growth of the total population of the country. It should be noted, besides, that in examining migration processes (to Russia or from Russia to other republics of the USSR), we shall compare the growth of the given peoples within the population of the Russian Federation and within the population of the USSR as a whole.

The Slavic Peoples (Russians, Ukrainians, Byelorussians, Poles, Bulgarians)

These peoples are as a whole characterized by a medium or low rate of natural growth connected with the completion (approximately by the mid-1930s) of the demographic transition.

The Russians. In 1937 the ratio of Russians in the Russian Federation equalled 82.1 percent; by 1989 it somewhat decreased, down to 81.5 percent. The proportion of the Russian population fell for a number of reasons: migration from Russia, the loss of the Crimea with its predominantly Russian inhabitants, and a rate of natural increase lower than for many other peoples of Russia.

Statistical data well demonstrate the role of migration in the changing numbers and proportion of the Russian population in Russia: from 1937 to 1989, the number of Russians in the Russian Federation increased only by 40.4 percent, whereas the respective figure for the Russian people in the USSR as a whole was 54.5 percent. It should be observed, however, that in the past 10 or 15 years, migration processes ceased to influence the numerical strength of the Russian population: from 1979 to 1989 it grew both in Russia and in the USSR by 5.6 percent. In other words, the balance of Russians who left for other republics and arrived from them to Russia approached zero. It should also be noted that the growth of the Russian population in Russia during this decade was somewhat less than the country's average (7.0 percent), which is due to a slower natural growth.

Speaking of the Russian population's growth, mention should be made of two more points. First, Russians so much surpass in number all other peoples of Russia that the demographic processes characteristic of other peoples have little effect on the proportion of Russians in Russia's population. Second, in the assimilation processes taking place in the country Russians usually appear as an active (assimilating) side.

Analysis of the data provided by the 1926 and 1989 censuses allows to draw interesting conclusions about the developments within the Russian population in the Russian Federation and the USSR.[2]

According to the 1926 census, the USSR had as its residents 77,791,124 ethnic Russians (distinguished "by nationality"), who made up 52.9 percent of the country's population. The Russian language was recognized as vernacular by 84,195,653 persons (57.3 percent of the population of the USSR). Thus, 4.4 percent of the country's citizens (6,404,529 people) were the so-called "Russian-language population" (ethnic non-Russians speaking the Russian language). This is 7.6 percent of the entire "Russian-speaking" population (regarding the Russian language as vernacular, including the Russians proper) and 8.2 percent as compared with the ethnic Russian population.

In 1989, the "Russian-language" population of the USSR totalled 18,809,765 people (6.6 percent of the country's entire population), which made up 11.5 percent of the "Russian-speaking" (163,645,476 people) and 13.0 percent as compared with the Russian population proper (145,155,489). Ethnic Russians equalled at that time 50.8 percent of the population of the USSR.

Let us compare these data with the census returns for the Russian Federation in the same year, 1989. Ethnic Russians totalled 81.5 percent of Russia's population (119,865,946). The "Russian-language" population reached in number 7,538,138 (5.1 percent of Russia's total population, 5.9 percent of the "Russian-speaking" and 6.3 percent as compared with the Russian population proper in the Federation).

It is noteworthy that the "Russian-language" population grew primarily not in the Russian Federation but in the other republics of the USSR, where the "Russian-language" population reached in 1989 the total of 11,271,627 (60.1 percent of the total "Russian-language" population of the USSR). This situation is due to two causes:

• Russia's national minorities, joining the streams of Russian migration from Russia, were quicker to begin to use the Russian language in their new place of residence in other republics of the USSR;
• the processes of linguistic russification of the native population in a number of Union republics supposedly went faster than similar processes in the autonomous republics of the Russian Federation.

Another remarkable fact is that although the proportion of ethnic Russians dropped in the USSR in the period from 1926 to 1989 from 52.9 percent to 50.8 percent, the proportion of the "Russian-speaking" population (i.e., all who regard the Russian language as vernacular) remained practically unchanged: 57.3 percent in 1926 and 57.4 percent in 1989. In other words, the difference in the rate of demographic growth between the non-Russian and Russian residents of the USSR was fully compensated owing to assimilation processes. According to all international standards, the millions of non-Russians by origin who regarded the Russian language as vernacular should be counted with the Russian people. Thus, its numbers in the countries of the former USSR outside Russia reach at least 35 million people.

The Ukrainians. The proportion of Ukrainians in Russia actually did not change from 1937 to 1989—it equals 2.97 percent. It should be pointed out that during this period of time the number of Ukrainians in the USSR was increasing considerably faster than in Russia: by 67.2 percent and 41.3 percent, respectively. The reason was the joining of the Western Ukraine to the Ukrainian Soviet Socialist Republic in 1939. Interestingly, from 1937 to 1979, (in 42 years), the increase of Ukrainians in Russia was quite low, 18.5 percent (compare with the increase of the Russians in the same period, 33.0 percent). Supposedly, such a small figure is due to two factors—the Ukrainians' participation in migrations from Russia, and assimilation on the part of the closely related Russian population. It is interesting to note, however, that during the decade between the 1979 and 1989 censuses, the number of Ukrainians in Russia was growing very fast and increased by 19.3 percent (compare with the growth of the Ukrainian population in the USSR as a whole—4.3 percent). This can mean only one thing—a considerable rise of Ukrainian migration to Russia (for example, to the Tyumen oil fields) from other republics, particularly from the Ukraine, during the past 10 to 15 years.

The Byelorussians. During the period under review the proportion of Byelorussians in Russia went up quite substantially from 0.34 percent to 0.82 percent. In the USSR, the number of Byelorussians from 1937 to 1989 increased by 105.9 percent, primarily not through natural growth, of course, but through the joining in 1939 of Western Byelorussia, and in 1940 of Lithuania, which also had a large Byelorussian population. Significantly enough, however, during the same period, the number of Byelorussians in Russia was rising even faster and increased by 245.4 percent. This can be explained only by intensive migration of Byelorussian population from Byelorussia, with migration processes continuing until very recently. Thus, from 1979 to 1989 the number of Byelorussians in the USSR grew by 6.1 percent and in Russia by 14.7 percent. The intensive Byelorussian migration considerably outstripped the assimilation processes (although in Russia Byelorussians are known to be assimilated by Russians).

The Poles. The number of Poles in Russia from 1937 to 1989 grew by only 2.7 percent, which is connected first of all with the assimilation of the greater part of increase of the Polish population by Russians. Therefore, the proportion of Poles in Russia's population fell during the 52 years from 0.09 percent to 0.06 percent. During the same period, Polish population in the USSR increased by 77 percent, which is due to the country's territorial expansion at the expense of areas which before 1939 were part of Poland, and also owing to Lithuania having been joined to the USSR. It should be mentioned that from 1979 to 1989, Polish population of the USSR decreased by 2.2 percent because of assimilation.

The Bulgarians. A considerable growth of the number of Bulgarians in the USSR (309.9 percent) is explainable by the joining in 1939–1940 of areas with a considerable Bulgarian population (Moldavia). From 1937 to 1989, the number of Bulgarians substantially increased in Russia as well—by 123.9 percent. This is due first of all to Bulgarians' migration to the territory of Russia from the areas of their traditional residence, but not to a high rate of natural growth (as regards Bulgarians it is low). Thus, the number of Bulgarians in the USSR increased from 1979 to 1989 by only 3.3 percent. This quite insignificant growth is also connected with Bulgarians' assimilation by the surrounding population—Russian, Ukrainian, Moldavian, Gagauz, and so on.

Thus, we see that population growth and the main demographic processes characterizing the five related Slavic peoples in Russia proceeded quite peculiarly. Whereas the two numerically small ethnic groups in Russia—the Poles and Bulgarians—had a largely common destiny (they lived on territories joined to the USSR and became the object of assimilation processes), the fate of the Ukrainians and Byelorussians was amazingly different.

The Finno-Ugrian Peoples (Mordovians, Udmurts, Mari, Komi, Komi-Permyaks, Karelians, Finns, Estonians, Veps, and Izhorians)

The Mordovians. The proportion of this people in Russia's population fell quite noticeably: from 1.17 percent in 1937 to 0.73 percent in 1989. This is one of the few peoples that decreased their absolute numbers in Russia, by 11.6 percent. The main reason is assimilation on the part of the surrounding Russian and other population among which Mordovians are dispersed. Another reason is Mordovians' participation in the Russian migration from Russia. Thus, in the USSR the proportion of Mordovians declined from 1937 to 1989 by only 7.6 percent, and considering that Mordovians' assimilation outside the Russian Federation proceeded even faster, it is obvious that the slower drop of Mordovian population in the USSR as compared with Russia is connected precisely with the migration factor. The assimilation of Mordovians continues: from 1979 to 1989 the numerical strength of this people declined in Russia by 3.4 percent and in the USSR by 3.2 percent. These figures also show that in the given decade Mordovians' departure from the Russian Federation to a considerable degree came to a halt.

The Udmurts. Although this people, unlike Mordovians, has not shown an absolute decrease in number, its proportion in Russia's population likewise fell from 0.54 percent to 0.49 percent. This people was distinguished by a lower rate of growth (from 1937 to 1989 the total population of Russia increased by 41.5 percent, and the Udmurt population only by 26.9 percent), which is due to both assimilation processes and migration to other republics of the USSR (in the USSR the number of Udmurts went up by

31.5 percent as against 26.9 percent in Russia). The rate of growth of Udmurt population was not high in the 1979 to 1989 period either—4.2 percent in Russia and 4.6 percent in the USSR (as compared with respective figures for the total population of Russia—7.0 percent, and for the USSR, 9.0 percent), although Udmurts' migration from the Russian Federation was not large.

The Mari. These are one of the few Finno-Ugrian peoples whose proportion in Russia's population noticeably increased—from 0.38 percent in 1937 to 0.44 percent in 1989. The growth of Russia's Mari population was appreciably higher than the growth of its population as a whole (respectively 61.5 percent and 41.5 percent). Mari but insignificantly participated in the outflow to other Union republics (the growth of the Mari population in the USSR totalled 67.3 percent). The increase of the Mari population in Russia from 1979 to 1989 was somewhat higher than of the total of her population (7.3 percent against 7.0 percent). This can probably be explained by a high natural growth and by the Mari's slight assimilation.

The Komi. The Komi's proportion in the population of the Russian Federation dwindled from 0.25 percent to 0.23 percent. The reduction is connected with the assimilation and migration processes: in Russia the number of Komi grew in the 1937 to 1989 period only by 29.7 percent, which is substantially lower than the growth of the republic's population as a whole. A higher level of the Komi's growth within the bounds of the USSR (31.2 percent) shows a certain migration from Russia. The same tendencies (especially assimilation processes) continued between the 1979 and 1989 censuses: The number of Komi in Russia increased by 5.1 percent (as compared with 5.6 percent for the Russians and 7.0 percent for the total population of the Federation).

The Komi-Permyaks. Their proportion in the population of the Russian Federation fell from 0.12 percent to 0.10 percent. On the whole, this people experienced the same processes as their nearest relatives, the Komi: assimilation and migration to other Union republics. Their number in Russia's territory increased by 21.0 percent, and in the territory of the USSR as a whole by 24.6 percent, which is twice lower than the average growth of population in Russia and thrice lower than the average for the USSR. It should be noted that in the past 10 to 15 years assimilation processes among the Komi-Permyaks have considerably quickened: Their growth in Russia has been but 0.9 percent.

The Karelians. This is another people, after the Mordovians, that absolutely decreased its number: It declined in Russia in 52 years by 46.0 percent, and in the USSR by 53.8 percent (the difference in figures points to the Karelians' slight migration to other republics). Accordingly, there was a substantial drop in the Karelians' proportion in the population of Russia—from 0.22 percent in 1937 to 0.09 percent in 1989. Very likely assimilation and migration involved above all the Tver Karelians (the group of Karelians, comprising almost half of the population of this people, who had resettled in Central Russia, leaving the Karelian isthmus in the 17th century). The above tendencies have continued in the recent past as well— in the period between the two latest censuses the number of Karelians in Russia decreased by 6.2 percent.

The Finns. They are also rapidly shrinking in number: the drop in Russia in 52 years totalled 68.1 percent; in the USSR, 53.8 percent. Assimilation and migration (largely forced, because the Ingermanland Finns were among the "repressed peoples"), as the main reasons of the Finnish population's decline, have continued in the past decade, when the Finnish population of the USSR diminished by 13.0 percent.

The Estonians. They were among the peoples included in the USSR in 1940, which meant that the number of Estonians in this country from 1937 to 1989 certainly rose tremendously. Despite this fact, however, the number of Estonians in Russia in the same period declined, and quite noticeably, by 48.2 percent. This was caused by Estonians' outflow from Russia, mostly to Estonia, and also by the assimilation of the small (46,000 persons in 1989) Estonian population in Russia. The reduction of the Estonian population in Russia from 1979 to 1989 by 16.5 percent (especially against the background of insignificant growth of the Estonian population in the USSR by 0.7 percent) shows that these processes continue at the present time as well.

The Veps. They thrice decreased their proportion in Russia's population: from 0.03 percent to 0.01 percent. This is due to the absolute decline in the number of Veps during the 52 years by 59 percent. This process was most intensive from the 1930s to the 1970s, when the Veps population fell (primarily through assimilation) by 74.5 percent. And reversely, recent decades exhibited a very intensive growth (by 60.8 percent from 1979 to 1989). This is supposedly the result not of natural growth but primarily of the growing national self-consciousness of the Veps people, the restored national self-identification, expressed, for example, in the projects of creation of a Veps autonomous area.

The Izhorians. The situation in which this small people finds itself is largely similar to the Veps' situation: the considerable assimilation which numerically reduced this people during the 52 years by 90.4 percent, is at present being replaced by the growing ethnic self-consciousness of the Izhorians, leading to a gradual rise of their numbers (by 9.6 percent in the period between the latest two censuses). This figure, which exceeds the average growth of Russia's total population (7.0 percent) may have two reasons: a restored national self-identification and a growing rate of natural increase.

The Letto-Lithuanian Peoples (Lithuanians and Letts)

The Lithuanians. The joining of Lithuania to the USSR in 1940 determined profuse migration of Lithuanian population to Russia. It grew here from 1937 to 1989 by 1,703.5 percent. In recent years the increase of Lithuanians in Russia (5.5 percent) was the same as the increase of the Russian population but was smaller than the growth of Russia's total population in the same period (1979–1989). The growth of Lithuanian population in the USSR (7.6 percent) was higher but likewise did not reach the figure for the population of the USSR as a whole (9.0 percent). These figures are possibly indicative of the following facts: (1) a lower natural increase of the Lithuanian people as compared with the total population of Russia and the USSR; (2) a definite migration of Lithuanians from Russia (to Lithuania first of all); (3) a certain assimilation of Lithuanians in Russia.

The Letts. Ethnodemographic processes typical of the Letts were nearer to the Estonian than the Lithuanian variety: after Latvia's having been joined to the USSR, part of Russia's Letts left for their native land, with the result that Lettish population in Russia fell in number from 1937 to 1989 by 30.4 percent (the assimilation factor, too, certainly had a role to play here). Interestingly, this process was initially a slow one. Thus, from 1937 to 1979 the Lettish population in Russia even increased by 23.4 percent. The difference between this figure and the growth of the country's total population during the same period (32.2 percent) can almost fully be attributed to assimilation and a low natural growth. In subsequent years, however, the decline in the number of Russia's Letts (by 14.1 percent from 1979 to 1989) appears to be connected primarily with repatriation, the Letts' return to Latvia.

We have examined the demographic behavior of the three Baltic peoples—the Estonians, Letts, and Lithuanians—and discovered three models. Why these differences? To our minds, they directly correlate with the level of economic development of the three republics: Estonia, Latvia, and Lithuania (enumerated in a descending order) in the prewar and present time. This factor, in our opinion, differently painted these countries' attractiveness for repatriates.

The Turkic Peoples (Tatars, Chuvash, Bashkirs, Kazakhs, Yakuts, Azerbaijanians, Kumyks, Tuvans, Karachaians and Balkars, Uzbeks, Nogais, Altaians, Khakass, Kirghiz and Turkmens, Shorians, Turks)

The Tatars. This people raised, although slightly, its proportion in Russia's population from 3.47 percent in 1937 to 3.76 percent in 1989. This people is Russia's second in number, with the rate of its growth higher than this country's average: during the above-mentioned period its population went up by 53.1 percent (against 41.5 percent of growth of all Russia's residents). This is due to the following reasons: (1) a higher natural increase; (2) consolidation of the Tatar people (inclusion in it of other Tatar-speaking groups of population); (3) Tatars' little assimilation by the Russian majority. The growth of the Tatar population in Russia would have been more noticeable if not for the Tatars' involvement in Russian migrations to other republics: In 52 years the population of Tatars in the USSR as a whole increased by 75.3 percent. Noteworthy is the important growth of Russia's Tatar population from 1979 to 1989 by 10.2 percent, which considerably exceeds the average for this country's population. A certain part seems to have been played here by Tatars' repatriation from other republics of the USSR, where the increase of Tatar population during this period was comparatively small (5.3 percent).

The Chuvash. Just as did the Tatars, the Chuvash increased their proportion in Russia's population, from 1.11 to 1.21 percent. The growth of Chuvash population from 1937 to 1989 in Russia was the same as Tatar— 53.1 percent, that is, quite high. It should be mentioned, however, that between the 1979 and 1989 censuses, Chuvash population in Russia grew insignificantly, only by 5.0 percent (which is below the average for Russia's population and even below the growth of the Russian people). The growth of Chuvash population was not, of course, influenced by such an important factor as repatriation (compare with the Tatars). A decline in natural growth and development of assimilation processes can also be assumed (assimilation is not hampered by the religious factor since Chuvash are Orthodox Christians).

The Bashkirs. As did most of the Turkic peoples, the Bashkirs became more noticeable in Russia's population—their proportion in 52 years increased from 0.72 percent to 0.91 percent. The growth of Bashkir population was higher than the growth of the Tatars, reaching 78.7 percent. At the same time, according to the two latest censuses, the growth of the Bashkir population slowed down a great deal, to 4.2 percent in 10 years. This fact, as we see it, can be explained by both the Bashkirs' lowered natural increase and the embracing by part of the Bashkirs (in Bashkiria and Tataria) of the Tatar self-consciousness.

The Kazakhs. They belong to the peoples whose demographic transition has not yet been accomplished and who retain a very high natural growth of population. The proportion of Kazakhs, therefore, in Russia's population from 1937 noticeably increased (from 0.28 percent to 0.43 percent), the same as the population of this people—by 111.7 percent. (It should be observed that in the areas adjoining Kazakhstan, Kazakhs can well be regarded as the "native" people). A higher growth of Kazakh population in the USSR as a whole (184.3 percent), just as the comparison of the growth of Kazakh population in Russia and in the USSR during the decade from 1979 to 1989 (22.7 percent and 24.1 percent respectively) may point to migration of part of the Kazakh population in Russia to Kazakhstan. These processes have been rapidly gaining strength in recent years, when Kazakhstan's President N. Nazarbayev officially announced encouragement of repatriation of Kazakhs from China and Russia.

The Yakuts. The proportion of this people in Russia's population went up from 0.23 percent to 0.26 percent (and its population in 52 years by 59.0 percent), thanks to a sufficiently high natural increase, insignificant assimilation, and little migration beyond Russia's borders. A high enough rate of growth remains to this day—16.4 percent in 10 years.

The Azerbaijanians. This people can in no way be considered one of the "native" peoples of Russia, but their proportion in the country's population became very noticeable, rising from 0.04 percent to 0.23 percent in 1989. This is due not to a comparatively high natural growth characteristic of the given people but to an extremely great migration of Azerbaijanians to Russia. Thus, from 1937 to 1989, Azerbaijan population in the USSR grew by 203.2 percent and in Russia by 787.2 percent. Intensive migration continued in the period between the latest two censuses, when the number of Azerbaijanians in the USSR increased by 18.1 percent and in Russia by 120.4 percent.

The Kumyks. This is one of the Turkic peoples of Daghestan, who are on the whole characterized by a high natural growth and insignificant migration activity. Its population from 1937 to 1989 grew in Russia by 166.7 percent and from 1979 to 1989 by 27.1 percent.

The Tuvans. The bulk of this people were included in the population of Russia only in 1944 when Tuva joined the USSR. Thanks to a high natural growth the proportion of this people in the country's population increased from 1959 to 1979 from 0.10 percent to 0.14 percent. The high rate of natural growth (coupled with the absence of assimilation and outflow beyond both Tuva's and Russia's borders) determined a considerable growth of the number of Tuvans from 1979 to 1989—by 24.6 percent (against 7.0 percent of growth of this country's total population).

The Karachaians and Balkars. These related peoples of the Northern Caucasus were combined in the 1937 census. During the period ending in 1989 their proportion in Russia's population noticeably increased from 0.10 percent to 0.16 percent, and their aggregate number grew by 110.8 percent. Although the natural growth of both peoples is high enough (their combined population increased from 1979 to 1989 by 21.9 percent), it is higher for the Balkars than for the Karachaians (in the above-mentioned period these peoples grew in number by 26.7 percent and 19.5 percent, respectively).

The Uzbeks. In the 1937 census the Uzbeks were not singled out among the peoples of Russia (their population over this country's territory was insignificant). Subsequently, however, Uzbeks became an appreciable component among Russia's residents: their proportion in the population went up from 1959 to 1989 from 0.03 percent to 0.09 percent, that is, tripled. This is connected, of course, not with the Uzbeks' characteristic high natural growth but with their migration to Russia. Thus, from 1979 to 1989 the number of Uzbeks in the USSR grew by 34.1 percent and in Russia by 75.3 percent.

The Nogais. They belong to the peoples which have not yet completed the demographic transition, therefore their population in 52 years increased quite substantially, by 123.3 percent. The high rate of natural growth has been retained by the Nogais at the present time as well: from 1979 to 1989 their number grew by 31.9 percent.

The Altaians. These are a "combined" group of related peoples of the Altai. These peoples increased their proportion in Russia's population from 0.04 percent to 0.05 percent (1937–1989), and their number went up by 50.4 percent. However, a considerable growth of the Altaians' population, characterized on the whole by "traditional" demographic behavior, was observed only in recent decades. Significantly enough, from 1937 to 1979 Altaians' population became larger only by 27.6 percent (against 32.2 percent of growth of Russia's entire population). This is due to the fact that intensive socioeconomic development of this area and its population began comparatively recently. Only from 1979 to 1989 Altaians' population growth (17.9 percent) surpassed the similar figure for Russia's population as a whole (7.0 percent). It was at the same period that the proportion of Altaians in Russia's population went up as well.

The Khakass. They experienced processes similar to those typical of the Altaians, although the Khakass' proportion in Russia's population remained at the level of 0.05 percent (with the growth of 63.7 percent from 1937 to 1989). However, the Khakass' growth from 1937 to 1979 was higher than the growth of Russia's population as a whole (44.4 percent) and considerably higher than the growth of the Altaians. While retaining a high rate of growth in the subsequent decade (13.4 percent), the Khakass, nevertheless, began yielding to the Altaians in this respect.

The Kirghiz and Turkmens. Comparatively few in Russia, these belong to the peoples with the traditional type of demographic behavior. Appreciable groups of these peoples appeared in Russia recently enough—in the past few decades. From 1979 to 1989 their populations in Russia increased by 178.0 percent and 78.2 percent, respectively (with their growth in the USSR as a whole by 32.7 percent and 34.6 percent). Naturally, population growth of these peoples in Russia can be explained above all by migration from the respective republics, although some groups of Turkmens (the so-called Trukhmens) resided in the Northern Caucasus back in the 19th century.

The Shorians. They are a small mountain people in Southern Siberia, whose proportion in Russia's population does not exceed 0.01 percent. The growth of Shorian population from 1937 to 1989 was quite insignificant,

4.7 percent, with the number of Shorians prior to 1979 rising by a mere 1.0 percent. Only in recent years (1979 to 1989) did their growth become noticeable (by 3.7 percent), which must be attributed to better medical care in Shoria today.

The Turks. These have appreciably increased in number from 1937 to 1989 both in the USSR (by 1,919.4 percent) and in Russia (1,078.8 percent). It is noteworthy that this process was to be observed in the USSR mostly from 1959 to 1989 (from 35,000 to 208,000 people). No natural increase (although it is sufficiently high for this people) could, of course, produce such growth of the Turkish population. It can be assumed that later censuses more precisely reflected the number of Turks in the USSR than the earlier ones. As to the Turkish population of Russia, it apparently formed primarily through migrations from other republics.

The Abkahzian-Adyghei Peoples (Kabardians, Adyghei and Cherkessians, Abazinians, and Abkhazians)

The Kabardians. In 52 years they appreciably increased their proportion in Russia's population from 0.14 percent to 0.26 percent, owing to a high natural growth (during this period their number rose by 156.9 percent), little migration outside Russia, and little involvement in assimilation processes. These tendencies continue at the present time: From 1979 to 1989 the number of Kabardians increased by 21.1 percent. Demographic processes within the other peoples of this group developed similarly.

The Adyghei and Cherkessians. Counted in the 1937 census together, they increased their aggregate proportion in Russia's population from 0.08 percent to 0.12 percent; their growth in 52 years was 122.0 percent. These peoples have retained a high natural growth to this day: 14.6 percent and 13.9 percent, respectively from 1979 to 1989.

The Abazinians. They numerically increased from 1937 to 1989 by 139.7 percent, and in the last decade of this period, by 25.8 percent.

The Abkhazians. These were mentioned as one of the peoples of Russia only by the latest census, when they totalled 7,200 persons. This is evidently the result of their comparatively recent migration from Abkhazia.

The Nakh-Daghestan Peoples (Chechens and Ingush, Avars, Darghinians, Lezghins, Laks, Tabasarans, Rutuls, Aguls, Tsakhurs)

The Chechens and Ingush. These two closely related peoples were counted in the 1937 census jointly. They then made up 0.42 percent of Russia's population, and by 1989 their aggregate proportion rose to 0.76 percent (the population increased by 155.6 percent). These peoples, as have the other Nakh-Daghestan peoples, have retained a high rate of natural increase, have a low migration mobility, and almost do not know assimilation.

The Avars. From 1937 to 1989 they grew in number by 148.1 percent, retaining a high rate of natural growth also in the last decade of this period (28.4 percent).

The Darghinians. They increased their population by 144.4 percent (from 1979 to 1989, by 29.6 percent).

The Lezghins. In Russia from 1937 to 1989 they grew in number by 152.7 percent (in the last decade, by 36.3 percent). As to the Lezghins in Azerbaijan, neither their precise numbers nor their status are known at present. There are grounds to believe that in the censuses their considerable part was counted as Azerbaijanians (i.e., was subjected to forcible assimilation).

The Laks. They increased in numbers during the 52 years by 112.3 percent, and in the last 10 years by 25.7 percent.

The Tabasarans. They swelled their size by 184.1 percent from 1937 to 1989, and by 30.5 percent during the last decade of this period.

The Rutuls, Aguls and Tsakhurs. These peoples were not taken into account by the 1937 census; it can only be surmised, therefore, that their numbers from 1937 to 1989 grew substantially, as did the numbers of the other Daghestan peoples. The surmise is based on the high growth of their population continuing between the two latest censuses: 36.5 percent, 54.7 percent, and 42.4 percent, respectively.

All the above-mentioned Nakh-Daghestan peoples (except the Chechens and Ingush), as well as the Kumyks and Nogais, constitute the so-called "peoples of Daghestan" forming this republic, that is, representing its "titular" nations. Mention should be made of a sizeable increase of the proportion of the peoples of Daghestan in Russia's population from 1937 to 1989: from 0.67 percent to 1.19 percent.

The Mongolian Peoples (Buryats and Kalmyks)

The Buryats. They increased their representation among the peoples of Russia from 0.21 percent to 0.28 percent during the 52 years, their numbers during this period having grown by 92.5 percent. They have retained their high naturic growth from 1979 to 1989 as well, increasing during this time by 19.3 percent.

The Kalmyks. These number among the "punished peoples," therefore, as the result of deportation, their numbers from 1937 to 1989 rose only by 34.1 percent (which is less than the figure for Russia as a whole) and their ratio in Russia's population fell from 0.12 percent to 0.11 percent. Characteristically, in the period from 1937 to 1959 there was a sizeable relative decline in Kalmyk population: Its proportion in Russia's population in 1959 was only 0.09 percent. Kalmyks, however, retained a high rate of natural growth (traditional demographic behavior); therefore, their number from 1979 to 1989 increased by 18.4 percent.

The Iranian Peoples (Ossetians, Tajiks, Tats, Mountain Judaists)

The Ossetians. In Russia they increased their proportion in this country's population from 0.17 percent to 0.27 percent, and their number went up from 1937 to 1989 by 132.2 percent. They are characterized by a comparatively high natural growth (their population increased from 1979 to 1989 by 14.3 percent), which is lower, however, than for many other peoples of the Northern Caucasus. In other words, the Ossetians are passing through the final stages of demographic transition. The number of Ossetians in Russia by the end of 1992 is hard to establish, owing to the appearance of refugees from Southern Ossetia (from the territory of Georgia). Estimates say that the number of refugees exceeds 100,000.

The Tajiks. In recent decades they have substantially increased their population in Russia, primarily as the result of recent migrations. Thus, from 1979 to 1989 the number of Tajiks in the USSR increased by 45.4 percent and in Russia by 113.9 percent.

The Tats. They are a small, Iranian-speaking mountain people (unrecorded by the 1937 census), with a characteristic traditional type of demographic behavior. Thus, the number of Tats grew from 1979 to 1989 by 52.3 percent but possibly this large growth reflects to some extent resettlement processes as well.

The Mountain Judaists. These increased their numbers in Russia from 1937 to 1989 by 226.9 percent. Such a sizeable growth can be explained by three factors: (1) traditional demographic behavior, (2) migration to Russia from other republics, and (3) improved collection of statistical data. Which of these factors should be given preference is unclear.

The Small Peoples of the North

Twenty-six nationalities of Russia, of diverse origin, are included in this group according to one criterion—they have preserved the relations of preclass society and a corresponding economic system. The 1937 census contains data only for some peoples of this group. On the whole, this category of peoples insignificantly increased its proportion in Russia's population from 1959 to 1989—from 0.11 percent to 0.12 percent. Their aggregate number went up accordingly. From 1979 to 1989 the population growth of this group of peoples surpassed this country's average, reaching 16.6 percent. During the 52 years a considerable numeric growth was shown by the Evens (largely, it seems, thanks to an improved collection of statistics), Selkups, and Yukagirs. A small growth of population was characteristic of the Chukchi, Koryaks, Mansi, Saami, and Kets. The Nenets, Evenks, and Khanty suffered a heavy loss in their populations. Groups of these peoples, separated from one another by tremendous distances, found themselves in quite different conditions, which determined different chances for their survival.

From 1979 to 1989 most of these peoples were characterized by a high rate of growth (from 7.1 percent for the Chukchi to 84.6 percent for the Itelmens). The latter figure, as the growth of the Nganasans' population (62.5 percent), is connected to a large extent with an improved statistical recording. The high population growth has resulted from most of the peoples of the North having preserved their traditional type of demographic behavior in the conditions of improved medical care. Nevertheless, the Khanty, Koryaks, Nivkhi, and Selkups showed during this period a low growth rate (4.8 percent, 3.8 percent, 4.5 percent, and 2.9 percent, respectively), and the Orochi absolutely declined in number (by 10 percent). It is probably connected with the continuing assimilation of these peoples.

The Peoples Not Included in the Above Ethnolinguistic Groups (Germans, Jews, Armenians, Moldavians, Gypsies, Georgians, Koreans, Greeks, and Assyrians)

The Germans. They decreased their proportion in Russia's population in 52 years from 0.63 percent to 0.57 percent, although their number grew somewhat (by 29.3 percent). The German population of the USSR grew on the whole during this period by 77.0 percent. Although German autonomy was done away with in 1941, the decline in the proportion of German population became noticeable after 1959, when it reached 0.7 percent of this country's population. This can be explained by two factors consequent on the deportation: repatriation to Germany and assimilation. From 1979 to 1989 the rate of growth of German population in Russia was higher than in the USSR (6.5 percent against 5.3 percent). These figures can be explained by Germans' migration to Russia from other republics, by a lesser extent of German repatriation from Russia as compared with other republics of the USSR, and a more rapid rate of Germans' assimilation outside Russia.

The Jews. In 52 years they substantially lowered their proportion in Russia's population: from 0.74 percent to 0.37 percent, as well as their numbers (by 30.6 percent). This was furthered by three factors: (1) a very low natural growth, (2) assimilation, and (3) emigration (including repatriation to Israel). On the whole these processes are more characteristic of the Jewish population outside Russia, where from 1937 to 1989 the number of this people declined by 48.4 percent. Noteworthy is the drop in the number of Jews in the USSR from 1937 to 1979 by 34.8 percent, whereas in Russia it fell only by 9.5 percent. These figures point to both the Nazi genocide during the war, which hit most of the Jewish population of the Ukraine and Byelorussia, and Jews' heavy migration to Russia in the above period of time. From 1979 to 1989, however, the situation changed: The outflow of Jewish population in Russia (30.6 percent) became more noticeable than in the USSR as a whole (21.8 percent). The most weighty factor here was, of course, intensive emigration (repatriation).

The Armenians. The people who traditionally had a vast diaspora within Russia's boundaries, during the 52 years the Armenians substantially increased their proportion in this country's population (from 0.16 percent to 0.36 percent). Their numbers in Russia during this period grew by 226.1 percent. Comparing these data with the growth of Armenian population in the USSR (134.8 percent), it is easy to see that there was intensive Armenian migration to the Russian Federation. It continued in recent years as well (1979–1989), when the Armenian population in Russia increased by 46.0 percent, while the growth of this people in the USSR as a whole totalled but 11.4 percent. It should be added that Russia has among its residents today a considerable number of Armenian refugees from the territory of Armenia and Azerbaijan (several hundreds of thousands), part of whom contemplate emigration.

The Moldavians. Back in 1937 they did not form a group of any importance in Russia, but at present reach 0.12 percent of its population (in 1959, 0.05 percent; in 1979, 0.07 percent). The intensive inflow of Moldavians is connected, of course, with the territorial acquisitions of the USSR in 1939–1940. Especially intensive Moldavian migration to Russia has occurred in recent decades, when the number of Moldavians in this country rose by 69.1 percent.

The Gypsies. The 1937 census clearly underestimated the number of Gypsies in Russia (1,800) and in the USSR (2,200), which determined extremely high figures of growth of the Gypsy people from 1937 to 1989. The high rate of Gypsies' growth from 1937 to 1959, however, was also due to the joining to the USSR of the Western Ukraine and Moldavia with their numerous Gypsy population. The proportion of Gypsies in Russia's population, thanks to the high rate of natural growth of this people and, possibly, to the migration factor, has grown incessantly—from 0.06 percent in 1959 to 0.1 percent in 1989. From 1979 to 1989 the increase of Gypsy population in Russia equalled 26.7 percent, and in the USSR, 25.4 percent. These figures may show the Gypsies' movement over the territory of Russia.

The Georgians. They sizeably increased their proportion in Russia's population from 0.01 percent to 0.09 percent. Their number in Russia went up in 52 years by 1,534.6 percent. Such growth can be explained exclusively by the factor of migration, which continued from 1979 to 1989 as well (Georgian population in the USSR rose by 11.5 percent and in Russia by 46.2 percent).

The Koreans. They were among the peoples who were subjected to reprisals. At the end of the 1930s they were removed from the Far East, primarily to Central Asia. In connection with deportation, Korean population in Russia decreased in 52 years by 36.0 percent, whereas in the USSR as a whole it grew by 161.3 percent. During this period the proportion of Koreans in the population of the Federation declined from 0.16 percent to 0.07 percent.

The Greeks. A people who suffered partly from deportation, their numbers and proportion in Russia's population (1937, 0.07 percent; 1959, 0.04 percent; 1979, 0.05 percent; and 1989, 0.06 percent) underwent substantial fluctuations. On the whole their number on the territory of Russia in 52 years increased by 22.7 percent (in the USSR, by 33.1 percent). The small growth of the Greek population is due not only to the fact of partial deportation but to assimilation and repatriation processes.

The Assyrians. In the territory of Russia they are not singled out by early censuses. In 1989, however, 9,600 Assyrians resided here, or more than one-third of the overall Assyrian population of the USSR. It should be noted that from 1937 to 1959 the number of Assyrians in the USSR increased by 587.3 percent, which is certainly due to an improved collection of statistical data. The small growth of Assyrians in the USSR from 1979 to 1989 (4.0 percent) is probably connected with the assimilation of this numerically small people.

Even a brief survey of ethnodemographic processes in Russia from 1937 to 1989 makes it possible to conclude that the country's ethnic structure underwent, during this period, substantial changes. They may appear inessential to those who focus their attention on the predominance of the Russian people (over 80 percent of the population). It will be recalled, however, that even a proportion of population amounting to 0.01 percent in 1989 equalled some 15,000 persons.

Of course, Russians and, more broadly, the Slavic group of peoples continue to predominate in the country, making up 85.38 percent of its population (in 1937, 85.55 percent). However, in the conditions of Russians' heavy migration from Russia and a low natural growth, stabilization of their relative numbers occurred primarily through the assimilation of other peoples.

An important factor in Russia's new ethnic structure is the appearance here of sizeable groups of "titular" peoples from the republics of the former USSR. Their proportion in the population increased from 1.26 percent to 5.3 percent. It is common knowledge that in any polyethnic entity of the imperial type the metropolis has always attracted population of the outlying areas.

A considerable numerical growth has been shown in Russia by the peoples of Trans-Caucasia and the Northern Caucasus (from 1.78 percent to 3.44 percent) and the peoples speaking Turkic languages (from 6.16 percent to 7.53 percent). At the same time, the Finnish-speaking peoples essentially lost their relative, and sometimes absolute numbers: Their proportion in the population dropped from 3.05 percent to 2.12 percent. In other words, Russia's population exhibited a substantial growth of ethnic groups that were culturally farther removed from the bulk of the population, and a decline in the proportion of ethnic groups culturally near to the main people.

This process can be described as *a growth of cultural heterogeneity in the ethnic structure of Russia*. It is confirmed by the changed ratio of peoples traditionally adhering to one worldwide confession or another: From 1937 to 1989 the proportion of "Christian" peoples dropped from 90.82 percent to 90.24 percent; the proportion of "Moslem" peoples went up from 5.93 percent to 7.90 percent; the proportion of peoples traditionally professing Buddhism increased from 0.49 percent to 0.61 percent.

RUSSIA'S NATIONAL REPUBLICS AND AUTONOMIES

Let us see now how the composition of the population of Russia's national republics and autonomies evolved. Arranged according to the Russian alphabetical order, they are called here as they officially are in the 1993 Constitution of the Russian Federation, with no mention of their former names or status.

The Republic of Adygheia, from 1922 (the year of its formation) to 1989, increased its population by 77.0 percent, which is a little more than Russia's average. Losses in population from 1922 to 1937 (by 7.8 percent) were compensated from 1937 to 1970 primarily through migration to its territory. In subsequent years migrations obviously did not influence the numerical strength of the republic's population. The proportion of Adyghei people in the population is not great (21.2 percent in 1970; 22.1 percent in 1989), which is due to remote historical factors: As the result of the Caucasian wars of the 19th century most of the Adyghei and the related Cherkessians left the Empire (the foreign diaspora of these peoples reaches five million people).[3] Russia's Adyghei, however, have retained a compact core in the territory of the republic: 81.6 percent of all Adyghei lived there in 1970, and 76.0 percent in 1989. The decline in the proportion is due primarily to migration of members of this people to other regions.

The Republic of Altai was created in 1922, and since then has increased its population by 112.2 percent. This increase is explained by mass migration to the territory of the republic from 1926 to 1940. Later on, there was an outflow of population from Gorny Altai to other regions. The proportion of the native population, initially not very large, in recent decades has gradually increased both through the exodus of "aliens" and through a higher natural growth of Altaians. Thus in 1970, Altaians constituted 27.9 percent of the republic of Altai's population; in 1989 their ratio rose to 31.0 percent. The compactness of Altaians' distribution within the republic has remained very high. In 1970, 91.6 percent of all Altaians lived there and in 1989, 83.1 percent.

The Republic of Bashkortostan was formed in 1919. According to the 1920 census, 32.4 percent of its population were Bashkirs. The 1926 census, however, already registered a fall of the Bashkirs' proportion to 23.5 percent. This was due to the creation in 1922 of the "bigger Bashkiria," which included, in part, the Ufa province with more Bashkirs residing in it than in the autonomy proper, but they constituted a mere 26.7 percent of the population. At present Bashkirs make up 21.9 percent of the republic's inhabitants, taking the third place, after Tatars and Russians. However, on the whole, between 1926 and 1989 the Bashkirs' proportion diminished slightly enough. On the other hand, the population growth from 1919 to 1989 was lower as compared to Russia's average. Today, Bashkirs have a compact ethnic core in their republic which totals 59.6 percent of this people. But during the Soviet period the compactness of their distribution suffered considerable decline: In 1926, 87.7 percent of all Bashkirs lived on their national territory. In other words, many of them migrated beyond the republic's borders.

The Republic of Buryatia was formed in 1923. In 1937, parts of it were cut off to make the *Aginsk Buryat Autonomous District* and *the Ust-Orda Buryat Autonomous District*. Population growth in the first two territorial units of the Buryat people substantially exceeded the average figures for Russia (during the period of existence, 196.6 percent and 129.0 percent respectively), whereas in the Ust-Orda district it was extremely low (6.3 percent). This is due first of all to the directions of migration streams and also to the Buryats' characteristic high rate of natural growth. By 1970 the native population of Buryatia made up only 22.0 percent of the total population, of the Aginsk district 50.2 percent (the only Buryat autonomy where the proportion of the local population exceeded 50 percent), and the Ust-Orda district 32.6 percent. Since that time, however, the proportion of Buryats in the respective autonomies was constantly rising, reaching in 1989 in the Republic of Buryatia 24.0 percent, in the Aginsk Autonomous District 54.9 percent, and in Ust-Orda Autonomous District 36.3 percent. This process is obviously connected with the dwindling migration stream to this region. Buryats as a whole belong to the peoples who have retained a compact core of their ethnos on the territory of their respective autonomies. The "three Buryatias" in 1970 accounted for 82.7 percent of all Buryats, and in 1989 for 81.0 percent. The insignificant decline in the compact core of the Buryat ethnos is probably due to the migration of part of the Buryats to other regions.

The Republic of Daghestan was formed in 1921, with the population having increased since by 153.8 percent (primarily due to a high natural growth of the native population and partly through migration). Daghestan is a republic where the population consists of predominantly "titular" peoples, whose proportion is gradually growing (74.2 percent in 1970, 80.2 percent in 1989). Most of the "titular" peoples of Daghestan have on the territory of the republic a compact ethnic core: Avars (1970, 88.1 percent; 1989, 85.5 percent); Darghinians (90.0 percent and 76.7 percent respectively); Kumyks (98.5 percent and 82.3 percent; Lezghins (50.2 percent and 43.8 percent; it will be recalled that a considerable part of Lezghins live in the adjoining areas of Azerbaijan); Laks (82.4 percent; 78.0 percent); Tabasarans (96.5 percent; 79.6 percent); Nogais (42.0 percent; 37.3 percent. A compact Nogai population is to be found in the bordering areas of Chechen and Ingush republics and the Stavropol Territory); Rutuls (97.7 percent; 75.0 percent); Aguls (97.9 percent; 73.7 percent); Tsakhurs (38.8 percent; 25.0 percent; part of the Tsakhurs live in the neighboring areas of Azerbaijan). Owing to migration processes the compact ethnic core of the Daghestan peoples has in recent decades been gradually eroding.

The Kabardian-Balkar Republic was formed in 1921 and sizeably (by 259.0 percent) increased its population by 1989. The main growth falls between 1926 and 1937 and between 1959 and 1970, which was probably connected with migration streams to the republic's territory. The two native peoples make up in their total the majority of its population (53.7 percent in 1970 and 57.8 percent in 1979), with the proportion of these peoples in the republic's population growing in recent decades. Both peoples have preserved on the territory of Kabarda-Balkaria their compact core: In 1970 the republic had 94.6 percent of all Kabardians and 86.3 percent of all Balkars; in 1989 the respective figures were 92.8 percent and 83.5 percent. As we see, in this case, too, the ethnic core of the peoples on the territory of their national-state unit was gradually diminishing.

The Republic of Kalmykia–Khalmg-Tangch was formed in 1920. During the Soviet years its population rose by 188.4 percent, with the more intensive growth taking place from 1920 to 1937 and from 1959 to 1970 through migration. The proportion of Kalmyks, however, considerably declined, from 75.6 percent in 1926 to 45.4 percent in 1989, which was due to both migration to the territory of the republic and the deportation of the Kalmyk people in the 1940s. Mention should be made of the growth of the Kalmyks' proportion in the population of Kalmykia during the past decade (by 3.9 percent), due to an interruption in migration and a higher natural growth of the Kalmyk people. A compact core of this ethnos permanently lives in Kalmykia. Thus, in 1926 there lived here 82.7 percent of Kalmyks and in 1989, 83.9 percent. The growing compactness of distribution of the Kalmyk people can be explained by both resettlement of part of Kalmyks in their native land and assimilation of the scattered groups of this people.

The Karachai-Cherkessian Republic was formed in 1922. Its high population growth (from 1922 to 1989 by 157.8 percent) can be explained by both a rapid natural increase characteristic of the native inhabitants and, partly, migratory additions. The proportion of the two native peoples in the population, which is not very high, is gradually rising (37.2 percent in 1970; 40.9 percent in 1989) owing to a high birthrate of the native inhabitants. Both peoples have on the territory of Karachai-Cherkessia a compact ethnic core (in 1970 the republic had 86.1 percent of all Karachaians and 78.4 percent of all Cherkes; in 1989 the figures were 82.7 percent and 76.9 percent, respectively).

The Republic of Karelia was formed in 1920. Mention should be made of a considerable increase of its population from 1920 to 1989 (by 222.4 percent), which can be explained above all by intensive (voluntary or involuntary) resettlement to its territory from other regions of the country. Peaks of migration activity fall from 1926 to 1959, when the forced type of migration predominated (prisoners' camps and deportations). It was at that time that Karelians became a national minority in their own republic, with the decline in the proportion of Karelian population continuing today (in 1920 Karelians made up 59.8 percent of the population; in 1926, 46.0 percent; in 1970, 11.8 percent; and in 1989, 10.0 percent). Mention should be made, however, of the constant rise in the Karelians' compactness, and a growing proportion of this people living in Karelia: In 1920 there were 38.7 percent of all Karelians, and in 1989, 60.3 percent. This is due primarily to Karelians' intensive assimilation outside the republic (especially Tver Karelians).

The Komi Republic was formed in 1921, and by 1989 increased its population by 558.4 percent. The period of especially rapid growth was from 1926 to 1959, when this territory was intensively used by the Soviet penitentiary system. Back in 1926, 93.6 percent of the republic's population were native inhabitants, while by 1970 already their ratio declined to 28.6 percent. At present it is equal to 23.3 percent. Thus, in Komi, as in Karelia, nonvoluntary migrations radically changed the ethnic composition of the population. However, these events had almost no influence on the compactness of Komi's distribution, who were able to preserve on the territory of the republic a powerful core of their people. Thus, in 1926, 82.9 percent of all Komi lived on this territory, and in 1989, 84.6 percent.

The Mari El Republic was created in 1920. During the years of Soviet power, the republic's population went up by 61.1 percent, in proportion to the growth of this country's population as a whole (61.6 percent). This shows that the republic was little involved in inter-regional migrations; at least the migration balance (the difference between the arrivals and leavers) approached zero. The proportion of native population, totalling in the republic in 1920 54.1 percent, fell relatively little (to 43.3 percent). The scattering of the people also occurred quite moderately: In 1926, 57.6 percent of all Mari lived on the territory of the republic; in 1989, 48.3 percent. In other words, the republic retained a compact Mari core.

The Republic of Mordovia, created in 1930 under the Soviet power, owing to intensive migration processes, lost by 1989 22.3 percent of its population. The process of Mordovians' dispersion that started prior to the revolution continued. At the present time (1989), Mordovians make up only 32.5 percent of the republic's total population, and only 27.1 percent of them live on its territory. Mordovians are one of the few peoples that do not have a compact core on the territory of the republic of the same name.

The Saha Republic (Yakutia) was created in 1922. Mostly owing to migrations, its population increased by 1989 by 280.0 percent. Accordingly, the proportion of the native population within Yakutia dropped to 43.0 percent in 1970; and 33.4 percent in 1989. However, the compact ethnic core of Yakuts on the territory of the republic remained: 96.5 percent of all Yakuts lived there in 1970 and 95.5 percent in 1989. These figures show a poor migratory mobility of Yakut population.

The North Ossetian Republic, formed in 1924, considerably (by 125.7 percent) increased its population in the years of Soviet power, primarily owing to a high natural growth of the North Caucasian peoples. The proportion of the republic's native inhabitants varied with the joining to it of territories with a numerous non-Ossetian population (Prigorodny district), but from 1970 it grew incessantly (1970, 48.8 percent; 1989, 53.0 percent). Most of the 100,000 to 110,000 Ossetian refugees from Georgia live today on the territory of North Ossetia. The republic has retained within its borders a compact core of the Ossetian people (in 1989, 83.3 percent of the Ossetians lived in North Ossetia).

The Republic of Tatarstan was created in 1920, and by 1989 its population had increased comparatively little, by 34.9 percent (less than Russia's average). This leads us to believe that there was a sizeable migratory outflow—in the 1920s and the 1940s and 1950s. However, due to a relatively high natural growth of the Tatars and, possibly, assimilation of other Turkic-speaking ethnic groups, the proportion of Tatar people in the republic's population rose from 41.6 percent (1920) to 48.5 percent (1989). During the same period the compactness of Tatars' distribution considerably decreased. Thus, in 1926 the republic accounted for 41.0 percent of all Russia's Tatars; in 1970, 26.6 percent; and in 1989, 26.5 percent. So the Tatar migration from the republic developing in the Soviet period led to a substantial contraction of the compact core of this people.

The Republic of Tuva was joined to the Soviet Union and Russia as recently as 1944. By 1989, its population substantially increased (by 225.3 percent), mostly through migrations (the main population growth was from the 1940s to the 1960s) and a high birthrate of the Tuvans. The proportion of native population fell by 1970, due to an inflow from outside, to 58.6 percent, but then was steadily rising (1989, 64.3 percent). Almost all Russia's Tuvans live in the territory of the republic (97.1 percent in 1970; 95.7 percent in 1989).

The *Udmurt Republic* was formed in 1920. Its population has been growing from 1920 to 1989 proportionately to that of Russia as a whole (65.6 percent), which indicates little involvement of the republic's territory in migration processes. A splash of migratory activity, though, was to be observed until 1940, with outflow from the republic prevailing until 1926 and inflow from 1926 to 1940. All this changed the ethnic composition of the population: In 1920, Udmurts made up 54.3 percent of the population of the republic; in 1970, 49.7 percent; and in 1989, 30.9 percent. Nevertheless, Udmurtia retained in its territory a compact core of the Udmurt people; in 1926, 77.9 percent of all Udmurts lived there; and in 1989, 66.5 percent. Obviously, the shrinkage of the ethnic core occurred as the result of Udmurts' migration from the republic.

The *Republic of Khakassia* was formed in 1930. The intensive increase of its population by 1989 (by 265.8 percent) is due to migratory additions from the 1930s to the 1950s and the 1970s to the 1980s. The result is that the proportion of the native population, already small, is gradually declining (12.3 percent in 1970; 11.1 percent in 1989). Khakass, however, have in the territory of the republic a compact ethnic core showing a relatively slow decline (1970, 82.1 percent; 1989, 78.8 percent).

The *Chechen-Ingush Republic* was formed in 1922. As its division into the Chechen Republic and the Ingush Republic (the both mentioned in the 1993 Constitution of the Russian Federation) is quite recent, data on the former "dual" republic are given here, by way of exception. Population growth equalled 205.3 percent by 1989, which is due to both a high natural increase and migrations to the territory of the republic (the peak years of migrations are 1926–1937 and 1959–1970). The reduction in the republic's population from 1940 to 1959 (by 4.4 percent) was due to the deportation of the Chechens. The republic retained prevalence of the native peoples, with their proportion growing (58.6 percent in 1970; 64.3 percent in 1989). Predominant parts of Chechens and Ingush resided compactly in the territory of the republic; however, the cores of these peoples are gradually decreasing through their migration from the republic. Thus in 1970, as many as 83.1 percent of Chechens and 72.1 percent of Ingush lived in Chechenia-Ingushetia; by 1989 the figures dropped to 76.8 percent and 69.2 percent.

The *Chuvash Republic* was created in 1920, and until 1989 its population growth was somewhat lower than that of the Russian Federation, with the 1926–1937 data testifying to an inflow into the republic, and the 1979–1989 data showing an outflow from the republic (its population increased by 3.7 percent against Russia's average of 6.9 percent). Chuvashia has preserved the numerical prevalence of native inhabitants but still their ratio declined (81.8 percent in 1920; 67.9 percent in 1989). The core of the Chuvash people, too, has remained in the territory of Chuvashia although in a reduced form. Thus in 1926, the republic had as its residents 59.3

percent of all Chuvash and in 1989, 49.2 percent. The smaller ethnic core is the consequence of Chuvash migration from the republic.

The Jewish Autonomous Region, created in 1934, can hardly be considered a national territorial unit of the Jewish people. Thus in 1970, Jews made up only 6.7 percent of the population of the region; and in 1989, 4.2 percent. Nor can it be said that here lives any appreciable part of the Jewish people of Russia (0.5 percent in 1970; 0.7 percent in 1989). In other words, the Jewish autonomous region should be regarded rather as a purely territorial formation, although the leading members of the Jewish national movement want to retain this region. It should be pointed out that its population from 1934 to 1989 increased very much through migrations (by 311.5 percent), with the main addition made from 1934 to 1937.

The Komi-Permyak Autonomous District, from 1925 (the year of creation) to 1989, had a decline in its population amounting to 7.0 percent. This is connected evidently with the outflow of its inhabitants. The only period of rapid growth of the region's population—1940 to 1959 (by 36.4 percent)—was probably due to the forcible migrations (camps for prisoners). Komi-Permyaks, however, still prevail in the population of this region (1926, 77.0 percent; 1989, 62.5 percent). Obviously, the decline in both the proportion of the Komi-Permyak people and its compactness was caused above all by migration processes.

The Koryak Autonomous District was created in 1930. The increase of its population by 1989 by 207.7 percent was due to a migratory influx most active from the 1930s to the 1950s. The percentage of Koryaks in the population is small and is gradually dropping (1970, 19.0 percent; 1989, 16.5 percent).

The Nenets Autonomous District, from 1929 to 1989, increased its population by 260.0 percent. This was due to the use of the district's territory for prisoners' camps (in the 1930s its population increased by 206.7 percent) and industrial development of the region in the 1970s, when its population grew by 20.5 percent (as compared with Russia's average of 5.7 percent). The proportion of Nenets population is small—15.1 percent in 1970; 11.9 in 1989. However, its compactness (i.e., the ratio of all Nenets living on the territory of the three districts of Nenets, Taimyr (Dolgan-Nenets), and Yamal-Nenets) is high and reached 89.3 percent in 1970 and 85.7 percent in 1989.

The Taimyr (Dolgan-Nenets) Autonomous District also considerably increased its population from its formation in 1930 to 1989 by 522.2 percent. From the 1930s to the 1950s population growth was stimulated primarily through the development of prisoners' camps; in the 1970s, through Taimyr's industrial development. A compact core of the Dolgan people—89.1 percent in 1970, and 71.0 percent in 1989—live on the territory of the district.

The Khanty-Mansi Autonomous District, created in 1930, showed by

1989 a gigantic growth of population amounting to 2,464.0 percent. The influx of migrants to this land was due to its industrial development in the years of Soviet power. The proportion of Khanty and Mansi in the district's population is trifling—7.0 percent in 1970 and 1.4 percent in 1989—which is due to the migration here from other regions of the country long before the revolution. It should be mentioned, however, that both peoples have retained a compact core on the territory of the district. Thus in 1970, there lived here 57.8 percent of all Khanty and 86.7 percent of Mansi; in 1989, 51.7 percent and 77.6 percent, respectively.

The Chukchi Autonomous District, formed in 1930, increased its population by 1989 by 1,071.4 percent. The main influx of population into the district was in the postwar decades and was connected with the development of the mining industry in the Chukot Peninsula and with the end of the notorious Dalstroi (The department which from the 1930s to the 1950s was in charge of forced labor in the Soviet Far East) rule in the Magadan region. The small proportion of native inhabitants in the district's population (10.9 percent in 1970 and 7.3 percent in 1989) is coupled, however, with a high compactness of the Chukchi people. Thus in 1970, as many as 80.9 percent and in 1989 as many as 79.3 percent of Chukchi lived in the territory of their autonomy.

The Evenk Autonomous District increased its population from 1930 to 1989, mostly through migration, by 316.7 percent. Migration peaks were in the 1930s (forcible migration) and in the 1970s and 1980s (industrial development). The proportion of the native people in the district's population fell, owing to migratory influx, from 24.6 percent in 1970 to 14.0 in 1989. It should be noted that Evenks are a people living extremely dispersedly and having no compact ethnic core on the territory of the district. In 1970 only 12.8 percent, and in 1989, 11.7 percent of all Evenks lived here.

The Yamal-Nenets Autonomous District, as were a number of other districts, was an arena of an extremely intensive influx of population. From 1930 to 1989 it grew by 2,052.2 percent, both through forcible migration in the early period of Soviet history and through the territory's industrial development in recent time. Therefore, the proportion of Nenets population here is constantly falling—from 21.9 percent in 1970 to 4.2 percent in 1989. It will be recalled, however, that the majority of the Nenets people are concentrated in the three Nenets territorial autonomies.

The above survey makes it possible to draw the conclusion that the territories of most of Russia's present-day republics and autonomies were, in the years of Soviet power, the arena of intensive ethnodemographic processes connected with forcible or voluntary migrations. The result was that the newly arrived population began to prevail in most of these territories. However, the overwhelming majority of Russia's national-state or national-territorial units retained within their borders a compact ethnic core, that is, by far a prevalent ratio of the people for whom the given republic or autonomy had been created. This fact was most important for the preservation of ethnic identity of the peoples and, consequently, for the process of national cultural revival that has made itself felt in recent years.

This thesis can be confirmed by the estimates we have made. We have calculated Spearman's coefficient of rank correlation[4] for twenty-six peoples of Russia: Russians, Tatars, Chuvash, Bashkirs, Mordovians, Chechens, Udmurts, Mari, Avars, Ossetians, Lezghins, Buryats, Kabardians, Yakuts, Komi, Kumyks, Darghinians, Ingush, Tuvans, Kalmyks, Karachaians, Permyaks, Karelians, Adyghei, Laks, Balkars; that is, the peoples having their own national-territorial units. Comparison was made of such indices as the number of the given people; compactness of its distribution (the proportion of those living within their national-territorial unit); knowledge of the mother tongue (the proportion of those regarding the language of their nationality as vernacular). The highest value of the coefficient (0.61)[5] pointed to the connection of compactness of the people's distribution within its republic or autonomy with a well-preserved national culture (the language above all). Dependence of the preservation of the national language on the number of the people, however, was not discovered (the coefficient value equal to 0.04). In other words, the preserved *ethnic core within the respective national-state or national-territorial unit is the major factor in maintaining the ethnic identity of a people.*

CULTURAL-LINGUISTIC PROCESSES

First of all, attention is attracted by the fact that most of the peoples of the USSR in 1926 well preserved their vernacular as the main national-cultural feature. By 1989 linguistic assimilation in many cases became noticeable, affecting first and foremost the peoples that did not have their own national-territorial units and also such a specific group of minorities as the small peoples of the North. The main pillar of linguistic and cultural traditions is the rural population, but the national-cultural revival reflected in a heightened interest in the mother tongue is more of an urban phenomenon. Mention should also be made of the widespread use by the peoples of Russia of the Russian language as a second vernacular.

The Russians. With regard to the subject of this section, mention should be made of a very poor knowledge by the Russian population of Russia of any languages of its peoples. On the whole, 99.38 percent of Russia's Russians are "unilingual," that is, do not know other languages spoken in the country. A somewhat appreciable proportion (more than one percent of the Russian population) of "bilingual" Russians is to be found in such republics as Daghestan, Komi, Mari, North Ossetia, Tataria, Udmurtia, Chuvashia, Yakutia, and in the Aginsk Buryat and the Komi-Permyak districts. This picture is typical of the dominating people in a multinational state. It is also due to a high migratory mobility of the Russian people. Nevertheless, it can be assumed that the sovereignty proclaimed by former autonomies within Russia and the respective policies of the republics' authorities (just as the eventual introduction of republican citizenship, declining migratory mobility, and other causes) may lead to a wider spread of bilingualism among the Russian population of the republics and autonomies. It should be observed that these national-territorial units, while occupying more than half of Russia's territory, have within their bounds less than 18 percent of its population. Bilingualism, consequently, will embrace, in any case, but a negligible part of the Russian people.

The Ukrainians. In 1926 there was an appreciable proportion of Ukrainians in the USSR who regarded not the Ukrainian language but Russian above all as their vernacular. Only 88.4 percent of the Ukrainian population spoke Ukrainian. In 1989 the Ukrainian language was seen as their vernacular only by 81.1 percent of Ukrainians in the USSR and 43.8 percent of Ukrainians in Russia. Ukrainian-Russian bilingualism was widespread: Russian as a second language was spoken by 56.2 percent of the Ukrainians of the USSR. In other words, the process of assimilation of the Ukrainians by the Russian people had gone quite far, especially in Russia. The rural Ukrainian population preserved their mother tongue to a greater extent. The decade between 1979 and 1989, however, saw a revival in Russia of Ukrainians' national culture, which more involved the urban inhabitants and the youth. Thus, in Russia's cities in 1979 the Ukrainian language was regarded as vernacular only by 39.8 percent of the Ukrainians. By 1989 the figure was 42.5 percent. In rural localities the process of reanimation of the Ukrainian language was most active among the youth (here and elsewhere this age group includes persons 16 to 19 years old). Thus in 1979, the Ukrainian language was considered vernacular by only 34.5 percent of Ukrainian young people, and in 1989 by 42.1 percent. It should be added that one of the components here may be the influence exerted on linguistic processes by the new wave of migrants from the Ukraine.

The Byelorussians have long been integrated into the Russian language environment. In 1926 only 73.1 percent of Byelorussians in the USSR regarded Byelorussian as vernacular; in 1989, 70.9 percent of Byelorussians in the USSR and 36.2 percent in Russia. Byelorussian-Russian bilingualism is widespread among this people. As with other peoples, their mother tongue has been better preserved by Byelorussian population in Russia's rural localities: In 1989 the Byelorussian language was regarded as vernacular by 34.9 percent of urban and 41.6 percent of rural Byelorussians. From 1979 to 1989 no splash of national-cultural revival was observed, either in towns or in the countryside, or among the young people. Rather, on the contrary, Byelorussians' assimilation increased. Thus in 1979, the Byelorussian language was regarded as vernacular by 39.4 percent of the Byelorussian urban youth in Russia, while in 1989 the figure dropped to 35.8 percent.

The Moldavians preserved their language and cultural traditions sufficiently well. Thus in 1926, the Moldavian language was seen as vernacular by 94.4 percent of Moldavians in the USSR and in 1989, by 92.6 percent; in Russia by 66.8 percent. At the same time Moldavian-Russian bilingualism attained a considerable level. In 1989 as many as 53.8 percent of Moldavians in the USSR and 61.7 percent in Russia spoke Russian as their second language.

The Lithuanians in the USSR in 1926 made up a numerically small and rather assimilated group of whom only 52.6 percent spoke Lithuanian. In 1989, however, in the USSR—which included the Lithuanian Soviet Socialist Republic—the degree of linguistic assimilation of this people was minimal: the mother tongue was spoken by 97.7 percent of Lithuanians, with only 37.9 percent of them knowing Russian as a second language. In other words, there existed a serious linguistic-cultural barrier between the Lithuanians and the other peoples of the USSR. As to Russia's Lithuanians, their assimilation was well advanced: 59.6 percent of them regarded Lithuanian as their vernacular; 39.5 percent, Russian; 56.6 percent spoke Russian as their second language.

The Letts, as did the Lithuanians, well preserved their linguistic identity in the Soviet years: in 1989, 94.8 percent of Letts in the USSR regarded the language of their nationality as their vernacular. Among them, however, bilingualism was more developed (64.4 percent considered Russian their second language) owing to a high proportion of Russians in Latvia's population. Russia's Letts experienced a greater linguistic assimilation than the Lithuanians: only 42.8 percent of them regarded Lettish as their vernacular.

The Estonians in many linguistic-cultural features resemble the Lithuanians (1989). These include a high degree of preservation by Estonians in the USSR of their mother tongue (95.4 percent), and an insignificant spread among them of Estonian-Russian bilingualism (33.9 percent). Estonians living in Russia, however, have been subjected to a greater linguistic-cultural assimilation than Lithuanians: only 41.5 percent of them consider Estonian their mother tongue. The different degree of preservation of their linguistic-cultural identity by the Estonians, Letts, and Lithuanians in Russia is due to the above-mentioned fact, namely, that the Lithuanian diaspora in this country is of a comparatively later origin. It was replenished by migrants from Lithuania in the postwar period.

The Poles in the USSR, even in 1926, were at a sufficiently high stage of linguistic-cultural assimilation: only 46.4 percent of them spoke their mother tongue. In 1989, only 30.6 percent of Poles in the USSR preserved Polish as their vernacular. In Russia this figure is substantially lower and reaches but 15.1 percent. In other words, Poles in Russia almost fully lost their ethnic originality.

The Germans in 1926 were almost not affected by linguistic-cultural assimilation: 96.3 percent of Germans in the USSR spoke German. In consequence of the liquidation of German autonomy and deportation of the German people in 1941, the German population of the USSR lost to a considerable degree their mother tongue—it was preserved by only 48.7 percent of Germans (in Russia by only 41.8 percent). More than half of the Germans passed to the Russian language, and German-Russian bilingualism became widespread. Assimilation processes can be stopped only through the restoration of German autonomy.

The Jews, back in 1926, still preserved in their overwhelming majority (72.5 percent of the Jewish population of the USSR) their mother tongue. At present the Jewish population in the main consider Russian their vernacular (86.5 percent of Jews in the USSR and 90.5 percent of Jews in Russia, 1989). The complete linguistic assimilation is connected with the absence in our country of the practice of cultural autonomy and with the fact that the overwhelming part of Jews are urban inhabitants. It should be mentioned that although the ratio of rural inhabitants among the Jews is very low, rural Jews in Russia preserved their mother tongue much better: in 1979, Jewish (mostly Yiddish) was regarded as their mother tongue by 21.7 percent of rural Jews; in 1989, by 26.8 percent. It was in the countryside that the process of national cultural revival had led, from 1979 to 1989, to statistically appreciable changes in the linguistic sphere. Interestingly, in the Jewish autonomous region the percentage of those who consider the Jewish language their vernacular is somewhat higher than among the entire Jewish population of Russia.

The Tatars in the USSR in 1926 fully preserved their mother tongue. Moreover, the Tatar language was also widely used by the other peoples of the Volga Belt. By 1989 the Tatars had almost not undergone linguistic russification. Note the following figures: Tatar was named as their mother tongue by 83.2 percent of Tatars in the USSR, 85.6 percent in Russia, and 96.6 percent in Tataria. In other words, with the widening of the Tatar diaspora's "circles" (Tatars in Russia outside Tataria, Tatars in the USSR outside Russia) the linguistic-cultural assimilation (russification) of the Tatar people is increasing. Thus, 16.1 percent of Tatars in the USSR, 14.2 percent of Tatars in Russia, and only 3.3 percent of Tatars in Tataria regarded the Russian language as their vernacular. Similar processes are also typical of other peoples in Russia having their own national-territorial units. Tatar-Russian bilingualism is widespread among this people: over 80 percent of its population use Russian as a second language or mother tongue. The Tatar language is preserved to a greater extent in rural localities: in 1989 as many as 81.0 percent of the urban and 94.5 percent of rural Tatars of Russia saw in their language the vernacular. It should be noted that linguistic statistics do not make it possible to conclude that a process of national-cultural revival of Tatars in Russia was taking place in

1989. On the contrary, in different groups of the Tatar people (city dwellers, rural population, the youth) the percentage of those who could speak the Tatar language somewhat declined.

The Chuvash in the USSR in 1926 spoke primarily their mother tongue (98.9 percent). The degree of linguistic assimilation of the Chuvash people by 1989 was somewhat higher than that of the Tatars, but the main tendencies were the same: the Chuvash language was regarded as vernacular by 76.4 percent of Chuvash in the USSR, by 77.5 percent in Russia, and 85.0 percent in Chuvashia. A better knowledge of their language was shown by the rural inhabitants (in 1989 by 90.8 percent against 64.2 percent of city dwellers). Revival in the national sphere from 1979 to 1989 was not observed either.

The Bashkirs in the USSR in 1926 spoke both Bashkir (55.2 percent) and Tatar. In 1989 the majority of Bashkirs considered their own language vernacular (in the USSR 72.3 percent, in Russia 72.8 percent, and in Bashkiria 74.7 percent). Bashkir-Russian bilingualism was widespread (over 80 percent of the Bashkir people spoke Russian as a second language or regarded it as vernacular). On the whole, the Bashkirs were subjected to a greater linguistic assimilation than the Tatars. Interestingly, however, linguistic assimilation (not only on the part of the Russians but also the Tatars) affected the Bashkir countryside to a greater extent than the town. Thus in 1979, the Bashkir language was regarded as vernacular by 73.6 percent of urban Bashkirs and by 63.3 percent of rurals. That was probably why the process of national-linguistic revival was taking place not in the cities but in the countryside. By 1989 already 75.7 percent of the rural inhabitants against the 72.8 percent of the town dwellers regarded Bashkir as their mother tongue. This process was faster among the rural young people.

The Mordovians in 1926 still spoke primarily Mordovian (94.5 percent). By 1989 the process of assimilation reached an appreciable (although not yet critical for the people) level: Mordovian was seen as their mother tongue by 67.1 percent of Mordovians in the USSR, 69.0 percent in Russia, and 88.5 percent in Mordovia. Mordovian-Russian bilingualism (the use of Russian as vernacular or a second language) embraced over 90 percent of this people. In rural localities the Mordovian language was preserved better than in towns (the respective figures for 1989 are: 83.5 percent against 55.7 percent). At the same time statistics do not show in recent years any signs of national-cultural revival of this people. On the contrary, there was observed a process of linguistic assimilation, especially among the urban Mordovian youth.

The Udmurts in the USSR in 1926 spoke primarily their mother tongue, which was used also among some other ethnic groups of the Volga Belt. By 1989, however, the Udmurts' linguistic assimilation became quite noticeable. Thus, in the USSR the Udmurt language was regarded as their mother tongue by 69.6 percent of representatives of this nationality, in Russia by 70.8 percent, and in Udmurtia by 75.7 percent. More than 90 percent of Udmurts knew Russian in one form or another. In the countryside the mother tongue was preserved by 83.8 percent of Udmurts (1989) and in the cities by 56.8 percent. From 1979 to 1989 the processes of linguistic-cultural assimilation continued.

The Mari underwent a very slight linguistic assimilation. In 1926 as many as 99.4 percent of Mari in the USSR spoke the Mari language. In 1989 the mother tongue was preserved by 80.8 percent of Mari in the USSR, by 81.9 percent in Russia, and 88.4 percent in the respective autonomy. About 90 percent of Mari (1989) could use the Russian language to some extent or other. As in other cases, the Mari language was better preserved in the countryside than in the cities (in 1989, 90.3 percent against 69.5 percent). From 1979 to 1989 statistics show a certain decline in the use of the Mari language.

The Komi, in the early post-revolutionary years (the 1926 census), spoke primarily their mother tongue (97.4 percent). During the years of Soviet power, however, the Komi language incurred certain losses: it was regarded as their mother tongue by 70.4 percent of Komi in the USSR, 71.0 percent in Russia, and 74.4 percent of the native population of the respective republic. The Komi, and all the Finno-Ugric peoples, are distinguished by a good knowledge of the Russian language (it is used as vernacular or a second language by over 90 percent of Komi). As in many other cases, the Komi language is better preserved among the rural population. The past decade has seen a process of linguistic assimilation, especially among the young people. Thus in 1989, the Komi language was considered vernacular by 55.8 percent of the city dwellers (among the younger ages by 41.2 percent) and by 85.5 percent of rural inhabitants (among the youth, by 76.8 percent). In other words, the Komi's linguistic assimilation will continue, at least in the near future.

The Komi-Permyaks exhibit a complete linguistic identity with the Komi proper (Zyrians). In 1926 the mother tongue was known by 96.2 percent of Permyaks, in 1989 in the USSR by 70.4 percent, in Russia by 71.1 percent, and in the Komi-Permyak Autonomous District by 82.9 percent. Russian was used as a second language or vernacular by over 90 percent of members of this people. The mother tongue was preserved by 82.5 percent of rural Permyaks and 53.9 percent of city dwellers. It is known by an appreciably smaller number of young people: in the countryside it is used by 75.1 percent of Komi-Permyaks aged 16 to 19, and in the cities by 51.8 percent.

The Karelians, during the Soviet period, were subjected to a considerable linguistic-cultural assimilation. In 1926, Karelian was spoken by 96.6 percent of Karelians, in 1989 in the USSR by 48.1 percent, in Russia by 48.6 percent, and in Karelia by 51.9 percent. Russian has become vernacular or a second language for the overwhelming majority of Karelians, considerably surpassing 90 percent. In 1989, Karelian was regarded as the mother tongue by 62.7 percent of the rural Karelians (among the young people, 34.4 percent) and 39.7 percent of urban Karelians (among the young people, 18.9 percent). The changes in the Karelian speakers' correlation from 1979 to 1989, as well as the poor knowledge of their mother tongue by the Karelian young people, indicate the rapid pace of Karelians' linguistic assimilation.

The Veps in the USSR in 1926 spoke primarily their mother tongue (94.9 percent). By 1989 the proportion of those who regarded Veps as vernacular declined in the USSR to 50.8 percent, in Russia to 51.3 percent. Almost all the Veps speak Russian as their mother tongue or a second language.

The Izhorians were counted by the 1926 census among the peoples speaking Finnish (the Finnish and Izhorian languages are closely related). By 1989 only 36.8 percent of Izhorians in the USSR and 50.7 percent in Russia regarded the Izhorian language as their mother tongue. Most of the Izhorians are Russian-speaking.

The Finns, in the first post-revolutionary years, spoke primarily their mother tongue. By 1989 it was preserved only by 34.6 percent of Finns in the USSR and 36.2 percent of Russia's Finns. The Finnish population in the main passed to the Russian language. Among all the peoples of Russia whose ethnic territory is within its bounds (the so-called "native peoples"), precisely the above four Baltic-Finnish ethnoses: the Karelians, Veps, Izhorians, and Finns (with the exception of the small peoples of the North) have undergone the greatest linguistic-cultural assimilation.

The Chechens have retained a good knowledge of their vernacular. It was regarded as the mother tongue in 1989 by 98.1 percent of Chechens in the USSR, 98.8 percent in Russia, and 99.8 percent in Chechenia-Ingushetia. Russian as a second language was spoken by over 70 percent of members of this people, which is a high level of bilingualism. It is to be observed that the mother tongue was known in both the cities and the countryside almost identically: by 97.0 percent and 99.5 percent, respectively. The Chechens have thus practically not been subjected to linguistic-cultural assimilation, although they have been able to enter the sphere of Russian culture through the knowledge of Russian as a second language.

The Ingush, in the linguistic sphere, do not differ from the Chechens. In 1989 the Ingush language was regarded as the mother tongue by 97.0 percent of them in the USSR, 98.2 percent in Russia, and 99.6 percent in Chechenia-Ingushetia. The Ingush-Russian bilingualism, however, is more developed than Chechen-Russian: more than 80 percent of Ingush knew Russian as a second language. Ingush of all ages living in cities knew their mother tongue almost as well as rural Ingush (96.6 percent and 99.2 percent, respectively). This state of the linguistic sphere is characteristic of practically all peoples of the Northern Caucasus.

The Karachaians, during the years of Soviet power, even increased their knowledge of the mother tongue. In 1926, Karachaian was spoken by 93.2 percent of this people. In 1989 the Karachaian language was regarded as vernacular by 96.8 percent of Karachaians in the USSR, 97.7 percent in Russia, and 99.2 percent in the respective autonomy. Moreover, up to 80 percent of Karachaians knew the Russian language as well. True, city dwellers knew their mother tongue less than rural inhabitants and young people less than representatives of the older ages, but these differences are not at all essential (ranging from 3 to 5 percent).

The Cherkes, by 1989, retained a very good knowledge of their mother tongue. It was named as vernacular by 90.4 percent of Cherkes in the USSR, 91.5 percent in Russia, and 97.9 percent in Karachai-Cherkessia. About 80 percent of Cherkes also knew the Russian language. Rural inhabitants knew their mother tongue somewhat better than city dwellers (94.9 percent and 85.7 percent, respectively). Differences between the younger and older people in the knowledge of the mother tongue were quite negligible.

The Kabardians have fully preserved their mother tongue. In 1989 it was known by 97.2 percent of Kabardians in the USSR, 97.6 percent in Russia, and 99.8 percent in Kabarda-Balkaria. Some 80 percent of Kabardians used Russian as a second language. A good, approximately the same, knowledge of the mother tongue is characteristic of the city dwellers and rural inhabitants of this nationality, in all age groups.

The Balkars, a people related to the Karachaians, in the linguistic sphere continue all the main tendencies of the North Caucasian peoples: a stable orientation to the mother tongue (it was used by 93.6 percent of Balkars in the USSR, 95.3 percent in Russia, and 98.4 percent in Balkaria); and a good knowledge of Russian (up to 80 percent of Balkars are bilingual in one form or another). As regards the degree of knowledge of the mother tongue, there are almost no differences between the city dwellers and rural population, in all age groups.

The example of the above-mentioned North Caucasian peoples is quite sufficient to judge the other native nationalities of this region: the Avars, Adyghei, Darghinians, Ossetians, Lezghins, Laks, Kumyks, Tabasarans, Nogais, Abazinians, Rutuls, Aguls, and Tsakhurs. All of them, primarily due to little dispersion, have practically not suffered linguistic assimilation. Most of them are bilingual, but the peoples of Daghestan know the Russian language appreciably less than the other North Caucasian peoples. The figure indicating the knowledge of the Russian language is the highest for the Laks and Nogais (about 80 percent in 1989) and the lowest for the Tsakhurs (23.5 percent of this people know Russian as a second language).

The Armenians in the USSR, in 1926, almost all spoke their mother tongue (94.1 percent). In 1989 as many as 91.7 percent of Armenians in the USSR considered Armenian their vernacular. In other words, linguistic assimilation had almost no influence on the Armenians in Armenia proper. Thus, only 47.1 percent of Armenians in the USSR knew Russian as a second language. The Armenian diaspora in Russia, however, is much more integrated in the Russian linguistic culture. Among them only 67.8 percent (1989) regard Armenian as their mother tongue, 31.8 percent are Russian-speaking, and 61.4 percent use Russian as a second language. Rural Armenians in Russia are the preservers of the national language: In 1989 it was considered vernacular by 83.5 percent of rural Armenians against 61.3 percent of the city dwellers. However, from 1979 to 1989 the rural Armenians showed certain losses in their knowledge of the mother tongue while the urban population showed gains, which possibly testifies to the beginning of the Russian Armenians' linguistic-cultural revival.

A situation similar to that of Russia's Armenians is characteristic of *the Georgians* and *Azerbaijanians* living on the territory of the Federation: The fully preserved vernacular and a poor knowledge of the Russian language in the respective republics; and certain indications of a linguistic-cultural assimilation of Georgians (to a greater extent) and Azerbaijanians (to a lesser extent) in Russia's territory. *The Abkhazians* in Abkhazia know the Russian language better (it was used by more than 80 percent of Abkhazian population in the USSR) and they have been more subjected to linguistic assimilation in Russia (only 65.6 percent of Russia's Abkhazians recognize the Abkhazian language as their mother tongue).

The Kara-Kalpaks, Kazakhs, Uzbeks, Tajiks, Turkmens, and *Kirghiz,* during the years of Soviet power, have practically not been affected by linguistic assimilation, preserving the knowledge of their mother tongue (1989) at the level of 95 to 98 percent of the numerical strength of the people. The Russian language in the respective republics did not play a part of any importance in everyday life. Russian as a second language is known best by the Kazakhs (60.4 percent), and least by the Kara-Kalpaks (20.5 percent). Members of these peoples in Russia have preserved their mother tongues (respective figures range from 80 to 90 percent), but have also developed bilingualism. Russian as the mother tongue or a second language was used in 1989 by approximately 90 percent of the members of these ethnoses. Russia's Kazakhs alone have an appreciable rural population, whereas the diaspora of the Central Asian peoples in Russia is represented by urban inhabitants. As in other similar cases, urban Kazakhs know their mother tongue less than the rural population (the respective figures for 1989 are 81.5 percent and 91.7 percent). During the ten years after 1979, the orientation of all groups of Russia's Kazakhs to their vernacular somewhat diminished (thus in 1979 it was spoken by 92.6 percent of the rural youth, while in 1989 the figure was 90.6 percent).

The Yakuts, whose language back in the 1920s was widespread in Siberia, have to this day been able to retain a high degree of knowledge of their mother tongue (94.0 percent of Russia's Yakuts, 95.1 percent of the

Yakuts of the respective republic). Russian, moreover, is used as a second language or the mother tongue by up to 70 percent of this people, which is a sufficiently high index of bilingualism. There is an appreciable difference in the knowledge of the mother tongue by rural and urban Yakuts (98.0 percent as against 83.8 percent).

The Kalmyks have well preserved their mother tongue (in 1989 it was used by 89.7 percent of Kalmyks in the USSR, 93.1 percent in Russia, and 96.1 percent in the respective republic). At the same time, Kalmyk-Russian bilingualism involved over 90 percent of the given people. Rural and urban Kalmyks have approximately the same knowledge of the mother tongue; in other words, the processes of linguistic assimilation have little affected the urban Kalmyk population as a whole. Certain tendencies toward a decline in the knowledge of the mother tongue, however, can be found among the Kalmyk youth in both the cities and the countryside.

The Buryats, have preserved their mother tongue somewhat less than the Kalmyks (in the USSR 86.5 percent of Buryats recognize the Buryat language as vernacular; in Russia, 86.6 percent; in Buryatia, 89.4 percent; in Aginsk district, 98.4 percent; and in Ust-Orda district, 90.0 percent). There is an appreciable group among the Buryats who have fully passed to the Russian language (it equals 10.0 to 13.0 percent of the Buryat population). More than 70 percent of Buryats use Russian as a second language. A difference between the urban and rural Buryats can be observed: the latter have preserved their mother tongue much better. Thus in 1989, as many as 94.0 percent of rural and 76.3 percent of urban Buryats were oriented to the Buryat language. In the past ten years a tendency to some curtailment of the sphere of usage of the Buryat language has appeared.

The Tuvans have fully preserved their vernacular (in Tuva it is used by 99.8 percent of Tuvans); the knowledge of Russian is at a comparatively low level (it is used by not more than 60 percent of the natives). The vernacular is almost equally widespread among the urban and rural Tuvans. This people has, for the most part, not been subjected to cultural-linguistic assimilation.

The Khakass in the USSR in 1926 were already appreciably affected by linguistic assimilation: the mother tongue was spoken by only 88.5 percent of this people. In the Soviet period this process continued, but on the whole the Khakass have preserved their mother tongue: 76.6 percent of Khakass in Russia and 83.2 percent in the respective republic are oriented to it. About a quarter of Khakass in Russia (and 16.7 percent of this people in Khakassia) are Russian-speakers, and together with those who know Russian as a second language this language is used by 90 percent of this people. The vernacular has been preserved to a greater extent by the rural Khakass (it is spoken by 84.7 percent in the countryside against 65.7 percent of Khakass in the cities). It should be noted that the process of transition to Russian has halted in the cities, while in the rural localities it continues.

Thus, among the young Khakass city dwellers the proportion of those who speak the vernacular is equal to this proportion in the entire urban Khakass population (66.0 percent), while in the countryside the Khakass young people are less oriented to the mother tongue (the respective proportion is 81.6 percent).

The Altaians have better preserved their mother tongue than the Khakass, although in the 1920s they were more subjected to linguistic-cultural assimilation. Thus in 1926, the Altaian language was spoken only by 82.8 percent of Altaians. By 1989 this proportion even increased: 84.3 percent of Altaians were oriented to the mother tongue in the USSR, 85.1 percent in Russia, and 89.6 percent in the respective autonomy. The Altaians have an appreciably smaller ratio of Russian-speakers (about 15.0 percent of all Russia's Altaians and about 10.0 percent of the respective population of Mountain Altai). On the whole, the Russian language is spoken by about 80 percent of this population. In 1989 rural inhabitants were appreciably ahead of the city dwellers in the knowledge of the vernacular: 89.8 percent against 64.2 percent. Of interest however, is the same correlation in the younger ages: 87.1 percent against 77.8 percent. The figures show that at the end of the 1970s and the beginning of the 1980s there began among the urban Altaians the process of linguistic-cultural revival, which, however, did not influence the rural localities.

The Shorians found themselves, toward 1989, in a state of much greater linguistic-cultural assimilation than their kith and kin, the Altaians and Khakass. Thus, the vernacular was known in Russia by only 57.5 percent of Shorians; 40.9 percent of them were Russian-speakers; 53.6 percent knew Russian as a second language. This situation developed when the Shorians did not have their own territorial autonomy.

The peoples of the North as a whole found themselves in hard linguistic-cultural circumstances fraught with the loss of their vernaculars. Thus in 1989, only 52.7 percent of representatives of these peoples preserved their mother tongue (taken in their totality), 36.4 percent were Russian-speakers, 50.5 percent spoke Russian as a second language. As regards individual peoples of this group, however, the situation varied. Good knowledge of their mother tongue (at the level exceeding 60.0 percent of the respective people) was characteristic of the Nenets, Nganasans, Dolgans, Khanty, and Chukchi. Poor knowledge of the mother tongue (less than 30.0 percent of the respective people) was exhibited by the Itelmens, Chuvans, Aleutians, Nivkhs, Udegheis, Orochi, Neghidals. Obviously, a better preservation of the mother tongue was helped by the existence of a national-territorial unit; at the same time, the absence of a territorial autonomy led to the loss of their vernacular by a number of peoples of the North.

Of course, the rural inhabitants have been the main preservers of the national languages of the peoples of this group. Data for the Northern peoples who have their territorial autonomies show that the 1980s saw a revival of national languages, that is, a splash of national self-consciousness among the urban population. This is evident in the growing orientation to national languages among these peoples' urban youth. Thus, among the urban Nenets a total of 56.5 percent were oriented to the Nenets language; and among the youth, 66.6 percent; figures for the Dolgans were 57.6 percent and 72.2 percent; for the Khanty, 42.9 percent and 63.5 percent; for the Mansi, 25.1 percent and 32.1 percent; the Evenks, 29.1 percent and 31.9 percent; the Chukchi, 47.1 percent against 53.6 percent.

Of the Northern peoples having their territorial autonomies the Koryaks were probably the only ones who did not exhibit a splash of linguistic-cultural revival in the 1980s.

The Koreans, after the deportation at the end of the 1930s, lost to a considerable extent their mother tongue and passed to Russian. In 1989, 49.4 percent of Koreans were oriented to their vernacular in the USSR and 36.5 percent in Russia. Almost all Koreans spoke Russian either as their mother tongue or as a second language. A similar linguistic situation is characteristic of *the Greeks* (94.8 percent of whom in 1926 spoke their mother tongue); *the Bulgarians* (their respective ratio was 95.3 percent) and *the Assyrians.* At present less than half of these peoples recognize the language of their nationality as their mother tongue: In the main they are oriented to the Russian language.

The Gypsies provide an especial example of linguistic-cultural situation. If the 1926 census is to be trusted, only 67.9 percent of Gypsies at that time preserved their mother tongue. By 1989 the proportion increased in the USSR to 77.5 percent and in Russia to 85.8 percent with a widely developed Gypsy–Russian bilingualism (77.3 percent of Gypsies in Russia used Russian as a second language). The proportion of Gypsies, however, who had fully passed to Russian was not high and ranged from 10.0 to 12.0 percent. If we are to believe statistical data (and with regard to the Gypsies they are often doubtful), this people in the Soviet years has been able almost fully to restore its language. Probably in this case the traditional peculiarities of the way of life of this people have played the same part in the preservation and reanimation of the mother tongue that territorial autonomy has for other peoples.

The main conclusion suggested here is that the preservation and development of the national language and other elements of culture essentially, if not mostly, depend on the possession by the given people of its own national-territorial (state or even administrative) unit, as well as the concentration in that unit of a compact core of the given people. In this sense the fundamental element of Soviet nationalities policy—the creation of national-territorial autonomies—should be recognized as having stood the test of time. Russia's further progress as a multinational state cannot be ensured without taking account of this fact.

Mention was made above of the growing cultural heterogeneity in the ethnic structure of Russia. This view, however, would be one-sided if consideration is not given to the widespread bilingualism (on the basis of the Russian language) in the country as a major channel of information exchange. It should be mentioned that bilingualism does not necessarily lead to linguistic assimilation. Moreover, in Russia only a few "native" peoples (Karelians, Veps, Izhorians, Finns, and part of the peoples of the North) are threatened with russification. Most of the peoples have retained their linguistic-cultural identity. Attention should be given to the need to develop a system of extraterritorial cultural autonomy in Russia to satisfy the linguistic-cultural requirements of the dispersed groups of peoples of newly born "foreign countries."

Statistics show that although the village population is the preserver of the linguistic-cultural traditions of a people, the reanimation and rebirth of these traditions is a phenomenon of urban life (only the Bashkirs are an exception). For a number of peoples of Russia the national-cultural (linguistic) revival became an accomplished fact at the end of the 1970s and the beginning of the 1980s.

The materials in this part of the book make it possible to assert that linguistic processes have not only ethnic but also regional links. Thus, among the peoples of the Northern Caucasus they had one form; among the peoples of the Volga Belt another; in Southern Siberia yet another variety was to be observed, and so on. The regional sameness of linguistic processes is largely connected not only with what ethnographers call "historico-ethnographic entity" (an area with similar cultural traditions) but also with a different level of socioeconomic development of different regions. This problem, however, requires additional study.

SOCIOECONOMIC PROCESSES

The modernization of Russia, that is, its transition from the traditional society to the modern industrial one, is primarily an event of the Soviet period. Thus, the 1897 census registered in the Russian Empire (without Poland, Finland, Bukhara, and Khiva) 12.6 percent of urban inhabitants within the total population. This is an extremely low index showing an agrarian character of Russian society. The 1920 census recorded in European Russia 14.6 percent of urban inhabitants within the entire population. Only in the 1960s did urban inhabitants exceed half of Russia's population; in 1970 their proportion reached 62.3 percent; by 1979, 69.1 percent; by 1989, 73.4 percent. From 1970 to 1989 the ratio of urban inhabitants increased by 17.8 percent. Russia joined the club of highly urbanized countries.

The demographic indices concerning Russia's population (1989) show that in its main demographic features it now differs little from the population of industrially developed countries of the world. These indices include the average age of the population (34.7 years), the average family size (3.2 persons), and the average number of births per one woman (1.8). From the demographic point of view, Russia's population as a whole is evidently living through the final stage of modernization, when the negative consequences of the demographic transition do not reveal themselves in full. Thus, the demographic structure of Russia's population has so far retained the prevalence of people of working ages, although their proportion is decreasing. In 1979 a total of 23.3 percent of the population were persons under working age; 60.4 percent were of working age; and 16.3 percent were persons who had passed the working age. In 1989 the respective age groups equalled 24.5 percent; 56.9 percent; and 18.5 percent. In other words, the process of aging of Russia's inhabitants was beginning to show. In 1989 a considerable influence of the countryside on demographic processes was still making itself felt. Although (owing to the "countryside–town" migrations) the average age of rural inhabitants was older than that of city residents by more than a year (35.8 years against 34.4 years), the countryside continued to be in the lead in birthrate (2.4 births per woman against 1.6 in the cities), preventing Russia's depopulation.

The 1979–1989 decade showed a noticeable rise in the education level of Russia's population, mostly through an increased proportion of persons with higher education (130 persons per every 1,000 against 94 persons in 1979) and with specialized secondary education (192 per 1,000 against 127 in 1979). The proportion of people with secondary education increased negligibly (484 persons per 1,000 inhabitants in 1989; 477 persons in 1979), although they totalled almost half of all Russia's citizens. There was a serious decline in the number of people with primary education or without any education. In 1979 they numbered 302 persons per 1,000; in 1989 a mere 194 persons per 1,000.

The decade from 1979 to 1989 saw the process of decline in the proportion of people employed in material production and a growth of those employed in nonmaterial branches of the national economy. Thus in 1979, as many as 75.8 percent of citizens worked in material production and 24.1 percent in nonmaterial. In 1989 the figures were 72.3 percent and 27.0 percent, respectively. Accordingly, the proportion of those engaged primarily in mental work was rising (31.2 percent in 1979; 35.1 percent in 1989) and the proportion of manual workers was falling (68.8 percent and 64.9 percent). However, in its employment structure Russia remains seriously behind the developed industrial countries of the world.

The sphere of material production showed during the same period a certain regrouping of labor resources: from industry, construction, agriculture, and forestry to transport and communications, to the services (trade, public catering, etc.). This movement of the labor force, however, can be appraised more as a tendency than a widespread process. In the sphere of nonmaterial production about half of the employees are concentrated in the education system, culture, art, and science (i.e., in the branches producing information). It can be repeated that the Russian structure of employment has retained quite an archaic nature, typical of the industrial countries before the accomplishment of the scientific and technological revolution (the 1950s and 1960s). Let us now examine how these processes developed among the various peoples of Russia.

In one of the previous chapters it was pointed out that most of the peoples in Russia had, by the beginning of the 20th century, primarily a peasant population. Among the relatively urbanized peoples having a higher proportion of urban population than the country's average (12.6 percent in 1897; 14.6 percent—European Russia's average—in 1920) were the Russians (the ratio of city dwellers in 1897 was 15.6 percent of the people; in 1920, 15.5 percent), the Letts (15.9 percent and 49.9 percent), the Germans (22.0 percent and 13.7 percent), the Greeks (17.9 percent; 63.6 percent), the Gypsies (14.8 percent; 50.8 percent), the Estonians (13.7 percent; 28.4 percent), the Finns (17.9 percent; 11.9 percent), the Uzbeks (17.4 percent in 1897), the Armenians (23.2 percent; 56.7 percent), the Jews (45.8 percent; 91.8 percent). Such sharp fluctuations in the percentages of urban population for a number of peoples are due to both the territorial changes that took place at that time and, probably, different methods used in the two censuses.

The Russians are a highly urbanized people. The percentage of city dwellers among the Russians (76.7 percent in 1989) is higher than Russia's overall average. It should be mentioned that from 1970 to 1989 this proportion rose by 17.1 percent (which is almost equal to the overall Russian rate of urbanization, 17.8 percent), but there was a fall in the proportion of Russians among the urban population of Russia. Thus in 1970, when the Russians were 65.5 percent urbanized, the ratio in the total of Russia's town dwellers was 87.3 percent. In 1989 it fell to 85.2 percent. Although it remains higher than the proportion of Russian people in Russia's population, nevertheless, polyethnicity of Russia's urban population is increasing through a higher rate of urbanization of other peoples.

Naturally, owing to the large numbers of the Russian people the demographic structure is practically identical to the structure of Russia's entire population. In other words, the Russians are only beginning to feel the consequences of the demographic transition. It will be observed that the Russians' birthrate, especially in the countryside (2.3 births per one woman), is somewhat lower than Russia's overall figure (2.4 births). This slight difference means that the greater part of Russia's peoples have considerably higher birthrates. As far as the demographic structure of the urban and rural Russians is concerned, the countryside has a considerably higher proportion of people of pensionable age because young people leave their villages.

The Russians' education level is somewhat higher than Russia's total owing to persons with higher and specialized secondary education. It is interesting that although the distribution of the employed Russian population between the branches of material production and the nonproduction sphere is identical with Russia's average (just as is the engagement primarily in manual labor or brain work), there is a definite "specialization" of the Russian people within material production. The percentage is much higher in industry and appreciably lower in agriculture. Both in Russia and in the former Union republics, Russians make up the bulk of industrial workers and engineers. In the nonproduction sphere statistics do not show any special "predilections" of the Russian people.

The Ukrainians are somewhat more urbanized than the Russians and Russia's population as a whole (in 1989 as many as 78.0 percent of the Ukrainians were city dwellers). Because of the high degree of urbanization, the Ukrainians exhibited from 1970 to 1989 a comparatively low rate of urbanization (the growth of city dwellers among the Ukrainians was 11.6 percent). Although Russia's Ukrainians have a birthrate somewhat higher than the average, the demographic structure of the people shows the prevalence of persons of working ages and pensioners, whose proportion is growing. This is undoubtedly the consequence of the recent Ukrainian migration to Russia, which included primarily people of working ages. The Ukrainians' recent labor migration to Russia also determined the family size, which is somewhat smaller than the average (2.9 persons, Russia's average being 3.2). The Ukrainians' education level is considerably higher than the country's average. The 1979–1989 data shows a substantial growth in the number of people with higher and specialized secondary education, with a consequent reduction in the proportion of people without education, with primary or even secondary education. Incidentally, this type of change in the education level of the population testifies to the people's achievement of a new quality in the way of modernization. This process is taking place in many economically developed countries.

Their high education level determines the Ukrainians' important representation in professions connected with brain work (40.4 percent against 35.1 percent as the country's average in 1989) and in nonproduction branches (30.5 percent against Russia's average of 27.0 percent). In the material production branches Ukrainians are well represented in construction (although their proportion in this branch from 1979 to 1989 fell), in transport, and in communications. Representatives of this people are less oriented to work in industry (although here there are concentrated on the whole over 40 percent of the Ukrainians employed in material production). In the nonproduction branches, Ukrainians are attracted by work in administrative bodies, the financial and credit system, and public organizations. Socioeconomic processes in the midst of Russia's *Byelorussians* are taking place in a similar way.

The Tatars, by 1989, did not reach the average Russian index of urbanization, although the proportion of urban population among this people is sufficiently high (65.7 percent). From 1970 to 1989 the Tatars' urbanization rate noticeably exceeded Russia's average (the increase of the urban population was 32.2 percent).

The Tatars' age structure differs little from the average for the population of Russia. The main differences are connected with Tatars' having a somewhat higher birthrate (2.1 births per woman), and consequently a somewhat larger family (3.3 persons) and a smaller ratio of people of pensionable ages in the population (16.6 percent). The latter figure may also be connected with a shorter life duration. As with most of the peoples that have not yet completed modernization, the Tatars' demographic structure shows differences between the city dwellers and rural inhabitants, though these differences substantially smoothed out from 1979 to 1989. Thus in 1979, the urban Tatars had among them 21.1 percent of persons under working age, 68.3 percent of persons of working age, and 10.6 percent of pensioners. For the rural inhabitants the figures were: 30 percent; 53.2 percent; and 16.8 percent, respectively. In 1989 the urban Tatars had among them 23.4 percent of people under working age, 62.9 percent of people of working age, and 13.7 percent of pensioners. In the countryside these groups were 25.4 percent; 52.6 percent; and 22.0 percent, respectively.

The Tatars' education level is lower than Russia's average. The Tatars have among them fewer people with higher and specialized secondary education and more people with the general secondary education. From 1979 to 1989 the Tatars' education level was growing through the rise in these three education groups.

Their employment likewise exhibits more archaic features as compared with the entire population of Russia. We should point out, however, an essential modernization in the employment structure from 1979 to 1989. Thus in 1979, as many as 22.5 percent of Tatars were engaged in brain work and 77.5 percent in manual labor (the respective ratios for the entire population were 31.2 percent and 68.8 percent). In 1989 there were among the Tatars 28.6 percent of brain workers and 71.4 percent of manual workers. The employment of Tatars in the branches of material (81.2 percent in 1979; 77.2 percent in 1989) and nonmaterial (18.7 percent in 1979; 22.3 percent in 1989) production changed accordingly. From 1979 to 1989, modernization of the Tatar people's professional structure of employment proceeded at a more rapid pace than these processes developed among the entire population of Russia and also among the Slavic ethnic groups. On the whole, modernization of the professional employment structure of a people, especially such a large group as the Tatars, has as its limit the professional structure of production existing in the country. These possibilities, fully utilized by the Russians, Ukrainians, and Byelorussians, are now being intensively mastered by the Tatar population of Russia.

In the material production branches Tatars are less than the country's average represented in industry, in transport, and the communications. Their proportion is higher in agriculture and forestry. The past few decades saw a shift of the workers of Tatar nationality from agriculture to industry, transport, and communications (i.e., to the branches requiring a higher skill). Of the nonmaterial production branches Tatars are better represented in the housing and communal services, the consumer services, and as well in education, culture, art, and science.

On the whole Tatars are living through the concluding stages of modernization, which follows from the data of their demographic structure, education level, and distribution in the branches of production. Similar tendencies are also characteristic of the other peoples in the Volga area: *the Chuvash, Bashkirs, Mordovians, Mari, Udmurts, Permyaks,* and *Komi,* among which the Tatars are distinguished by the most pronounced modernization processes.

The Kabardians well exemplify the peoples of the Northern Caucasus in their main socioeconomic indices. They are characterized by a low level of urbanization (44.3 percent of urban population) coupled with a high rate of urbanization (the growth of urban population from 1979 to 1989 was 89.3 percent). The age structure of the Kabardians shows a high proportion of young age groups (in 1989 as many as 32.4 percent of the population) and an insignificant proportion of people of pensionable age (9.9 percent). This is the result of a high birthrate, especially in the countryside (2.6 births per woman), where the bulk of the population lives.

The Kabardians' education level is somewhat lower than in Russia as a whole but higher than the level of education of the Tatars and most of the other peoples in the Volga Belt. This is due to two factors, the first of which is the compulsory secondary education. The peoples having more young persons in their composition (the Kabardians' average age is 28.5 years against 33.8 years for the Tatars) automatically have a higher education level. Second, there is the prestige of higher education and the ranks and positions it offers among the peoples in the process of socioeconomic modernization. This is a form of the so-called "prestigious consumption" existing among most of the peoples of this type. "Prestigious consumption" can be considered one of the sociopsychological mechanisms of modernization.

The education level has a noticeable influence on the distribution of representatives of the given people among occupations of brain work or manual labor. The Kabardians' level here is lower than Russia's as a whole but higher than that achieved by the Tatars and many other peoples of the Volga Belt. In 1989, 30.5 percent of them were engaged in brain work and 69.5 percent in manual labor. Accordingly, they have better "achievements" in the ratio of those who are employed in nonmaterial (25.1 percent) and material (74.2 percent) production than the Volga Belt peoples, but still this correlation is more archaic than Russia's average.

Quite specific is the distribution of working Kabardians among the material production branches. Mention should be made of their poor representation in industry, construction, transport, and communications, but their good one in agriculture, trade, and public catering. Such a structure of employment is typical, for example, of the peoples of Central Asia. It is due to the agrarian nature of settlement and to the jobs in industry, construction, transport, and communications being held by other peoples (Russians first of all). "Cultural division of labor" (American anthropologist M. Hechter's term), that is, concentration of workers of different nationalities in different branches of production, is more important for the peoples involved in the process of modernization than for peoples like the Tatars and other ethnic groups of the Volga Belt experiencing its final stages.

As regards their socioeconomic indices, therefore, the Kabardians belong to the category of peoples undergoing modernization but still far from its completion. In their main parameters and pronounced tendencies they have as their kith and kin the *Kalmyks, Chechens, Ingush, Karachaians, Cherkes, Adyghei, Balkars, Avars, Lezghins, Darghinians, Kumyks* and other peoples of the Northern Caucasus. The level of socioeconomic development of *the Ossetians,* however, is considerably higher as regards a number of indices.

The Yakuts can serve as an example of large Turkic- and Mongolian-speaking peoples of Siberia. Their level of urbanization is on the whole somewhat lower than that of the peoples of the Caucasus (in 1989, 27.7 percent of city dwellers); the urbanization rate is also considerably lower than for the peoples of the Northern Caucasus (from 1979 to 1989 the number of city dwellers increased by 33.2 percent). The demographic structure of the Yakuts and the other peoples of Siberia, however, is approximately the same as the structure of the peoples of the Northern Caucasus—the same high proportion of the youth under working age (33.5 percent in 1989) and a high birthrate (2.7 births per woman). Mention should be made of a substantial difference in the demographic structure of the urban and rural population. Thus, of the Yakuts residing in cities in 1989, 25.3 percent were under working age, 65.7 percent were of working age, and 9.8 percent were pensioners. For the rural population the figures were: 36.8 percent; 53.8 percent; 9.4 percent, respectively. These figures show that the rural Yakut population is affected by the modernization processes to a very slight degree. There is an obvious gap between rural inhabitants and city dwellers. It should be pointed out that the peoples of the Northern Caucasus do not exhibit such disproportion, and modernization processes develop side-by-side in the countryside and in the cities.

The Yakuts' level of education is high enough, and their percentage of persons with higher education (143 persons with higher education per

1,000 population) is even larger than the figure for Russia as a whole. In this group of peoples, however, a high education level exists, besides the Yakuts, only among the Buryats, while among the others it is extremely low. As was mentioned above, the education level determines the distribution of the employed among the manual labor and brain work occupations and also among the production and nonproduction branches. Therefore, the described group of peoples shows different indices of distribution by the spheres of activity. Thus, the nonproduction branches in 1989 included 38.5 percent of Yakuts (which is considerably higher than Russia's average) and only 26.7 percent of Altaians. Engaged in brain work are 36.0 percent of Yakuts and 27.7 percent of Altaians. It can be surmised that prestige of higher education is of great importance for the most numerous peoples of this group, the Yakuts and Buryats.

This group of peoples is considerably smaller than the peoples of the Northern Caucasus represented in industry, construction, transport, and communications. An enormous proportion of these peoples is concentrated in agriculture and forestry (57 percent of Yakuts and 66 percent of Altaians employed in material production). Interestingly, as for the branches of nonmaterial production the majority are employed in education, culture, art, and science (60 percent of Yakuts and 58 percent of Altaians employed in nonmaterial production). These data testify to an extremely distorted socioprofessional structure of the peoples of the given group, including two dominating sections—agricultural workers and creative intellectuals. To repeat it, the Yakut type of modernization is largely characteristic of such peoples as *Buryats, Tuvans, Khakass, Altaians, Shorians.* The more "advanced" in this group of peoples are the Yakuts and Buryats.

The Nenets can here be examined as an example of the small peoples of the North. This people is characterized by an extremely low degree of urbanization: In 1989 the proportion of Nenets city dwellers constituted but 17.1 percent. For this group of peoples as a whole the proportion of city dwellers has reached 25.9 percent, which is a very low index. True, the urbanization rate for the Nenets from 1979 to 1989 was relatively large (30.5 percent; and 48.0 percent for the entire group of peoples), but urbanization did not proceed at such a rapid pace as among the majority of the peoples of the Northern Caucasus.

The Nenets' demographic structure is distinguished by a high proportion of persons under working age (37.5 percent)—owing to a comparatively high birthrate (2.5 births per woman) and, what is most important, a short duration of life (the Nenets' average age is 25.6 years). Importantly, the demographic structure of the urban and rural population appreciably differs (the city dwellers comprise 28.1 percent of young people, and the rurals, 39.5 percent; in the cities there are 1.4 births per woman and in the countryside, 2.8 births).

As for their education level the Nenets and other peoples of the North lag considerably behind the rest. Thus, the Nenets have only 29 persons with higher education and 102 persons with specialized secondary education per 1,000. Naturally, this gap in the education level with the bulk of Russia's population is due to the low urbanization of the Nenets and other peoples of this group. Hence only 14.3 percent of Nenets were, in 1989, occupied in brain work while the majority (85.7 percent) were manual workers. However, the influence of the low education level was less felt in the distribution of population between material production and nonproduction branches.

The dominant branch of material production is agriculture (it accounts for 57 percent of the Nenets population working in this sphere). However, the peoples of the North living in the regions of intensive industrial development (the Khanty and Mansi) are appreciably represented as industrial workers. The major branches in nonmaterial production are education, culture, art, and science (they employ 62 percent of the Nenets working outside material production). As in the Yakuts' example, the small peoples of the North have in their socioprofessional structure two dominating groups—agricultural workers and creative intellectuals.

We have thus examined the socioeconomic processes taking place within the main groups of the peoples of Russia. Evidently, the majority of this country's population, the most numerous ethnic groups (the Russians, Ukrainians, etc.) have completed the socioeconomic modernization within the limits determined by the structure of Russia's national economy. Incorporated in this group of peoples is the numerous diaspora of the main peoples of the former Union republics. It should be pointed out that the leading position in all socioeconomic indices here is held by the Jews. But Russia's Jewish population, whose average age is 49.7 years, may in the nearest future find itself on the verge of disappearance (this is due to both emigration and an extremely low birthrate).

The peoples of the Volga Belt, with the Tatars leading among them as regards most of the indices, are at the final stages of socioeconomic modernization. The peoples of the Northern Caucasus are characterized by quite a high rate of modernization process but on the whole it is still far from completion. The peoples of Siberia lag behind the majority of the country's population in all indices—this applies to both the big peoples of the region and the small peoples of the North. The modernization process here has not yet gained strength, and these peoples are living through its initial stages.

With a certain degree of relativity the groups of peoples can be ranged, as it has been done (also see Chapter 3), according to the stages through which the modernization pass. No less interesting, however, is the very fact of regional timing of the processes of modernization. Moreover, it is possible to single out three types of this process on the territory of Russia, conventionally speaking, the "Volga Belt," "North-Caucasian," and "Siberian" types. The main difference between them consists in the degree of this process being an integral whole.

For the Volga Belt mention should be made of a high integration of modernization, the gradual "assimilation" by the peoples of the region of the entire existing socioeconomic "spectrum": educational and professional opportunities offered by the structure of Russia's national economy.

The North-Caucasian type is characterized by lesser integration, emphasis on prestigious patterns (in education and employment), and the existence of the cultural division of labor. At the same time this group of peoples does not exhibit any substantial distance between the urban and rural inhabitants.

The Siberian type of modernization is quite inorganic. The main feature here is a deep split[6] in the population, whose principal empirical manifestation can be seen in the concentration of representatives of these peoples primarily in agriculture and in creative professions. This type of modernization is, in prospect, too much fraught with conflict.

It should be noted that the conclusion regarding the modernization types is a substantiated hypothesis and needs a thorough empirical verification.

NOTES

1. Thus, according to experts' estimates, in 1992 alone forced migration to Russia can reach 500,000 persons.

2. See: V.P. Shibayev, *Etnicheskii sostav naseleniya Evropeiskoi chasti Soyuza SSR* (The ethnic composition of the population of the European part of the USSR) (Leningrad: Izdatelstvo AN SSR, 1930); *Natsionalny sostav naseleniya SSSR. Po dannym Vsesoyuznoi perepisi naseleniya 1989 g.* (The national composition of the population of the USSR. Based on the data of the All-Union Census of 1989) (Moscow: Academia Nauk, 1991).

3. *Rossiiskaya gazeta* (Russia's daily), October 12, 1992, p. 2.

4. See: *Rabochaya kniga sotsiologa* (Sociologist's workbook), 2nd ed. (Moscow: Nauka, 1983), pp. 183–184.

5. The values of the coefficient range between +1 and −1. Its values approaching 0 means that phenomena are totally unconnected.

6. Analysis of the philosophical conception of the split, see in: A.S. Akhiezer, *Rossiya: kritika istoricheskogo opyta* (Russia: Criticism of historical experience) (Moscow: Filosofskoye Obshchestvo, 1991), vols. 1–3.

5

The Main National-Political and Socioeconomic Problems of Russia at the Present Stage

After the disintegration of the USSR in December 1991, Russia, just as the other former Union republics, found itself at the turning point of socioeconomic and political development, which cannot but affect the national-political processes within the Russian Federation. That is why it is necessary to analyze the present national problems of the country, especially in this context. It is appropriate, to our mind, to preface a concrete (regional) analysis with a "general" survey.

In 1992–1993, the country was characterized by the following main phenomena in the sociopolitical sphere:

1. Conflict between the legislative and executive branches of power developing at all levels, from the Supreme Soviet to the local Soviets, from the government of the Russian Federation to the prefectures and executive committees of the local Soviets. In many civilized countries such a confrontation is a normal element of the political process. In our case, however, this confrontation happens in the absence of a stable division of powers—both by "branches" (legislative, executive, and judicial) and territorially (the federal and regional authorities). There was a struggle for power at the top, fraught with losses for the society as a whole, whoever might win. Concentration of excessive power in the hands of legislators spells substantial losses in the control of all processes and aspects of the country's life. The executive authorities' uncontrolled rule makes it absolute and destroys the society's back influence on the administrators.

The judicial authorities in Russia are historically underdeveloped, and the courts lead a miserable existence. A radical judicial reform is, in our opinion, a top priority task in the setting up of a proper state structure.

Unfortunately, the course of events shows that so far the ruling circles have not realized the importance of the judicature for any state. It is one of the reasons for the eventual persistence of destructive confrontation between the legislators and executors.

2. Growing political and other activity of directors of state-owned economic units (plants, state farms, etc.). Their principal kinds of action are: lobbying the parliament, direct pressure on the government, and creation of their own parties. The objectives of this social group are the following: tactical, to retain state subsidies to enterprise; strategical, effecting privatization of state-owned property in their favor.

3. There was an impetuous rise of political forces adhering to the great-power and nationalistic positions. Such convictions are often shared by the managers, too. Chauvinistic ideas have a certain influence also among high officials. Generally, it is an inevitable process: turning to the national ideals and values after the failure of communist ideology. Quite probably the peak of these moods is still ahead. However, it can causee problems both throughout the Commonwealth of Independent States and within Russia proper.

4. The country's federalization started in 1990–1991 with the declaration of sovereignty by many of Russia's autonomies. The Federative Treaty signed in 1992 and even the adoption of the new Constitution in 1993 did not complete this process. The problem is very serious: a federative system is incompatible with the socioeconomic relations (forms of ownership and distribution) still existing in the country. All this presupposes an extremely complicated and even painful process of implementing a new model of state organization.

Let us see now how the economy of the Russian Federation has been developing.

The economic reform started in January 1992 with the liberalization of prices, which was to accomplish three main tasks: (1) to bring internal prices in line with the world prices; (2) to compel producers to assimilate market-type behavior; (3) to reduce budget deficit by curtailing public investments in industry. The side effect reformers hoped for was a considerable reduction (through inflation) of the savings of the population exerting pressure on the market. The more or less remote objectives included macroeconomic stabilization, internal convertibility of the ruble and also restoration of the economy. Taxation policy (heavy taxation of commodity producers—taxes on value added) was chosen as the main instrument of state economic policy. The reformers deliberately accepted the eventuality of a considerable recession in the country.

As a result, inflation has exceeded the expected level, mostly because of the failure of all attempts to restrain the growth of the mass of money: (1) the inappropriate taxation strategy has led to not more than half of the taxes being collected in the country and, consequently, to the remaining

practice of subsidizing public enterprises by means of an excessive (inflationary) emission; (2) massive privatization has not become reality: The
enterprises don't secure promissory notes with their property. High inflationary expectations (coupled with the State Bank's fallacious policy) lead
to the incessantly sinking exchange-value of the ruble versus hard currency.

The population's savings, which exerted pressure on the market, have
practically been eliminated by inflation. Due to this, first of all, consumer
goods have become less scarce. On the other hand, enormous sums of
money are being accumulated in the hands of a limited group of persons,
directors in particular. Conditions have thereby been created for a "nomenclature privatization." The unfavorable political and economic situation in the country leads to the outflow of hard currency.

The task of balancing the budget, too, has not been fulfilled, mainly
because of industry still being subsidized by the state and the high tax rates
which provoke tax evasion.

The decline of the living standard has continued because of the high
inflation rate, the growing budget deficit, and so on. In parallel, there was
the tremendous socioeconomic stratification of Russia's population, due
first of all to intolerable disparities in the income and consumption levels
of various socioprofessional groups.

By the autumn of 1993 the public dissatisfaction with mass pauperization, corruption at all levels of the administration, and unprecedented rise
of crime became quite pronounced. The conservative majority of the parliament and leftist and rightist extremist movements of communist and
chauvinistic nature came out as "protectors of the people."

On September 21, 1993, the president of Russia, Boris Yeltsin, took a
step which formally contradicted the existing Constitution. He dissolved
the Supreme Council (the parliament) accusing it of opposition to the reforms and to the adoption of new Constitution. The parliament in fact
provided reasons for such accusations. A number of deputies refused to
leave and voted for the president's impeachment. Two weeks later the leaders of the above-mentioned movements along with the members of parliament tried to seize the TV Center in Moscow and the City Council by
military force.

The revolt was suppressed and the parliament building was stormed.
According to official data, the number of victims reached 150. The leaders
of the opposition were arrested, their political parties and movements
banned.

However, general elections that took place on December 12 held an un-
pleasant surprise for Yeltsin and his team. It turned out that the voting on
the party lists had been a success of the so-called Liberal-Democratic Party
headed by Vladimir Zhirinovsky. His eccentric views are identified as fascist
by many observers in Russia and abroad. That was the price of public
dissatisfaction with reforms.

A number of reformist groups and parties received less than a third of all votes. New opposition in the lower chamber of parliament—the State Duma—is represented along with supporters of Zhirinovsky by the communists and by the "agrarians," belonging to the previous generation of agricultural managers.

Several weeks later almost all reformists left the government or were forced to. Nobody is denying the need for reforms but their future is not clear. As for the new parliament, one of its first political decisions was the one on the amnesty of the leaders of the 1991 putsch and the revolt of October 1993.

The referendum on the Constitution, considerably widening the powers of the president, took place simultaneously with the elections. More than half of the electorate took part in the voting while a little more than half of it adopted the draft of the Constitution. So, the Constitution has come into effect. We have described its provisions concerning the federative structure of Russia in Chapter 2.

The chances of the country's economic revival directly depend on the pace of privatization. It is unclear now which route privatization will take: whether the actual proprietors will be large sections of the population or whether the property is doomed to be concentrated in the hands of a limited group of persons, consisting of some of the former and new high officials. Without privatization in some form, however, further progress is impossible.

Privatization will aid in demonopolization, since the giant monopolies, in order to be privatized, will have to be divided into smaller enterprises.

Structural reorganization of the economy is so far conducted (or planned to be conducted) in the inflationary way, through budgetary subsidies to a number of the military industrial complex enterprises that are most up-to-date in technological achievements. (Structural reorganization, however, always requires enormous investments.) Without preserving these enterprises (and their personnel), without their entering the international market, further development will require much greater expenses. It should be mentioned also that the country's progress is likewise impossible without preserving the system of education and science, which are now in a critical state.

Finally, the most important aspect of the forthcoming stage of the reform is connected with its regionalization, that is, the shifting of the weight of the reform to the republics and regions.[1] Since each region has its own peculiar conditions for socioeconomic revival (economic, geographical, sociopolitical, ethnocultural, etc.), the correction of the general course should be made precisely in the respective localities in accordance with the concrete situations. Regionalization of the reform will make it possible to lay a considerable part of the responsibility for it on the local authorities, to use their initiative and to attract the local resources (good work in this respect has been done in Nizhni Novgorod). Of course, regionalization is fraught with the potential danger of separatism, but at the same time it provides a foundation for a further, firmer integration of the republics and lands within the bounds of the Russian Federation.

Let us turn now to Russia's national-political problems.

The conclusion that a system of values lies at the foundation of individuals' behavioral mechanism is commonplace in the world and in Russian sociology and ethnology. Nevertheless, information of this kind is by far too rarely used in forecasting the countries' socioeconomic and political evolution. Nor was the Soviet Union an exception, with its disintegration predetermined, in the period of radical socioeconomic reforms, by the authorities' inattention to the conflict of value systems aggravated by the country's democratization. A similar situation has now taken shape in the Russian Federation, whose existence as an integrated state will be decided above all "in the heads" of its citizens.

The question is: Are there universal national cultural values naturally manifesting themselves in typical historical situations; or is the value system of any people unique, originating from the peculiarities of its history and the specificity of its cultural and religious life? We make bold to assert that the system of values of any people includes both universal and nationally specific features. In the critical (transitional) conditions, timed, of course, with definite stages of socioeconomic development of society, the universal set of national cultural values manifests itself quite logically and in full measure.

Through an analysis of texts (especially of a political nature) from various national groups, programs, and statements by leaders of some national political movements and parties; speeches by members of governmental structures; and opinions of experts in national relations and nationalities policy, we found the following structure of national values characteristic of Russia's society.

1. *The value of national identity (the problem of national cultural revival).* In the present conditions, the value of reviving national culture (above all the national language) as a premise for consolidating national identity is characteristic of all the peoples of the Russian Federation, representing a number of sociopolitical types. The rise of such a frame of mind is logical for the industrial period of development of society with its standardization of life, uniformity of interpersonal relations (including the widespread use of one language which is not the mother tongue for many peoples), and intensive migrations "rarefying" the ethnic mass. The national cultural revival should be interpreted as a search by the people (ethnic group) with a foothold in the past for a spurt forward.

Probably for a good decade to come, Russia's administrative structures will have to confront the problem of national-cultural revival as a most important factor of human moods and behavior. In what can it be primarily expressed? In a sharply negative attitude toward projects leading to a transformation (often destruction) of the traditional environment, intensive influx of populations of a different nationality, changing the way of life of whole ethnic groups. It can be expressed in the demands for more extensive introduction of national languages in the sphere of education, culture, and the mass media; and in the efforts to use national forms of organization of citizens within the framework of modern political, economic, and other institutions. Under such circumstances the main task of the government is, to our mind, to remove the problem of national-cultural revival from the sphere of political actions. This is possible with a broad development of national-cultural autonomy and local self-government at all levels of the hierarchy of territorial units.

2. *National statehood as a value.* The national cultural revival, as can be seen from the experience of our own and many other countries, is a basic mass prerequisite of nationalism—the ideology having as its aim to create and consolidate the national state. Nationalism is a political interpretation of the value of national-cultural revival.

The striving for national statehood should be recognized as a major national value of our society. What is the content of this value orientation? First, it implies that only within its own state can a people preserve and successfully develop its culture and national identity. Second, the ideology of national statehood operates with the idea of exceptional ties attaching a people to the territory on which it lives. Both ideas have rational foundations, but in such a categorical form they are incorrect.

What are, and will be, the political consequences of the widespread value of national state? They include the growth of separatism in any form— from the declaration of independence to conflicts between the republican and federal authorities, caused by actual or imaginary infringements upon sovereignty; frontier disputes between peoples (republics) concerning the ownership of territories; striving for political unification of different parts of one people.

The best remedy against nationalism and separatism in our conditions is the development of the federative principle in the Russian State system. Objectively, most of the peoples and national-state units in Russia do not have, for various reasons, essential potentialities for independent existence. If the Russian Federation, however, wants to preserve its territorial integrity, it should revise the federal authorities' attitude toward the republics and autonomies within it. This involves, especially, the necessity of optimizing the division of functions between the central and local authorities and of strictly respecting the terms of the Federative Treaty. (By Russia's territorial integrity we mean here not a value pattern but a vital need dictated by the present-day socioeconomic and political situation).

3. *The value of unity.* As was mentioned above, in the context of the

minorities' rising nationalism and separatism leaning on the values of national culture and national statehood, a certain strength is being gained by the value of territorial integrity of the multinational state, with this issue especially accentuated by the prevalent people and its sociopolitical movements, by the functionaries of the federal government bodies. In Russia the value of preservation of the country's territorial integrity is particularly often proclaimed by representatives of the so-called "state-oriented" wing of the sociopolitical forces. It should be mentioned that the desire to preserve the territorial integrity of the Russian Federation is usually combined with the calls to restore the Soviet Union and often goes together with the calls for the national-cultural revival of the Russian people.

The value of the country's territorial unity is inherent in peoples already having "their own" statehood. In practice it is coupled with the negation of federalism as a method of administrative-territorial organization of national life. The proponents of this value desire the creation of a unitary, "one and indivisible" state. At the stage of national-cultural revival the main collision is the struggle between the desire of the minorities to create national states and the desire of the majority to preserve the country's territorial unity. This struggle often degenerates into armed clashes, as it was demonstrated by many of the CIS countries. It should be noted with satisfaction that although separatist movements do exist on Russia's territory as well, the central administration has so far not used military force for their suppression. Nor is it possible to suppress them (an example is furnished by Chechenia, which has firmly taken the stand of secession from the Russian Federation precisely after the attempt at armed intervention in the late autumn of 1991). The main task is to channel the conflict of values from an armed to a peaceful form.

4. *The development of a democratic, law-governed state as a national value.* In the period of national-cultural revival and the development of nationalism, the arising value collisions have no resolution on their own ground. The victory of the unitarian or the separatist line in this situation depends on a concrete correlation of forces in their crude physical (military) expression. At the present time, as is clear from the experience of former Yugoslavia, this spells an obvious blind alley in political actions, detrimental to both the unitarians and the separatists.

The political history of the most developed region in the world, Western Europe, knew two periods: centralism (the period of multinational empires of the 18th century to the early 19th century) and nationalism (the late 19th century to the early 20th century). Today, after the two world wars connected with the creation and development of national states in Europe, a third period has set in, the period of the democratic, law-governed state.

Russia and many other countries that have been delayed in their progress are only now approaching the period of nationalism. The main task of the Russian administrative structures at the present time is to go through this period with the least losses for the country and its population, relying on the values of a democratic, law-governed state. Russia's survival as an integrated state and the lowering of a degree of conflict in the country can be achieved by evolving a constant dialogue (negotiation process) between the "social actors," the proponents of the above national values.

Obviously, the country's regions most deserving a detailed analysis are the Northern Caucasus and the Volga Belt. It is here that the most intensive national-political processes are taking place and the situation is fraught with conflict. This is due to a number of factors. First, in the Caucasus and in the Volga Belt the larger and more compactly residing masses of the native population are concentrated, whereas Siberia is populated in the main by Russians. Second, the autochthonous population of the two said regions of European Russia has advanced further toward modernization and attained the industrial level of socioeconomic development correlating with the formation of their own national states. Third and last, the population and its density in the Siberian region is such that all sociopolitical processes here are slower than in the European part of the country. It is our deep conviction that precisely in the European regions of Russia the question is now being decided whether the Russian Federation will retain its integrity and in what form it will further exist as a state. This is why we intend to analyze the situation in the Volga Belt and in the Northern Caucasus in more detail while examining Yakutia alone as an example of one of the regions east of the Urals.

PRESENT SOCIOECONOMIC AND POLITICAL SITUATION IN THE VOLGA BELT

The socioeconomic geography of the Volga Belt is usually seen to include the Mordovian, Mari-El, Chuvash, Kalmykia–Khalmg-Tangch, and Tatar republics, and also the Kirov, Nizhni-Novgorod, Astrakhan, Volgograd, Samara, Penza, Saratov, and Ulianovsk regions. But when this regionalization is approached from the standpoint of the Volga's actual history and cultural background, it is clear that the Komi, Udmurt, and Bashkir republics also belong here.

This belt is characterized by features which distinguish it from the other "national" regions of the Russian Federation. First of all, there is the pertinent fact that it was incorporated in the Russian State as early as the 16th century and so may be considered an integral part of Russia. At the same time it was here that the states (Volga Bulgaria and Kazan Khanate) sprang up on Russian soil—and were subsequently "swallowed up" in the course of Moscow's territorial expansion.

The area is distinguished by another inherent or "inner" feature: it lacks common borders with other states, some within the frame of the CIS. At the same time it serves as a highly important transportation link between western Russia and its east and south, and even the Central Asian republics.

And yet the exceptionally diverse multinational composition of the Volga area (in a way comparable in ethnic multiformity with the North Caucasus) has not made it a hotbed of inter-ethnic animosities. Certain forms of co-existence among its many peoples have become habitual here, as befits such a heterogeneous population with so many groups so widely dispersed and yet tending to cling together in ethnic solidarity around chosen occupational sites, and they weaken potential tensions.

The world's three great religions also coexist normally here: the Russian Orthodox Church with its Christian congregations of Slavs, Chuvash, all the Finno-Ugric peoples and some Tatars; Islam among the majority of Tatars and Bashkirs; and Lamaism among the Kalmyks.

It is true that the proportion of Russians in almost every republic of the Volga Belt is quite large: sometimes they are as many or even more than the "indigenous" people whose name the republic bears. Still these republics are rightly conceded to be national states, for most of them contain the overwhelming majority of the "titular" ethnos. Some specific problems have arisen as a result of the diaspora of autochthonous groups to neighboring republics and regions. The most widely dispersed of the Volga peoples remain the Mordovians, Tatars, Mari, and Chuvash.

As for the economic contours of the Volga area, it specializes in oil extraction and refinement (Tataria accounts for over 6 percent of Russia's oil), and also in machine building. Military production has been assigned no small role in its economy. Agriculture and the Astrakhan fishing industry are also well developed.

In level of economic and social development, the Volga republics and regions may be divided into two groups: (1) those that are highly developed by Russian standards (Volgograd, Saratov, Nizhni Novgorod, Kirov, and Ulianovsk regions, the Tatar Republic), and (2) the medium developed group (Udmurt, Bashkir, Mari, Mordovian, Komi, and Chuvash republics; Penza and Astrakhan regions). The Kalmyk Republic stands alone as a poorly developed area.

Obviously, the share of federal subsidy of the income side of the republican and regional budgets depends on their economic level: the less economically developed a member of the Federation is, the more financial injections it needs.

As regards the republics, Tataria, Bashkiria, Komi, and Udmurtia are the least dependent on federal aid which provides 0.99 percent, 7.5 percent, and 5.5 percent of their respective budget incomes. It is clear that this circumstance has had a lot to do with the nature of Tatar or Bashkir political relations with the federal government and the course the economic reform program is taking there.

In our view, the redistribution of enormous sums through the federal budget is an extremely archaic practice peculiar to the socialist type of economy. Only those resources received in the form of taxes and emissions should be concentrated in the federal budget, which should also include the funds necessary for it to perform its function as defined in the Federative Treaty (plus an emergency fund for special exigencies). All other resources should accumulate in the budgets of the republics and the regional and central banks. In the event that local administrators find themselves in need of cash to cover budget outlays, they can borrow it on the currency market and repay it plus the agreed interest on the loan by a fixed date. Such a system makes it incumbent on a republic or region to give more careful thought to the formation of its budget. Ways of increasing profits on investments are bound to suggest themselves; the formation of regional integration systems is ensured as new financial relations begin to replace the old republican or regional administrative bonds.

Of course, it will take some time for the members of the Federation to accommodate themselves to this transition from centralized allocation of resources to independent financing. It must be accomplished by stages as the role of the federal budget gradually recedes and local budgets are worked out.

The economic decline typical of the whole country also affected the Volga Belt, but to a less severe degree than the average for the rest of the Russian Federation. The least developed of the Volga republics and most in need of help, Kalmykia, had evidently the poorest economic results.

The general standard of living in the Volga republics and regions is unrelated to the results of their economic activity. Paradoxically, Kalmykia's population enjoy the highest cash per capita income. Nizhni Novgorod region and Tataria show the best economic results, yet the living standards of their inhabitants are the same as in Russia as a whole. That state of affairs is apparently the result of the considerable redistribution of their resources through the federal budget—a problem we have mentioned before. Naturally, such a situation can hardly be to the liking of the more advanced members of the Federation.

How have the republics and regions of the Volga area reacted to the present state of affairs and tried to rectify it? Actually, we are dealing here with two distinct strategies of which Nizhni Novgorod and Tataria are striking examples. Whereas Nizhni Novgorod sought to solve its problems by expediting economic reforms, Tataria (or its leadership) chose, on the contrary, to slow down reform by fixing consumer prices and confining its domestic market. In its ultimate form the latter stands for the creation of an internal customs zone, regulation of commodity and monetary exchange.

But the trend toward economic autarchy within the Russian Federation may, under present conditions, have a deleterious effect on the domestic economies of the regions and republics that choose that road. It is a road that cannot be consistently followed. Russia's galloping inflation will continually overturn Tataria's domestic market.

Generally speaking, as regards the advancement of economic reform, the Volga Belt republics and regions may be divided into four groups:

1. Economic reform is making comparatively rapid headway both in the cities and the villages. This group includes the Mordovian and Bashkir republics and also the Nizhni Novgorod, Volgograd, Penza, Astrakhan, Samara, and Ulianovsk regions.

2. Reform is proceeding at a slow pace in both cities and villages: the Tatar, Komi, Udmurt republics and Kirov region.

3. Economic reform has affected the countryside more than the cities: Mari-El and Chuvash republics and Saratov region.

4. Economic changes are more pronounced in the cities than in rural vicinities: the Kalmyk republic.

Our conclusion is that, compared to Russia, economic reform is making satisfactory progress in the Volga republics and regions as a whole, with the exception of those that come under Type 2. We may therefore reiterate our conviction that reform is being hampered by political rather than economic considerations.

We shall now proceed to review the politico-economic situation in each of the Volga republics.

The Chuvash Republic

The Supreme Soviet of the Chuvash Republic with its 200 deputies (here and elsewhere, data of this kind concern the period before March 1994, when following new elections, all legislative, executive, and local administrative structures radically changed) did not differ substantially in social composition from its counterparts elsewhere. It functions fairly well, although public opinion throughout the republic concurs in the view that its main function is to belatedly copy the decisions of Russia's lawmakers.

Presidential elections were held in the republic during November and December 1991, a period which may be viewed as the high point of its political life. But no one was elected: the vote for A. Khuzangai, candidate of the Chuvash Party of National Rebirth (PNR), was several percentage points short of the necessary majority that would have made him president.

Executive power was divided mainly between the chairman of the Supreme Soviet, Kubarev, regarded as the acting president, and the head of the Council of Ministers, Victorov. The Russian Federation president's representative, Zaitsev, wielded less influence in the government.

After overcoming a good deal of initial friction and bickering, the "triumvirate" was to all appearances laboring amicably in the economic domain. Their efforts boiled down mostly to trying to "milk" Moscow for whatever privileges and help they could wrangle from it and prolong the same time-honored domestic and foreign trade contacts to which each member of the triumvirate enjoys wide access. At the same time these leaders have been wary of committing themselves to an out-and-out pro-Moscow stance for fear of antagonizing the republic's nationalistic elements.

Only two outright power conflicts have taken place in the republic. After rather violent clashes in the beginning, the conflict between the Supreme Soviet and the Cheboksary's Soviet assumed a more subdued, protracted form. It was not a politically motivated conflict; it hinged rather on the settlement of certain property rights.

The conflict with the Alatyr and Polesiye districts started in the autumn of 1991 during the election campaign, when the press carried articles calling for the creation of a "Greater Chuvashia" and "Great Bulgaria." Alatyr and Polesiye are primarily Russian-speaking districts, as is Shumerliya— and their Soviets have repeatedly threatened to break away from the Chuvash Republic and merge with the Ulianovsk Region. The leaders of the republic have chosen to ignore the threat and maintain that it merely reflects the economic interests of a few deputies.

The two chief exponents of the nationalist movement in the republic are the Chuvash Party of National Rebirth (CPNR) and the Chuvash Socio-Cultural Center (CSCC). Various small groups dedicated to cultural enlightenment have appeared but do not play a notable role in political life, CPNR's is the most influential political voice. Its chairman is the university professor Lukianov and its ideologist is A.P. Khuzangai (son of the outstanding Chuvash poet and philologist Pyotr Khuzangai in whose honor one of Cheboksary's avenues has been named), deputy to the Supreme Soviet and chairman of its permanent Committee on Culture, Language and International Relations.

It is in the main a party of the intelligentsia led by prominent and highly respected citizens of unsullied reputation. Unlike similar organizations in neighboring republics, CPNR cannot be charged with having communist roots. This party has no staff headquarters or publications, but the newspaper *Hypar* (circulation 73,000) as well as the republic's TV programs may be said to be CPNR-oriented.

The tactics of its leaders remain extremely cautious. They are hardly for taking ill-considered steps likely to discredit CPNR in the eyes of either the Chuvash or Russian public. CPNR has openly affirmed its sympathy with the Tatar "Ittifak" party, not a little on the grounds of the higher standard of living in neighboring Tatarstan—"a result of its genuine sovereignty." At the same time, it has not committed itself to any declaration of political sovereignty. Its only weakness today is its hostile attitude toward CSCC— so far to the embarrassment of the latter.

Nevertheless, CSCC remains the republic's second largest important social and cultural center. It is more a political party in essence; as a matter of fact, CSCC and CPNR actually uphold almost identical political ideas. The CSCC chairman, Mishi (Mikhail) Yukhma, an author and member of the former Writers' Union of the RSFSR, was one of the signers of the "anti-Perestroika" letter of 73 writers, after which he transferred his allegiance to Yevtushenko's writers' organization. Now he has formed an alternative Union of Chuvash authors aligned with the CSCC platform.

CSCC came out for awhile in a political bloc with the neo-Communists. Now it is backing the Chuvash democratic movement, specifically the "Union in defense of country and freedom." It publishes a newspaper in Chuvash (with occasional Russian items) called *Vuchakh,* meaning "Hearth," which has a circulation of 3,000. Lately, there has been a rift in the organization; most of its leaders demand real participation in the task of national rebirth, a task which can only be realized in close cooperation with CPNR.

Should CPNR take power, a smaller-scale "Kazan scenario" might take the stage—were it not for the fact that Chuvashia's national leaders would probably hesitate to form a close union with Tataria because of the latter's territorial claims on Chuvashia and their different religions (practically all native Chuvash are Christians of Orthodox Russian persuasion). Chuvashia has every reason to put forth its own territorial claims, especially as concerns the territory of Ulianovsk Region, for when the Chuvash Autonomous Soviet Socialist Republic was first set up its administrative center was to have been Simbirsk; only the fact that it was Lenin's birthplace placed that city outside the bounds of the new republic.

Of its various parties and democratic movements, its one realistic force is the Chuvash Republican Union in defense of country and freedom," an organization which grew out of a "voters club" formed in 1989 and was renamed on May 26, 1990 as "The Democratic Alternative" (republican first registered civic organization). In March 1992 that body rejected the idea of joint membership and was reregistered as "The Chuvash Republican Union in Defense of Country and Freedom." It regards itself as a collective affiliate of CSCC.

There are several other democratically oriented political parties and also a few small Left parties.

Turning now to an analysis of the republic's economic status, we find that Chuvashia has no mineral resources. Its chief source of income is hop growing. Since the collapse of the USSR, it figures as Russia's monopoly producer of hop (the top producer used to be the Ukraine). But on the market the price of hop is low.

Chuvashia holds third or fourth place in Russia for density of population. Its land is not very fertile and its tillable soil measures only 0.6 of a hectare per person, which means that the republic can only feed itself by raising stock. It grows mostly grain for fodder—and not enough of that.

Its industry is concentrated in Cheboksary, but there are also several rather large factories in Novocheboksarsk and Alatyr. Its largest enterprise is the Cheboksary Industrial Tractor Plant. For the rest, it produces mostly electrotechnical equipment and machine tools, in which fields the local administration claims it can satisfy the market demand from Moscow to the Urals.

So far the social atmosphere in Cheboksary has been calm and undisturbed by strikes or public unrest. The most serious event was the setting up of a roadblock when the savings banks ran out of cash.

The standard of living is much lower in the villages than in the cities. With so little land available the prospects for private farming are dim. The Peasants' Union remains a powerful organization that wields considerable authority throughout the republic and is well represented in all its districts. It has demonstrated its ability to exert effective economic and sometimes even political pressure on the republic's leaders. The latter have not developed any relatively integrated economic program; the privatization plan they have outlined for the republic is generally regarded as a mere formality.

The general orientation of the Chuvash leadership boils down to dependence on Russian subsidies. It is clear that there can be no question yet of the republic's being economically independent. Nevertheless, there may be attempts (though this seems rather unlikely) to play the national card under pressure from the nationalist political movement.

Thus, Chuvashia's chief problem today concerns its economy rather than its national policy. The process of the cultural rebirth of its people has as yet been developing more or less calmly. It is clear, of course, that the political elite have hardly managed to get their bearings in the current atmosphere of countrywide economic and political change. But the republic may soon begin to show an interest in achieving economic integration with the whole Volga Belt.

The Mari El Republic

Mari El is a republic which had presidential rule. Its president headed the government and formed the cabinet with the concurrence of the Supreme Soviet. No conflicts had taken place between him and the chairman of the Supreme Soviet. The government's every proposal had been dutifully accepted by a Supreme Soviet whose deputies were prone to being rather inactive. The general shortage of trained managers in the republic is a problem which has been further aggravated by the decision of the president, a Mountain Mari, to make up his team entirely of fellow Mari nationals—

an unprecedented practice for a republic which had rarely ever promoted national cadres before, least of all to top levels.

The Mari Republic signed the Russian Federative Treaty without hesitation or reservations. There have been no conflicts between any of its administrative bodies. The president of the Russian Federation has no representative in this republic, where the status of the top leadership is stable itself.

In "The Land of the Mari" (Mari El) the Mari people constitute a minority; Russians make up the majority, Tatars 5.9 percent, Chuvash, 1.3 percent of the population. In Paranga District there are compact settlements of Tatars.

The Mari, who call themselves "Oshmari" or "White Mari," are divided into at least two ethnic groups known as Mountain Mari and Meadow Mari; these names reflect the historical division of their territory between two clans, one of which settled on the right or mountainous bank of the Volga, and the other on its left meadowlands. The dividing line between the two groups is not very rigid, however, and Mountain Mari also inhabit the left bank. There is another group called Eastern Mari made up of those who live in the East (Bashkiria). Meadow Mari is officially considered the true Mari language, and Mountain Mari a dialect. Linguists are endeavoring today to have Mountain Mari recognized as a separate language, since those who speak either of the two tongues find it hard to understand each other. All in all there are 671,000 Mari in Russia, and 346,500 or 51.7 percent reside outside Mari El, some in Russia's Kirov, Perm, and Ekaterinburg regions, others in Tataria and Bashkiria.

The Mari are mostly villagers. Only 36.6 percent are considered urbanized, compared to the figure of 62 percent for urbanization of the republic as a whole. Spokesmen of the national-political movement have pointed out that only 15 percent of the Mari who live in the city of Yoshkar-Ola (republican capital) have received modern flats; the rest have no choice but to share "communal" apartments or live in dormitories. From 85 to 90 percent work in the field of community services or trade.

This is a republic practically without an autochthonous intellectual or working class, without medium range leaders—a republic where the number of Mari factory directors can be counted on the fingers of one hand, where only 30 percent of the heads of its collective and state farms are native Mari, even though the latter make up 63.4 percent of the rural population (as compared to only 18.6 percent of Russians). Its few native engineers or scientific workers do not usually reside in Mari El proper.

The Russian majority does not seem to be perturbed by the nationalistic sentiments echoed in the Mari programs of the republican television and radio stations.

One-third of the Mari who live in the republic, and even 45 percent of its intellectuals, speak only Russian with their children. Seven percent of the native population is entirely unfamiliar with the language; 20 percent cannot read it, 27 percent cannot write it. In the cities a third of all young Mari between the ages of 18 and 30 never speak it and 80 percent converse with their children only in Russian. It is actually a rarity to hear the sound of the Mari tongue being spoken on the streets of Yoshkar-Ola.

Teaching that language has now become a burning problem. The only two places where teachers are being trained (50 a year) in the language and literature of their republic are the Mari State University and the Mari Ped-agogical Institute. Of its previous six teacher-training secondary schools, none are still functioning. In Yoshkar-Ola there is not a single school where teaching is conducted in the native language.

The most far-sighted leaders of the national movement realize that the only real chance there is of perpetuating the Mari ethnos is to give the Mari countryside all-out support. Only there, in the villages, can an attempt be successfully made to conserve the living tongue, the culture and customs of the people.

There is a movement afoot in the republic called "Mari Ushem" or "Union of the Mari People," a name taken from an analogous organization founded in 1917. This new movement, which held its organizational con-gress and adopted a charter and program in April 1990, is reputed to have been set up originally under the auspices of the former Regional Committee of the CPSU. Today "Mari-Ushem" maintains quite close ties with Eston-ia's nationalistic institutions, even to the extent of imitating their tactics, documents, and lexicon, although it doesn't publicize the fact. Instead, it has been playing up its relations with the Tatar organizations: the Tatar Civic Center and "Ittifak," though said relations cannot be called more than friendly. No doubt this is a concession to the admiration in which the wide public holds neighboring Tatarstan for its higher standard of living.

The organization's highest body is the "Mari Ushem" Congress which meets in plenary session once in two years. Between congresses, its Central Council meets at least twice a year, while the Board of the Central Council is chaired by A. S. Patrushev of the Mari Musical Theatre. Since 1990, "Mari Ushem" has been publishing a newspaper called *Mari Chang,* with occasional articles in Russian, which comes out in 3,000 copies.

"Mari Ushem" is registered as a "democratic public society," but in structure, aims, and activity it is obviously striving to become a potent political force in the republic. So far it can hardly count realistically on exercising any serious influence. There is not a single striking personality in the whole organization, no one capable of influencing the political pro-cess. Most of the people who support it are solely interested in its cultural aspect.

In 1990 a group of radical intellectuals inaugurated "Kugeze Mlande" ("Land of our Fathers"), formally registered in February 1991. The aim this organization has exposed is the separation of Mari El from Russia, adoption of harsh laws against migration, and similar measures. Its members have achieved notoriety in the republic mostly due to their scandalous picketing and demonstrating with banners bearing nationalistic slogans. The extremely low level of its adherents' political thinking has prevented "Kugeze Mlande" from playing anything like a serious role in the life of the republic.

A true religious revival is plainly on the upsurge in the republic today. A religious movement which calls itself "Oshmari Chimari" or "The White Mari Are the True Believers" has been spurred on by the prominent writer A. Uzikain, and with him has proclaimed its purpose to be the revival of the pagan religion of the people. Uzikain has made it his personal mission to resurrect and save from oblivion the ancient ceremonies and prayers of his people and has appointed himself their High Priest. Their heathen creed is being openly propagated, their prayers are being published, including the whole annual calendar of ancient incantations still extant. Simple folk here are shedding their orthodox religious beliefs just as they have divested themselves of communist ideas—a changeover facilitated by the tolerant attitude the new religion has shown in allowing its converts to attend conventional church ceremonies.

Nationalistic slogans hardly exert any influence, whether on Mari countryfolk with their ingrained passivity, or in the town where the process of assimilation has made great headway. Under present conditions a nationalistic takeover is unrealistic. The government has not expressed disapproval of the activities of the nationalists. Nationalistic trends are hamstrung by the fact that relations between the Mountain and Meadow Mari are even worse than those between the Mari and the Russians.

Political activity in Mari El is at a standstill—a conclusion warranted by the traditional passivity of the populace and the absence of an acceptable political prospectus. Left organizations of either patriotic or neo-Communist orientation are conspicuous by their absence.

The republic has few natural resources: sand and forestland, the latter occupying 58 percent of its territory. But it has no woodworking industry or energy sources. It gets most of its electricity from the Balakov atomic energy station and a little from Tataria. Yoshkar-Ola, its industrial hub, specializes in some branches of military production, such as electronics and machine building.

Agriculture is poorly developed in the republic; such are its soil and natural conditions that it can only satisfy its own needs in the products of livestock breeding. Its problems have been aggravated by the commissioning of the Cheboksary hydroelectric station, from which it has not received an iota of energy, but which has flooded its most valuable river valley. And every acre in this republic is priceless.

The conversion of military enterprises is hardly making any better headway here than in other parts of the country. The only plant that can show progress in respect to conversion is the Yoshkar-Ola former rocket-hull manufactory which now makes bicycles. There has been little progress at other large plants, whether the Mari Mechanical Works (which formerly specialized in rocket technology) or "Contact" and "Electroautomatics," where the situation may be considered grave. As for "Electronika," whose output of semiconductors is still in demand, production has been brought to a relative standstill by the disruption of the country's economic ties. The Mari government has not developed a serious conversion program.

A program for the privatization of state and municipal enterprises was adopted in March 1992, but was postponed by decision of the Supreme Soviet as being no more than recommendatory.

In the referendum held on March 17, 1991, the citizens of what was still the Mari Autonomous Soviet Socialist Republic were asked to express their opinion as to whether they considered private ownership of the land desirable. The majority of the people said no, it was not. Today's government takes every opportunity to recall and quote the results of that referendum. The stand taken by "Mari Ushem" on the question is not altogether clear.

The Mari El government is making an intensive but rather unsystematic search for foreign partners. It has engaged in negotiations at various levels with representatives of South Africa, Turkey, China, and others. It has also signed an agreement with Estonia. One thing is clear in all the high-sounding phraseology surrounding these negotiations, and that is that its foreign partners are interested in the Mari Republic's timberland. On the whole the government's economic policy, though unsystematic, remains largely Russia-oriented. It still looks to Moscow's subsidies as the solution to all its economic troubles, and in its sober evaluation of its present position sees no likelihood of either political or economic sovereignty. It goes without saying that the republic is interested in developing economic ties within the frame of Volga integration.

The Mordovian Republic

From December 1991 to the spring of 1993, Mordovia was under presidential rule: Its president was invested with great nominal power, including the right to appoint all the members of his government except the ministers of Internal Affairs, Security, Finance, and Justice—posts which must be approved by the Supreme Soviet.

The president, Gusliannikov, was formerly the chairman of the regional section of "Democratic Russia." His opponent took every opportunity to criticize him for his lack of experience in state affairs and to expose his many missteps.

Neither were the Democratic, neo-Communist, or old nomenclature factions well-disposed toward the president, more because of his lack of professionalism than because of concrete political issues.

Ethnically, the Mordovians comprise two groups: Erzyan and Mokshan, each with its own language. Mordovians are the third largest Finno-Ugric nation in the world, and between the sixth and seventh largest nationality in Russia, numbering 1,154,000 (and declining steadily ever since the 1930s), of whom only 27 percent reside in Mordovia proper. The Erzyans and Mokshans in fact constitute only 20 percent of the republic's approximately one million inhabitants. In Saransk, with a population of 312,000, only 20 percent are ethnic Mordovians.

Mordovians are now mainly resettled in the Samara, Orenburg, Ulianovsk, Nizhni Novgorod, and Penza regions, in Tataria and Bashkiria. There is not a single administrative territory where they constitute a majority.

Their nationalistic elements are grouped around the "Mastorava" or "Mother Earth" society, the status of which is rather vague. Essentially, it is a political organization. Its leader is Professor D. Nadkin of the Mordovian State University. "Mastorava" does not issue any publications.

The Society's public activity has increased since the First All-Russian Congress of the Mordovian People was held in March 1992. In its documents the Congress has demanded that the president be a person who can speak the Mordovian language; that it be granted the right to submit legislative proposals, including a law on migration; and that it be endowed with the status of a legislative body. "Mastorava's" Chairman Nadkin, after a visit to Finland, has come home convinced that the Mordovian people need a Protestant Church.

Although the leaders of "Mastorava" try to muffle their differences, attention has been called, on the one hand, to the squabble between Nadkin and the Russian Orthodox Churchman Father Varsonophy (prior of the Saransk Cathedral), and between the anti-Communists and the pro-Communists on the other hand. The nationalists also stand divided between adherents of the "One Mordovia" trend and those who are calling for the separation of the Erzyans and Mokshans. All this political activity has attracted a good deal of public attention, due only to demonstrations regularly organized by students of the Mordovian State University.

Relations between Russians and Mordovians are normal; nationality does not play any role to speak of in their personal contacts. The assimilation process is far advanced. More and more Mordovians are becoming urbanites, more are migrating to other parts of the country. Not a single school in Saransk conducts teaching in the national tongue. Only half an hour a day is devoted to radio programs in the two local languages, and even less (10 minutes) to television programs in those languages. The "Moksha Pravda" (4,700 copies) and "Erzya Pravda" (3,000 copies) are distributed and read mostly in the villages.

There is no clearly targeted national policy and the government seems hardly concerned with the national problem. No group of deputies can be said to have rallied to the banners of the Mordovian national movement. That has further antagonized the extremist elements that are all too prominent in the national camp. It is no easy task to preserve the Mordovian ethnos and ensure its cultural rebirth. If the present situation persists, frequent small-scale extremist acts may be increasingly instigated by the nationalists.

The political influence of the democratic parties and movements has fallen since their most active exponents have joined the government. The Democrats have no newspapers of their own and rarely trouble to explain their views in other papers.

Almost all the republic's Left organizations have rallied since April 1992 around the "popular patriotic" movement "For Union and Justice" uniting local branches of the Communist (Bolshevik) Party, the Mordovian Workers' Socialist Party, and the Liberal Democratic Party.

The trade unions play quite a prominent role in Mordovia's life. They have launched their own newspaper, *Position,* which is doing much to sway public opinion and government action in the direction of economic change. With the backing of the Left bloc it has been tirelessly bringing stiff pressure to bear on the country's leaders, who have had to respond to the call that they "do something." Under this pressure the government introduced a project of a law adopted by the Supreme Soviet on help for the underprivileged sections of the populace. Unfortunately, the government does not have the necessary resources to implement that law.

On the whole the political life of the republic is highlighted by growing activity on the part of both the neo-Communists and the Federation of Free Mordovian Trade Unions. This trend was further accented when the head of the Liberal Democratic Party, Vladimir Zhirinovsky, visited Saransk early in June 1992, a visit which aroused great interest.

So far, the social climate in the republic is peaceful. No cuts in the labor force have taken place in its large industrial enterprises. The average earnings of its workers are slightly above those in neighboring areas, while prices on basic food products are comparatively low.

Mordovia has hardly any natural resources, and no minerals. Most of its industries are located in Saransk. Obviously, Mordovia has much to gain by participating in a Volga integrational set-up.

The Udmurt Republic

After adopting a law on the election of a president, his election was blocked for lack of a law regulating the procedural aspects of the matter. A group of nationalistically oriented deputies tried to push through a motion requiring the president to know the Udmurt language—a motion fiercely opposed by the Democrats. Neither side has gained. Given the present low level of activity in the Supreme Soviet, all they can do is thwart each other. There are no promising candidates for the presidency, a reflection of the absence of strong figures generally on the political proscenium. Nor has an exact dividing line been drawn between the functions of the head of the Supreme Soviet and those of the chairman of the Council of Ministers. Important decisions are jointly signed and sealed by both. Overall leadership is exercised by the Council of Ministers and Presidium of the Supreme Soviet, but the exact functions of either remain undefined. As a result there is no republican center capable of making cardinal decisions.

A Treaty on Friendship and Cooperation with the Republic of Tatarstan was concluded, for instance, but the motive behind its conclusion is wrapped in a fog. The only plausible explanation offered so far was deputy N. Nagornikh's remark that "they are accustomed to friendship with everybody, and so they signed it."

There are no conflicts for power at the top; relations between the leaders of the republic and the capital Izhevsk cannot be called either good or bad—it is better to say they are nonexistent. There have been no clashes between the Supreme Soviet and Izhevsk municipality on the division of property, probably because they have nothing to divide: The top leadership has little real authority, and the city administration even less. There has been only one local conflict, which flared up when the Sarapul City Soviet began to collect signatures in favor of merging with Kirov Region. Sarapul happens to be a town that was incorporated in the Udmurt Republic in the 1940s, and few Udmurts reside there. Sarapul's complaint was that it was regularly omitted from the list of cities entitled to financial aid. The conflict was promptly regulated.

The political climate may be described as traditionally calm and stable. Neither the Democrats nor the Left enjoy much prestige in a region with a population made politically inert by decades of social conditioning directed toward that very end.

As far as the Democratic movement in Udmurtia goes, it is euphonic to speak of it as a "bloc"—it is too atypical and amorphous. The most that can be said for the Democrats is that they have managed to avoid factionalism and disagreements—a reflection of the fact, no doubt, that the movement lacks charismatic leaders who have strong political convictions.

The Left can boast of two other parties or movements of a vague nature. One is the "Union of Udmurt Workers and Peasants" led by R. Galeyev, a stovemaker in the town of Mozhga, who in addition heads a movement launched in January 1992 under the name of "Toiling Udmurtia." The members of both organizations are hard put to explain in what ways they differ. Nor must we forget to mention the branch of the Liberal-Democratic Party which has appeared in the town of Glazov.

The majority in the republic's total population of one and a half million are Russians. Next come the Udmurts with 34 percent of the total, the Tatars with about 10 percent, and finally the Mari. Each nationality can point to its own compactly settled neighborhoods. There are four Udmurt and two Russian civic organizations, and many cultural associations (Tatar, Russian, Mari, Ukrainian, Bessermanian), all duly registered.

Udmurts comprise the fourth largest Finno-Ugric nationality in the world (from 700,000 to 800,000). Two-thirds live here, in the republic, but fairly large Udmurt settlements are also found in Ekaterinburg and Perm regions and the republics of Tatarstan and Bashkortostan. As a nation they are divided into two segments, the Northern and Southern Udmurts, who differ mostly as to language; a difference the republic's nationalists are inclined to minimize in spite of the fact that the Northern and Southern Udmurts barely understand each other. The Northern speech reveals more Russian and Komi strains, the Southern is more under the influence of the Tatars.

The most serious association of nationalists is "Udmurt Kenesh"—the Udmurt word "Kenesh" harking back to a traditional national self-governing body. This association pursues mostly political aims, in which it has had the support of the government. Its president, M. Shishkin, is an economist who once served as the Second Secretary of the regional committee of the CPSU. Both the personality of the man and his policies have aroused the displeasure of many supporters of the national movement. Held against him are both his Communist background and the objectionable way, in the opinion of his nationally oriented opponents, he has been playing up to the Democrats. "Kenesh" has clearly announced its desire to create a parallel structure of power similar to Tatarstan's Milli-Mezhlis in an attempt to be allied with the government. It has also been making overtures to the "Society of Udmurt Culture" in order to bring the Society under its wing. So far, its tactics have been moderate and restrained.

Second to it in significance is "Demen" or "The Society of Udmurt Culture," founded in 1990. It started out with quite an active political program, but now is focusing its attention on culture. Its new leaders, especially its present chairman, the writer P. Chernov, are opposed to any merger with "Udmurt Kenesh," largely because they distrust the policies and personality of leader M. Shishkin.

In April 1992 an Udmurt youth league called "Shundy" ("Sun") was formed with the backing of "The Society of Udmurt Culture" in order to "promote the political, cultural, and economic interests of the young." Exactly how it intends to realize that aim is not yet clear.

In October 1991 a new party called "Udmurt Kalyk" (Udmurt People's Party) made its debut. Its slogan is democracy plus complete economic and political sovereignty for Udmurtia, for which reason it has not found common ground with either the Democrats, who are generally opposed to the idea of sovereignty, or with the nationalists, who feel that it is not the right time to raise the issue of sovereignty. "Udmurt Kalyk" still does not play much of a role in the life of the republic.

The Union of Udmurt Businessmen, formed early in July 1992 under the auspices of "Udmurt Kenesh," proposes to set up a business center, a chamber of trade, and a national bank.

Relations between Russians and Udmurts are peaceful enough, and yet no observer can fail to notice the slight air of contempt with which a good many Russians regard their Udmurtian fellows. Occasionally, quarrels break out on buses or streetcars when someone speaking Udmurtian is insultingly called a "Votyak" or "gray mouse." Evidently, even the uneducated are aware of Russia's historical role in the destiny of the Udmurt people, on whose bones (as every inhabitant of Izhevsk knows) that city was built.

At the turn of the century, Udmurts comprised 80 percent of the population of Votsk territory; today they represent a stable minority. Since there is no manifest influx migrational trend, the proportion of Udmurts is slowly increasing. Assimilation has made less pronounced inroads here than among the related Mari and Mordovian peoples. The government has put no obstacles in the way of the nation's cultural rebirth—the real barrier is the widespread apathy of the public. The situation here is not very different from that which prevails in the other Volga republics. Only the Tatars are actively promoting their cultural autonomy.

Tatars, numerically the third largest nationality in Udmurtia, dwell in the Alnash area and the Lenin arrondissement of Izhevsk, where they have practically monopolized the field of trade and its adjuncts at high levels.

Historically, relations between Tatars and Udmurts have always been rather strained. The Tatar Civic Center (TCC) is not supposed to engage in political activity. Actually, its leaders have intervened in the affairs of the nationalities, less as concerns the Tatars than with regard to Russian-Udmurt relations. Spokesmen of the Udmurt national movement accuse TCC of constantly inciting tensions with the Democrats. As an example, they cite the draft resolution TCC submitted at the Congress of Finno-Ugric Peoples, which proved far too radical to be considered.

In response to the emergence of the above-mentioned Udmurt and Tatar national associations, a "Society of Russian Culture" was set up in 1991 by a "patriotic" group to promote Russian cultural contacts. The "Russian League," organized by a group of radical "patriots," has taken a rather extremist stand in favor of rapprochement with the neo-Communists.

On July 2, 1992, the Presidium of the Udmurt Supreme Soviet adopted a decision to restore the historical name of the Bessermanian people. Until then all who belonged to that nationality were registered as Udmurts.

The Bessermanians are a small rural people who inhabit a few scattered villages and dress in a style distinctly their own. Their language is close to Udmurtian, but their folkways and culture relate them to the Volga Bulgars

from whom they trace their origin. In July 1992 they formed a Bessermanian Society with the aim of restoring their cultural and national identity.
The Society's moving spirits are for the most part representative of the
humanitarian intelligentsia; the thrust of their activity is anti-Udmurtian.

Many Germans (an estimated 5,000) live in Sarapul. They hark back to
the time when German war prisoners were left behind at the close of hos-
tilities and when deported Germans arrived here from their former autonomous republic. Although these Sarapul Germans do not have any
organization of their own, they are prominent citizens.

Udmurts have always been known as good farmers. This is generally held
to be a republic that can feed itself. Yet the head of its Council of Ministers
gave the figure for the republic's self-sufficiency in food supplies at no more
than 25 percent.

Udmurtia has four large industrial centers: the cities of Izhevsk, Votkinsk,
Sarapul, and Glazov. They engage mostly in the sphere of military production (officially, it is 85 percent of the republic's economy). The only
large enterprise not connected with military production is Izhevsk "Bum-
machine" which produces paper-making machinery. Among the plants that
make arms, the best known are the Izhevsk gunnery and the Votkinsk
medium and close-range rocket plants. In addition, there are sundry radio
and electromechanical works in Izhevsk, Sarapul, and Glazov. The output
of Izhevsk's automobile plant comes to more than 30,000 motorcycles and
100,000 automobiles annually.

Some 10 million tons of oil are extracted annually in Udmurtia, of which
80 percent finds its way to Russia. Bashkir diggers also make off with 2
million tons a year from its Kambarka district, where most of the deposits
are concentrated, near the border of Bashkiria. Evidently, that situation is
beyond the control of the government, which promises at every Supreme
Soviet session "to look into it." Although the republic has such rich stores
of oil, it has no oil-refining industry to speak of.

Its natural resources also include lumber, which according to government
estimates is exported to the tune of about one million cubic meters a year,
half by official sanction and the rest haphazardly by whoever can carry it
out.

The Udmurt government takes hardly any part in the direction of the
armaments industry. The largest plants in the republic have always been
administered directly by Moscow. Now that direct orders from Moscow
are no longer forthcoming, the industry has been left to its own devices.
The Udmurt government's feeble attempts to exercise some authority have
been to no avail. Given strong leadership, the industry could well rule the
roost in Udmurtia, but its heads are not organized and their efforts are not
integrated. They have not adopted a clearly enunciated economic program
or taken a definite political stand. They have no realistic conversion program and are limping along as best they can. There is only one shop, where

double-cassette magnitophones are made, in operation at the Izhevsk plant; the Votkinsk plant is making electric washing machines, and so on.

Udmurtia's largest new economic structures are its regional commodity-exchange stock market "KAMA," and the Eurasian Bank of Economic Development. Originally created by the republic's Council of Ministers, the "KAMA" stock exchange is now an independent set-up; it holds sixth place among Russia's exchanges. Among its many activities is the training of commercial cadres. In April 1992 a Glazov broker sponsored the visit of V. Zhirinovsky to his city. This was not so much a political act as an expression of his fellow entrepreneurs' desire to popularize their activities. The Eurasian Bank of Economic Development is one of the largest banks in Russia.

An adverse ecological situation has developed in the Kambarkan area where much of the soil has been ravaged by the oil diggings. To make matters worse, a great deal of poisonous material is stored in the same district (15–16 percent of the total USSR reserve), and the problem of re-processing it is causing great concern. Local inhabitants have protested publicly against the construction of a reprocessing plant in the vicinity; they have been promised the support of the local authorities in preventing its construction, even if such is the president's order.

And so—although Udmurtia has great economic potentialities it also has much to gain from participation in the complex division of labor in the whole Volga area. Such integration will help it to resolve many of its economic and ecological problems; it will also expedite the solution of the conversion problem, at the same time ensuring the future of the Volga Belt's vital military-industrial complex.

The Republic of Bashkortostan

Bashkiria today has not formed an authoritarian center of power as has, for instance, Tataria. The reason is a strong national opposition to the republican executive authorities, concentrated both in the official (the Supreme Soviet) and public institutions. The national opposition reflects the complex ethnic composition of the population. Manifestations of the opposition activities are different. Thus, Bashkiria's leaders were subjected to severest criticism by the Bashskir and Tatar national-political movements after the signing of the Federative Treaty (although the latter had a supplement sharply extending the republic's economic rights). The Moslem clergy takes an active part in the political processes in the republic.

The complicacy (political above all) of the ethnic composition of the republic's population stems from the fact that none of the three main ethnic groups—Russians (39 percent of the population), Tatars (28 percent) and Bashkirs proper (22 percent)—has an absolute numerical prevalence. Besides these ethnic groups there live here Mari and Chuvash (approximately

3 percent of each). There are areas compactly populated by these ethnic groups: a considerable part of the Tatars live in the northwest of the republic near the border with Tataria (the Tatar nationalists have already voiced the demand for joining these areas to Tatarstan); the areas in the southwest and the northeast of the republic (together with the city of Ufa) have a primarily Russian population. In such circumstances, some observers point to the danger of either the disintegration of Bashkiria or its unification with Tataria (the Tatars and Bashkirs are two closely related peoples).[2] To us this danger appears somewhat exaggerated since most of the real politicians in the region cannot but be aware of what danger territorial redivisions represent at the present time.

According to the 1989 census, 585,000 Bashkirs (40.4 percent of the people) resided outside the republic: in Chelyabinsk region (161,000), Orenburg region (53,000), and a little less in Perm, Ekaterinburg, Tyumen regions, Kazakhstan, and Uzbekistan.

The Chelyabinsk group of Bashkirs came into being in 1934, when Chelyabinsk Region was formed and it received from Bashkiria the Argayash and Kunashak areas inhabited primarily by Bashkirs (today Bashkirs make up respectively 60 percent and 47 percent of their populations). It should be mentioned that these districts of Chelyabinsk Region are in a difficult ecological situation owing to the development here of atomic industry enterprises. This, just as does the process of assimilation of Chelyabinsk Bashkirs, engenders their national political activity (in 1991, for example, there was formed the Chelyabinsk Regional Bashkir People's Center). The solution to the problem of Chelyabinsk Bashkirs, as of the other dispersed groups of the Bashkir people, excepting the unrealistic recarving of the borders, can take two forms: extraterritorial cultural autonomy and the creation of territorial autonomous units.

A wide range of sociopolitical movements that formed in Bashkiria by the beginning of the 1990s reflect the interests of the different ethnic groups: in addition to the above-mentioned, the Ukrainian, German, and Jewish groups and their national-political movements. There exist, besides, movements of a general democratic nature akin to the Russian sociopolitical associations.

The "Ural" Bashkir People's Center (BPC) was established in December 1989 at the first congress of representatives of the Bashkir people. It has its branches in all districts of the republic. The Center assigns primary importance to the strengthening of Bashkortostan's sovereignty. The "Ural" ideological system gives prominence to the principle of the "native people," of Bashkiria as a territory belonging exclusively to the Bashkir ethnos, and the principle of the "national right." On the basis of "national right" the Bashkir People's Center demands for the Bashkirs in the republic practically a monopoly on the institutions of political power, preference in receiving property (land above all) and its possession. To citizens of the republic who disagree with such objectives, the Bashkir People's Center activists address quite severe statements.

"Ural" is the backbone of the mass national Bashkir movement in the republic. Besides the Bashkir People's Center, there are the Bashkir People's Party, Bashkir Women Society, Union of Bashkir Youth, and the Bashkir Cossack cultural-historical society "Severnye Amury," which fulfil the functions of sections of one movement headed by "Ural" rather than act as independent entities on the political scene.

In December 1991, the 6th Congress of the Bashskir People's Center, held in the atmosphere of disintegration of the USSR, advanced the idea of creation of a Bashkir National Congress, which was "in certain circumstances to claim the role of an alternative government." In other words, "Ural" has chosen the course of struggle for political power in the republic. For this purpose the Center has started a drive for influence on the non-Bashkir population of the republic, organizing, back in September 1991, the Congress of Democratic Forces of Bashkortostan. Most of the democratic societies in the republic, however, ignored this endeavor.

The Tatar Civic Center was created in Ufa in January 1989. It has no official membership. According to some estimates, the TCC includes about 600 activists carrying on work among the Tatar population, using, in part, the nonperiodical publication *Tatar Press Digest*. The TCC program advances to the forefront the following questions: reestablishment of the constitutional status of the Tatar language as official, along with Bashkir and Russian; greater opportunities of tuition in the Tatar language; promotion of the press and radio broadcasting in the Tatar language, and so on. The TCC is the main political opponent of the BPC, with the contradiction involved not only on the culturological plans (for instance, the status of the Tatar language). The BPC vigorously opposes "Tatarization" of Bashkirs and "the right of the Tatars to self-determination within the bounds of Bashkortostan."

The TCC therefore is becoming ever more politicized. A radical wing has formed in the organization. In July 1991, the Center's plenary meeting adopted a resolution recognizing as futile the attempt to solve national and economic problems within the framework of Bashkiria and admitting the need to create (reestablish)—on a constitutional basis, by holding a referendum, within the borders of the former Ufa Province—an Ufa Region (Republic) as part of the Russian Soviet Federative Socialist Republic.

The TCC is, second to "Ural," the most important, numerous, and ramified organization in the political system of Bashkiria. It can claim the role of a serious parliamentary party—after the elections to the organs of state power. So far, unfortunately, there has been no serious dialogue between the TCC, on the one hand, the state organs of Bashkiria, and "Ural," on the other.

Among other Tatar civil movements mention should be made of the Tatar Democratic Party "Idel-Ural," and the Union of Tatar Youth "Aza-tlyk." The Tatar national-political organizations of Bashkiria have strong contacts in Tataria.

The republic has also sufficiently developed Russian national-political movements, in which some radical-minded representatives of the Bashkir community see almost "the instrument of the Bashkirs' ethno-death." The reason is not only the process of russification of Bashkirs but also because Russians are concentrated mostly in the industries that have grossly upset the traditional way of life of the Bashkir people.

Until recently, the majority of politically active representatives of the Russian population were members of the Communist Party of the Soviet Union (CPSU). After its having been banned, the Russian population of the republic found themselves to a certain extent disorganized. The Ufa His-torico-Patriotic Assembly alone (created in 1990) raises "purely Russian" questions. The other sociopolitical movements, which attract the Russian population, emphasize in their activities primarily issues of a "universal" sociopolitical nature. This is why they are joined by part of the Tatars, Bashkirs, and representatives of the other nationalities of the republic.

The program of the Ufa Historico-Patriotic Assembly is based on the idea of a "single and indivisible" Russia within its historical boundaries. The Assembly is against the sovereignization of the national republics. The organization advances Russia's revival on the foundations that were inter-rupted in 1917. At the same time, the Assembly has among its slogans the creation of a "multiparty democratic system with an active participation in it of nonparty movements." The Assembly's leaders do not accept the political stand of both the BPC and TCC.

Mention might also be made of the Volga Cossacks (Tabyn Cossacks) Association, an organization formed in 1991 and upholding the interests of the Cossacks of Bashkiria. The positive contacts between the Russian and Bashkir Cossacks are to be stressed.

The Congress of Democratic Forces of Bashkortostan was formed in Sep-tember 1991. It is a bloc of movements defending the interests of alien peoples of the republic. Most influential and active in the Congress are the TCC and the Democratic Party of Russia.

The republic has national-cultural movements and societies of Chuvash, Mari, Ukrainians, Germans, and Jews, whose aims are to ensure conditions for a national-cultural revival of these ethnic groups.

Worthy of attention among the "left-wing" (socialist) organizations in Bashkiria are the regional association of the Social-Democratic Party and the Democratic Union. The republic, with its unfavorable ecological situ-ation, has ecological movements. Various organizations of producers have been formed, such as the Association of Industrialists of Bashkortostan, the Union of Tenants and Employers of Bashkortostan, the Agrarian League, and others.

Thus the republic has an extremely complicated sociopolitical situation with a manifest or potential confrontation of the various ethnic groups. For the level of political activity of its population, Bashkiria is apparently second (after Tataria) in the Volga Belt.

In the past few decades Bashkiria has become an industrially developed republic possessing 99 industries out of the 110 listed by the State Statistics Committee. Of the total of gross national product, industry accounts here for 60 percent, with the bulk of output coming from the heavy industry (production of means of production). The agrarian sector accounts for approximately 17 percent of the gross national product. All this shows that the republic cannot at the present time provide itself with consumer goods (farm and light industry products).

Intense dissatisfaction with both the government bodies and public movements of Bashkiria is evoked by the redistribution by the federal authorities of a considerable part of the wealth produced in the republic: first of all, the oil and gold (about two tons annually) mined here. This is why the declaration of the republic's sovereignty was approved in September 1990 by the overwhelming majority of parliament members (by 245 votes, with one against and four abstainers).

The republic's intensive industrial development has brought about a grave deterioration of the ecological situation owing to the increased oil production, oil refining, and other branches of chemical industry (the republic accounts for 60 percent of the herbicides and 30 percent of the soda produced in the territory of the former USSR). Typical of Bashkiria are frequent accidents at chemical enterprises (the so-called "phenol disasters").

Bashkiria is supposedly interested in the promotion of economic integration in the region. This is due to both the peculiarities of its economic condition (dependence on the deliveries of consumer goods and Siberian oil for the oil refineries) and the specificity of its national-political situation (aid in the minorities' national-cultural revival from the respective republics in the Volga Belt). Bashkiria, besides, needs assistance to normalize its ecological situation.

The Republic of Kalmykia–Khalmg Tangch

The Republic of Kalmykia is confronted primarily by the following problems: (1) a low level of socioeconomic development and mainly agrarian orientation of the republic's economy (leading to the outflow of part of the Russian population); (2) territorial rehabilitation of the Kalmyk people; and (3) ecological calamities connected with the arid climate and soil erosion.

In contrast to Bashkiria, the "native" population of the republic represents a numerically large group of the population (45 percent), incessantly growing due to a high natural increase. The proportion of Russians reaches 38 percent of the republic's population. Yet another appreciable ethnic group here are the "Caucasians" (mostly Darghinians, Chechens, and Avars), making up together 9 percent of the population. While Russian-Kalmyk relations, both in the past and today, have, on the whole, been free of conflict, a growing collision is to be observed between the "Caucasians," on the one hand, and the other inhabitants of the republic, on the other. The causes of the collision are to be found, in our opinion, both in the appreciable difference of behavioral stereotypes and in the "Caucasian"-Kalmyk rivalry in the sphere of employment (both the former and the latter specialize in distant-pasture cattle rearing).

A serious problem for the republic is the realization of the Law of the Russian Federation "On the Rehabilitation of Repressed Peoples." The fact is that, after the reestablishment of the Kalmyk Republic (Autonomous Soviet Socialist Republic), it did not receive the lands in the lower reaches of the Volga, which form at present parts of Astrakhan Region and Daghestan. The Kalmyk population in these areas is quite small; nevertheless, Kalmykia's authorities insist on the return of the lost territories.

In this case, as in many other similar cases, territorial rehabilitation of the peoples repressed in the years of Soviet power is extremely difficult, for it encounters resistance on the part of the people now living on the disputed lands. To our mind, in the case of Kalmykia the disputed territories issue can be resolved if the republic agrees to waive the territorial claims in exchange for a massive federal economic aid. Such aid is intended by the Decision of the Government of the Russian Federation of January 3, 1993, "On Urgent Measures for Support by the State of Socio-Economic Development of the Republic of Kalmykia–Khalmg Tangch."

The Komi Republic

The Komi-Zyrians and Permyaks (the latter concentrated in the Komi-Permyak Autonomous District and Perm Region) are one of the peoples who have undergone intensive assimilation by the Russian population. The number of Komi-Zyrians in the republic does not reach even a quarter of its population. Of course, this people, too, gradually joins the process of national-cultural revival, but at the present time it is impossible to speak of a developed confrontation between the Komi and Russian population in the republic. Yet, as shown by the poll conducted among the delegates of the First Congress of the Komi People in January 1991, relations among the nationalities were changing for the worse. It should be observed that the Congress oriented the Komi national movements to constructive efforts to solve social, economic, and cultural problems of the republic by constitutional methods.[3]

The Congress, arranged at the initiative of the "Komi kotyr" society (the republic's most influential political force), adopted a resolution "On the National Policy in the Field of the Language and National Culture." The main ideas of the document are apparently the following: it is the Komi people which is the source of the state system; therefore the administration of the republic must make every effort to develop the culture of the Komi people; the immediate task is to grant to the Komi language official status along with the Russian language. The same ideas were written down in "The Declaration of the State Sovereignty of the Komi Soviet Socialist Republic" (August 29, 1990). The latter document does not contain, on the whole, statements that can be defined as discriminatory with regard to "alien" population.

The political spectrum of the republic includes also strongly pronounced radical nationalist movements demanding the creation of an ethnocratic administration. One of these is the party "Biarmiya," formally succeeding the national party of the Komi people formed in 1917. Among its political tasks, according to the Rules, the party enumerates the achievement of independence by the Komi state incorporating all speakers of the Perm branch of the Finno-Ugric languages (the Zyrians, Permyaks, and Udmurts); orientation to a confederative union with the other Finno-Ugric peoples (Estonians, Finns, etc.). To be a citizen of this state, according to "Biarmiya," one must necessarily know the Komi language; Russians and people of other nationalities living in the republic, who do not know the Komi language, should be included, the party says, in the category of "foreign workers." As far as we know, the "Biarmiya" party does not have much political weight in the republic.

Komi is a sufficiently developed republic possessing good resources of oil, gas, and timber. A specific branch of the republic's economy, actively opposed by the national political forces, is the prisoner-cap facilities (i.e., reformatory labor institutions). Owing to its peripheral location, the Republic of Komi tends least of all to economic integration with the republics of the Volga Belt. The northern, near-arctic situation of the republic confronts it with a number of problems common, for example, with the problems of the Arkhangelsk Region, Karelia, or Yakutia.

The Republic of Tatarstan

National-Political Situation in the Republic. The Tatar republic is inhabited by two large ethnic groups of almost equal size, Tatars comprising 48.5 percent and Russians 43.4 percent of the population. Other ethnic groups include the Chuvash (3.7 percent) and Mordovians (0.8 percent).

The Tatars are a widely dispersed nation. They form a large section (1,121,000 persons) of the Bashkiria population. Tatar communities number from tens to hundreds of thousands in the Tyumen, Chelyabinsk, Ekaterinburg, Ulyanovsk, Orenburg, Kuibyshev, Moscow (including the city of Moscow), Perm, Astrakhan, Kemerovo, Nizhni Novgorod, Saratov, Omsk, Kirov, Leningrad (including St. Petersburg), and Penza regions, as well as the Krasnoyarsk Territory, and the Udmurt, Mordovian, Mari El, and Chuvash republics.

Tatars have struck roots in practically all the republics of the former USSR; 468,000 live in Uzbekistan, 328,000 in Kazakhstan. Recently, in response to much pressure from below, a Tatar (Kamyshin) administrative area was formed in Samara Region on the border with Tatarstan, and local radicals are now calling for it to be reunited "with its historical homeland."

Not excluded is the eventuality of a territorial conflict with Bashkiria, should the question arise of the annexation of its western part, populated mostly by Tatars, to Tataria. Reverting to the plan adopted in 1918 by the People's Commissariat for Nationalities Affairs of the RSFSR on the formation of a Tatar-Bashkir Republic, or to an analogous (non-Bolshevik) project on the creation of an "Idel-Ural" state, Tatar nationalists (the N. Mansurov group) have suggested various forms of Tatar-Bashkir union—that of a confederation, for instance. Today these projects appear to be at odds with the aspirations of the Bashkir nationalists and local leaders for various reasons: such a union would inevitably reduce Bashkiria to the status of a lesser partner, aside from the fact that it would complicate relations with Moscow. Others point out that cutting off the Tatar part of Bashkiria and joining it to Tataria would greatly increase the proportion of Tatars there; still others object that resurrecting the idea of an Idel-Ural Republic (and on an even larger scale) would reduce the proportion of ethnic Tatars in such a new republic.

Against the general background of growing Tatar influence, it remains that the dispersion of the Tatars is increasing; their numbers are growing in the Ulianovsk, Saratov, Astrakhan, Chelyabinsk, Ekaterinburg, Perm, Samara, and Orenburg regions, and the Udmurt and Bashkir republics.

Simultaneously, Russian voices are making themselves heard; people in the border towns of Nurlat, Bugulma, Yalabuga, and Zelenodolsk, which are populated mostly by Russians, are demanding to be separated from the Tatar Republic should the latter leave the Federation. There is very little likelihood of these territorial problems being resolved by force in the near future, especially since the position of Tataria's leaders on the question remains circumspect.

Having adopted a course directed toward state sovereignty, Tataria's rulers have managed to keep to it and even strengthen that position. The three basic political forces in the republic—its governing apparatus, its national political movements, and the Russian democrats—have failed so far to evolve political forms of action adequately expressing their particular interests.

Considering that the rule of the CPSU in Tataria did not expire and give up the ghost of its own volition, but was simply extinguished "by a telegraphed order" from the Russian government, the purely nominal dismantling of the old political structure did not lead to any significant changes, least of all with respect to personnel; most of the previous Party function-aries simply switched over to the president's staff and Cabinet of Ministers, or to key positions in the Supreme Soviet. At the same time, the growing emphasis on "Tatarization" at the top levels has provoked some muffled grumbling on the part of the Russians in high posts who are worried about their futures. All this stands today in the way of the formation of a con-solidated political body representing the interests of the republic's multi-national nomenclature. However, such a prospect looms now with the emergence of the Tatar Republican Party.

The government's principal ally is the All-Tatar Civic Center "ATCC," especially its moderate wing. In the autumn of 1991 serious differences cropped up in the national camp, presaging the division of ATCC into a moderate wing and a radical wing. The radical wing embraces "Ittifak" ("Sovereignty"), and "Azatlyk," as well as the "Marzhani Society." Its in-fluence on the young Tatar careerists whose interests are no longer directly tied to the old Party machine has grown. The radicals are all for the im-mediate proclamation of full independence for Tatarstan and a share in the wealth of the Union.

This confrontation ended in a schism when the radicals, bypassing both the ATCC leadership and the president, convened in February 1992 a "Ko-rultai" or Congress of the Tatar people and elected a national parliament or "Milli Mejlis," which was proclaimed as the only legitimate voice of the Tatar people, endowed with full rights to enact laws and issue orders bind-ing on the whole nation. In opposition to the Milli Mejlis the government and ATCC organized a World Congress of Tatars which called itself "an authoritative forum speaking for Tatars all over the world," and ridiculed the above-mentioned "impostors." When 150 delegates from Milli Mejlis tried to attend the Congress, they were not admitted. The head of Milli Mejlis, deputy T. Abdullin, was given the floor at the Congress, but his speech amounted to an admission of defeat.

There is no gain-saying the fact that the Tatar national-political move-ment has the decided support of the Tatar government. For instance, when hundreds of "activists" decided to assemble in Kazan, their trips were or-ganized and financed by their employers on orders from the government and its executives; the delegates were allowed generous transportation fees and access to the media, while the political activities of small enterprises, cooperatives, and various foundations were granted tax exemptions and sundry other privileges.

Peculiar to the political movement in Tatarstan is the fact that the idea of its union as a state with the Russian Federation is supported only by a small mixed cohort of Democrats without the least encouragement from Russia's officialdom or the directors of the republic's state or private en-terprises. As in the rest of Russia, Democracy in Tatarstan is many-sided and draws its inspiration from divergent political trends and organizations;

lacking resources, it abounds in actual or prospective leaders but cannot point to any "great names." It is obstructed by wide opposition from the masses.

Only by playing up the spread of dissatisfaction among the Russian and Russian-speaking section of the population, especially in the cities, have the Democrats managed to prolong their existence. Without real support from the Russian state and its representative bodies, from all of the other Russian democratic parties and organizations, Tatarstan's Democrats can hardly wage an effective political struggle.

Another attempt to unite the Russia-oriented Democrats of the republic was the creation in June 1992 of an electoral bloc called "Equality and Legality" which hoped to repeat the electoral triumph of 1989–1990 when not a single Tatar nationalist won a seat in the parliament in Kazan.

December 23, 1991 saw the formation in Kazan of "The Fund for Democratic Initiative" whose aim is to organize and finance the framing of laws and legislative acts, to provide expertise on and organize the study of public opinion, to analyze current social and economic problems, to further establishment of independent democratic channels of mass information, to train skilled personnel, to hold seminars and conferences on political and economic problems, and to give financial and material help to programs for developing small businesses and small private farms. The Fund and its founders are not interested in its commercial potential; all its profits are to be devoted to the realization of its charter goals. The chairman of its Council of Directors is a deputy, I. Grachev, whose many duties include coordinating the work of the parliamentary groups "People's Rule" and "Concord" and chairing the electoral bloc "For Equality and Legality." Today, political power in the republic is still in the hands of the ex-Party bosses. Present chances of the Tatar radicals seizing power are not great, for all that some sort of an alliance between them and the Party bosses already exists.

The national Russian movement is undeveloped. Most Democrats favor the growth of market relations and Tataria's remaining a part of Russia. But the fact remains that no potent consolidation, political or economic, of its market forces has taken place yet.

The republic's political course is being charted today by the group under the leadership of President Shaimiyev. The support tendered him by the majority of the population is a correlate of such elements of the nation's socioeconomic life as the granting of food cards and slightly lower prices for foodstuffs. To be sure, discontent has been growing lately because of the fact that wage rates here lag behind wages in the Russian Federation. The rampage of crime, corruption, and extortionism is another cause of discontent.

Tataria happens to be a testing ground of Russian regionalization. If the policy of separatism proves viable, even only temporarily, its example might be followed by other regions. Failure of the policy of separatism could spoil the desire of other regions to follow its example.

Meanwhile, the leadership are supported by the moderate nationalists (actually the majority of nationalists); they control much of the countryside through the agro-industrial complex; they have won over the wide public with food tickets and comparatively low food prices; they have also been unsparing of promises to the industrialists. They are doing their best to win over to their side the necessary leaders, the antimarketeers and anti-Yeltsinites. The sum total of all these efforts is that 60 to 70 percent of the populace support the government. Today, the Democrats are unable to gain the support of the people because of the popular opposition to the market program. As for the national radicals, they cannot count on more than a 15 percent vote in their favor. Yet, significantly enough, the leaders of the republic have not risked openly raising the question of separation from the Russian Federation; the opinion polls have told them that the majority of their countrymen are opposed to such a break.

In March 1992, a referendum was held in the republic on the following issue: "Do you agree that the republic of Tatarstan is a sovereign state, a subject of international law which is building its relations with the Russian Federation and other republics on the basis of equitable treaties?" The majority of those who participated in the referendum (61.4 percent) said "Yes."

Having set the compass toward real sovereignty, the Tatar government has taken the following course:

1. Under the slogan "Tatarstan is the cradle of the Tatar nation and its function is to unite the whole Tatar diaspora and so influence the national policy of Russia" (M. Shaimiyev), a World Congress of Tatars was convened in June 1992 which was attended by over 1,100 delegates from the other newly independent republics of the CIS, the Baltic republics, the United States, Finland, Austria, the Federal German Republic, Turkey, and other countries. The Congress appealed to all the countries of the world as well as the United Nations to recognize Tatarstan's independence. It created an Executive Committee of twenty-five members and elected as its chairman the Kazan University professor I. Tagirov, one of the ideologists of Tatar sovereignty (in the past a member of the Tatar Republic's Communist nomenclature). One of his three vice-chairmen is R. Valeyev, editor in chief of the newspaper *Denya,* and former editor of the journal *Agitator.* The Executive Committee of the Congress defined its aim as "all-round encouragement and help for the socioeconomic, ethnocultural and political development of the Republic of Tatarstan, intermediation in the solution of Tatar ethnoregional problems" and other cultural undertakings.

The authorities are abetting the creation and activization of various public organizations aimed at uniting all the Turkic and Moslem peoples on the basis of their inherited traditions—albeit with an outspoken anti-

Russian political bias, such as the Turkic Young People's Association and others of the same tenor.

2. Marked activation of inter-republican ties through the agreements and treaties it began to conclude in the middle of 1991 with the Baltic States, the CIS republics of Bashkiria, Udmurtia, and Mari El, and the Kemerovo and Astrakhan regions. These agreements have usually contained offers of separate terms and help from the republic in providing cultural services for the Tatar populations of the other areas. A decision has also been adopted on the exchange of missions by mutual agreement between Tatarstan and other CIS republics (Shaimiyiev's decree of April 4, 1992).

Economic agreements have been signed with the Ukrainian and Uzbek republics, as well as the former Soviet republics of Lithuania and Latvia and a number of regions and other republics of the Russian Federation. The authorities in Tatarstan are not interested in concluding regional treaties of a "Greater Volga" or "Volga Belt" type on the grounds that such treaties would lower its standing as an independent republic. Nevertheless, the city of Kazan signed a treaty in July 1992 with a number of cities (headed by Ulianovsk) in that Belt.

3. By building its relations with the Russian Federation exclusively on the basis of an agreement by which its powers of authority are delegated "from below" to the Russian government, and are exercised by the latter only to the degree set by treaty between the two republics and the provisions of their Constitutions (many of which are mutually exclusive), the republic was trying to realize the idea of a state associated with the Russian Federation, and succeeded in doing it. The bilateral Treaty (signed in February 1994) proceeds from the principles of Russia's territorial integrity, Tatarstan's sovereignty, and a Tatar-Russian alliance.

"Even if we imagine for a moment that Tatarstan became an independent state, no more than a week or month would go by before we'd be seeking rapprochement with Russia again," said the Tatar Prime Minister M. Sabirov. "Our republics cannot survive without each other. Nowadays some very courageous politicians keep shouting about independence, but do they really have the strength to lift such a heavy burden? Perhaps it would be better to share it with Russia?"

4. Although the international legal recognition of Tataria can only follow upon the regulation of its relations with the Russian Federation, the republic's leaders have, in a one-sided declaration, protested that it is not merely a participant in international relations, but a subject of such relations. The official press has been actively boosting the government's contacts with foreign officials, firms, and organizations which promised to give to Tataria their economic and technical assistance in different fields. Great hopes are pinned on the prospect of help from businessmen of Tatar nationality now abroad. In Tatarstan itself, the necessary legal base to warrant large foreign investments is still lacking, in the light of which the

hullabaloo of publicity which followed the above negotiations with foreign firms was really inspired by little more than the signing of protocols outlining intentions. The republic's most intensive political and cultural ties are with Turkey.

In addition to political and economic activity on the foreign stage, the republic's leaders are pursuing a purposeful policy of strengthening their prestige by a well-coordinated program of ideologically shaping public opinion. The elements of this program may be summed up as follows:

- complete control of the local radio, television, and press;
- popularizing the "right" stereotypes (for example, everything in Russia is bad, whereas we are protecting your true interests) of psychological paternalism and the idealization of Tatarstan as the true motherland;
- conditioning of the young from grade school on in the spirit of loyalty not to Russia, but to "their own" country, Tatarstan;
- individual work (not unsuccessful) with the creative and scientific intelligentsia to persuade them to support the republic's political course, or at least not to oppose it;
- ousting of Russians from influential managerial or social spheres, and particularly the mass media, the fields of culture and education;
- surrounding the republic's present leaders with a "personality cult"; at the same time the opposition has no republic-wide tribune and can only make itself heard in Kazan;
- the living and working conditions of officials, administrators, industrials managers, creative workers, scientists, and journalists have been made to depend on support for the political course proclaimed by the republic's leaders.

Characteristics of the Republic's Economy in Brief. In 1992 Tataria accounted for 7 percent (28 million tons) of the Russian Federation's output of oil. The leading branches of the republic's economy are the oil industry, petroleum production, automobile, airplane, and machine building industries, and machine-tool production for the military industry. The scientific and technical center of the republic is Kazan where the main intellectual potential of the republic is concentrated.

Of particular importance to Russia's economy are the products of some enterprises of Tataria, but the breakdown of economic ties and financial blockade of its industries will of course have a worse effect on the economy of Tatarstan than that of Russia. At the same time, Tatarstan's territory remains an avenue of much of the country's railway, automobile, and river communication. Major oil pipelines pass through its territory. In a crisis the republic's leaders could resort to economic blackmail.

There is no market substructure to speak of in the republic. Such commercial ventures as have been started are held in the grip of former Party officials. The Cabinet of Ministers has declared practically all Tatarstan's leading enterprises to be monopolies whose operation is to be controlled as heretofore by the state. As for the creation of a market substructure, the republic lags far behind the rest of the Russian Federation. Of the few promising beginnings it has made in that direction, the largest are the Tatar "Commercial Bank" and the Volga-Kama Exchange and Bank. Its Russian banks (savings banks excluded), stock exchanges, insurance and joint stock companies may be said to be practically inoperative. Nor has there been any noticeable penetration of Tatar economic ventures into the Russian Federation's economy.

Tatarstan's leaders believe that it is to their advantage to dissociate themselves from the Russian Federation when it comes to repaying the debts of the former USSR. They would rather attract foreign capital for themselves independently of Russia's programs—and not through IMF credits or policies, but in the form of direct investments in their economy, so far without success.

In general, the situation in the republic's industrial complex, which is preponderantly a military industrial complex, may be described as quite poor. Without its own mighty constructors' bureaus or modern technological base it can hardly solve its structural reconstruction problems. The dimensions mass unemployment reaches in the republic will depend to a great extent on how well Russia supplies it with orders and keeps its plants in operation.

The economic course chosen by Tatarstan's leadership is based on the following pattern: independent sale of oil for dollars plus purchase of rubles at the current exchange rate equal enough to take care of all its budgetary problems. Its leaders are also counting on complete control of the republic's production potential.

At the same time, there are many pitfalls, many things that may engender popular discontent with their economic course such as price liberalization, growing unemployment if Russia defaults with its orders, agriculture's need of subsidies, urban population growth, the appearance of internal regional political groups or a technocratic oppositional bloc, transportation hold-ups in Kazan, curtailment of home building, the prospect of the republic's becoming a low wage zone.

Oil is the key to the republic's policies and the bulwark of its sovereignty. Oil continues as always to focus the leadership's thinking and planning. Oil is indeed the republic's chief source of wealth and its great reserve in the event of a general deterioration of the situation. Of course, the situation is not as simple as that. The republic itself requires approximately 8 million tons a year for its own needs. Its critical export limit is 15 million tons given its usual level of output. If output drops, so will exports. What's more, it has to buy its gas in Orenburg, and coal from Kuzbas to keep the Zainsk hydroelectric station in operation. The oil has to be shipped to

Moscow for refining. Having rejected the idea of building an atomic power station, and confronted now with the need to lower the level of the dam at the Nizhnekamsk hydroelectric station, it will have to use more oil to satisfy its own energy needs. The calculations on this chain of expenditures: oil-coal-gas-electric energy—are still to be worked out.

Tataria has adopted a course of complete independence as concerns its oil policy. All its hard currency oil transactions take place under its own jurisdiction. In that respect it boasts all the necessary technological structures as well as its own personnel. Tataria is also conducting negotiations with Bashkiria concerning oil refining (the republic's weak spot), and is projecting a refinery of its own with a capacity of 7 million tons annually. Plans are being drawn up to build a republican oil tanker flotilla.

Formerly, the republic produced a good deal of grain, but lately it has had to import 30 percent of its requirements. Its grain and sugar purchases are oriented on foreign sources, particularly on the Ukraine. Stock breeding (sustained by imported combined forage) has been developed for the production of milk and meat. But the influence of Tatarstan's agricultural output on the food situation in Russia has been minimal: Both exports and imports have been negligible.

The following are the economic and social problems of the republic that need to be solved.

- Power—experts forecast a power shortage by 1996; electric station equipment is worn out and no new stations are being built.
- Oil—if the present reduction of output continues, it will drop to below 20 million tons annually by the year 2000, and the republic's export potential will fall, followed by the problem of finding jobs for the unemployed oil workers.
- Elaz—(the Yelabuga auto plant): the source of its financing is not clear; construction has stopped.
- Kazan—the problem of conversion of its military enterprises, its dependence on Russian orders; unemployment.
- The Market Substructure—it is very weak and is not backed by the authorities.
- Demography—the young continue to migrate from the villages, the population is aging: There are more than 800 thousand pensioners in a total population of 3.7 million.

As we can see, the Republic of Tatarstan confronts the Russian authorities with their most serious problem in the whole Volga region. Obviously, there are also weak and strong points in the position of the republican leadership. In our view nothing good can come of confrontation between the two. Everything points to the conclusion that the Tatar situation is to a great extent a consequence of the fact that Russia itself still does not have a wholly viable conception of its own future. The experiment of Tataria's leaders may be said to have been forced on them to no small extent. At the same time, it is important that Tataria is a testing ground of Russia's new forms of statehood. If its experiment proves successful, other members of the Federation will follow suit.

CONTEMPORARY SITUATION IN THE NORTH CAUCASUS: SOME GENERAL CHARACTERISTICS

In socioeconomic regional composition the North Caucasus includes the Ingush, Chechen, North-Ossetian, Adygei, Daghestan, Kabardino-Balkarian, and Karachai-Cherkessian Republics, as well as Stavropol and Krasnodar territories, and Rostov Region.

Rostov Region, of course, shares only indirectly in the national and political processes taking place in the area—that is to say, only to the extent that this is a region to which the tide of refugees and displaced persons heads from the Caucasus. For that reason Rostov Region will not be discussed here.

The Caucasus as a whole is chronologically one of the last territorial acquisitions of the Russian Crown. Its "subjugation" lasted until the second half of the 19th century, and so its integration with Russia may be said to be relatively recent. A strong tradition of military resistance to Russian domination persisted for a long time here. Further, during the years of Soviet government some of the Caucasian peoples were subjected to arbitrary persecution and deportation without sanction of law: the Cossacks in the 1920s, the Chechen, Ingush, Karachay, and Balkar peoples in the 1940s. The memory of these injustices lives in the minds of the peoples of the Region.

At the same time, the information, acquired as a result of a March 1992 poll (conducted by the Analytical Center of the North Caucasian Council of the "Senejh Forum," and embracing 1402 Avars, Adygeis, Balkars, Darghins, Ingush, Kabardinians, Karachaians, Kumyks, Laks, Lezghins, Nogais, Ossetians, Tabasarans, Cherkes, and Chechens) shows that most of the non-Russian peoples living in the North Caucasus wanted to remain within the Russian Federation (64.7 percent of the respondents as against the 18.7 percent who want their republics to be independent of Russia). The authors of the study conclude: "The reform of the national states of the North Caucasus must be accomplished in a constructive manner, a reform based not on confrontation, but on cooperation between both the republican and the Russian national movements and ruling bodies at all levels."[4]

Speaking of the population of the North Caucasus, it is necessary to keep in mind the predominantly autochthonous composition of practically each republic, the extremely mosaic composition of the area, the uniqueness of the culture of each of the native peoples, so different from the culture of the Russian-speaking settlers who later arrived in this area of predominantly Moslem Sunnites. At the same time, the region remains a distinct ethnographic historical area, the North Caucasus, whose local inhabitants share many common traditions and cultural traits.

The North Caucasus as a whole may be classified as one of Russia's industrially backward regions, where agricultural production exceeds industrial output. Most of its republics are weakly developed, like the region as a whole, whose social and economic level is only semideveloped. The share of heavy industry (machine building and metal working) in its total industrial output is lower than in the country as a whole. The only exception is perhaps Northern Ossetia, which according to the methodological criteria we follow belongs socially and economically among our highly developed republics in the northern part of the region—Rostov area, representing the most highly developed industrial area.

The North Caucasian economic area is comparatively rich in mineral resources. It is a source of natural gas and oil, of wolfram, molybden, coal, and rock salt. It produces electric energy at its own heat and hydroelectric stations (TES and HES), which together form a unified power system. The area's output of gas, oil, rock salt, and power came to 3 to 7 percent of the former USSR's. The region is also a monopoly source of aviation fuel; 90 percent of the country's needs was supplied by Grozny. At the same time, our statistics reveal that the North Caucasus has only an insignificant number of high-technology enterprises, even as concerns the military production complex.

On the other hand, the agrarian specialization of the area is of the greatest importance to the country. It accounted for 10 percent of the total agricultural output of the former USSR; its share in the output of canned vegetables and kitchen oil amounted to a fifth of the national total. By developing practically all aspects of stock breeding, it made significant contributions to the nation's larder.

Mention must be made of the singular role of the North Caucasus as a recreational area, indeed, the most attractive one in the country. Its principal centers are Sochi and Anapa on the Black Sea coast; the mineral watering spas of Kislovodsk, Essentuki, and others; the Elbrus mountain resorts of Nalchik, Dombai, and Tiberda, and also Talgi in Daghestan. It goes without saying that economically the potential of the region is extremely great. However, it can only be fully realized under stable political conditions.

The importance of the region as a transportation avenue must also be stressed. It connects European Russia and the East European countries with Trans-Caucasia and the lands of the Near East via the Great Caucasian Mountain Range—through which, by the way, there are only a few passageways. Thus, the main branch of the North Caucasian railway which links the republics and regions of the whole area (Rostov-Tikhoretsk-

Table 5.1
Share of Federal Resources in Budget Intake of Republics and Regions of North Caucasus (in millions of rubles)

	1992	1993
Republic of North Ossetia	42.8	41.8
Adyghei Republic	32.8	32.1
Daghestan Republic	76.4	70.5
Kabardino-Balkaria Republic	45.5	63.9
Karachai-Cherkessian Republic	37.3	45.4
Chechen Republic	72.7	32.4
Ingush Republic	79.2	92.9
Krasnodar Territory	8.8	11.1
Stavropol Territory	5.5	37.3
Rostov Region	2.4	—

Source: Pokazateli byudzhetov i economicheskogo razvitiya respublic, avtonomnykh oblastei i okrugov Rossiiskoi Federatsii za 1992 god i prognos na 1993 god (Budget and Economic Development Indices of the Republics and Autonomous Regions of the Russian Federation for 1992 and prognosis for 1933) (Moscow: Goskomstat, 1993).

Zelenchuk-Minvody-Prokhladnaya-Gudermes-Shamkhal-Makhachkala-Derbent-Samur) is the most important "gateway" in all Trans-Caucasia.

Major gas pipelines pass through its territory to Central Russia, the Ukraine, the Volga Belt, and all Trans-Caucasia. Its oil pipes reach the Volga Belt and Siberia. Three special automobile highways connect it with the Sukhumi, Ossetian, and Georgian Zones.

The North Caucasus economic area is divided into three geographical zones: steppeland, alpine meadowlands, and mountains; the first two occupy four-fifths of its territory.

Practically all its regions, as the statistics presented in Table 5.1 show, form their budgets with the help of federal resources; only a few territories draw a small share of their budgets from the federal budget. It goes without saying that the given situation is the result of the comparatively underdeveloped industrial status of the area. The 1992 fall in industrial output throughout the region, reflected in Table 5.2, was more drastic than the average for all of Russia. It is perhaps only in the percentage of unprofitable enterprises that it looks better than Russia. That is evidently a reflection of the fact that the region boasts more light and food industries whose products are in great demand on the market.

Against the all-Russian background the figures in Table 5.3 show that cash income exceeded cash expenditure and the rate of income growth was greater than the rise in consumer-goods prices, but it can hardly be taken as proof that living conditions in the given areas had improved. The decline in the turnover of retail goods was greater than for Russia as a whole. In

Table 5.2
1992: Results of Economic Activity of Republics and Regions of North Caucasus

	% of unprofitable enterprises	Retail trade (sum total vs. 1991 %)	% of housing construction vs. 1991	Consumer goods output % (in real prices) vs. 1991
Russian Federation	17.0	60.9	11.0	85.0
Republic of North Ossetia	7.3	31.6	69.0	71.3
Adyghei Republic	19.5	45.2	64.0	87.2
Daghestan Republic	8.3	33.9	38.0	81.2
Kabardino-Balkaria Republic	20.5	53.2	52.0	70.4
Karachai-Cherkessian Republic	11.8	48.6	50.0	70.4
Chechen-Ingush Republic	17.9	32.3	29.0	60.7
Krasnodar Territory	17.8	68.1	79.0	82.1
Stavropol Territory	12.1	44.8	84.0	80.6
Rostov Region	10.6	51.5	68.0	76.5

Source: O razvitii ekonomicheskih reform v Rossiskoi Federatsii (dopolnitelnye dannye) v 1992 godu (Additional data on Progress of Economic Reform in Russian Federation for 1992) (Moscow: Goskomstat, 1993).

fact, the figures indicate that the great mass of people in the region were not able to buy goods for their money.

It is interesting to note that in the republics and regions of the North Caucasus, the pace of economic reform relating to privatization has proven to be faster than in Russia as a whole (see Table 5.4). That is true in both the cities and the countryside. Despite the comparatively rapid rise in the number of individual farms, most collective and state farms have retained their previous status.

Karachai-Cherkessia

Karachai-Cherkessia became a republic only recently. In November 1990, following a session of the Regional Council of People's Deputies, it applied to the Supreme Soviet of Russia to be granted the status of a republic—a request which met with a positive response from the Russian government on July 3, 1991. Thus, after having functioned as an Autonomous Region until July 1991, its status as a republic was confirmed by the Russian Federative Treaty in March 1992.

The economy of the region has well-developed agrarian and industrial

Table 5.3
Standard of Living in the Republics and Regions of North Caucasus

	Ratio: cash incomes to consumers' outlays in December 1992 per capita % population	Rate of growth of factory and office workers' wages as against consumer goods prices: % November vs. October 1992
Russian Federation	1.7	0.95
Republic of North Ossetia	4.4	1.10
Adyghei Republic	1.7	—
Daghestan Republic	3.8	0.90
Kabardino-Balkaria Republic	2.4	1.00
Karachai-Cherkessian Republic	2.2	—
Chechen-Ingush Republic	2.9	0.96
Krasnodar Territory	2.0	1.10
Stavropol Territory	2.0	1.00
Rostov Region	2.3	0.98

Source: O razvitii ekonomicheskih reform v Rossiiskoi Federatsii (dopolnitelnye dannye) v 1992 godu (Additional Data on Progress of Economic Reform in Russian Federation for 1992) (Moscow: Goskomstat, 1993), pp. 36–37, 42–43.

spheres. Important among them are its chemical and oil-refining plants, which account for a third of GNP, its food industry (20 percent GNP) and its light industries. Its hydroelectric station on the Kuban River supplies it with electricity. Machine-building, metal- and woodworking, mining, and production of ores prolong the list of its industries, most of which are concentrated in Cherkessk. Its agricultural specialties are the production of grain, meat, and dairy products, and sheep raising. Its farming area is divided almost equally between cultivated and pasture lands.

The main political problem of the republic hinges on the separatist processes which have been accentuated lately; Karachaiyans, Cherkessians, Abazinians, Cossacks of the Zelenchuk and Urup districts all proclaiming "their republics." In the greater part of its expanses these self-proclaimed "republics" overlap one another, causing mutual friction. Then there is the problem of the Nogaians (3 percent of the population) who are seeking their own autonomous status in the North Caucasus.

The most acute problem, of course, is that of the Karachaiyans and their striving for their own statehood. A mass Karachaiyan movement was launched at a congress held in October 1989, where the demand for separation from the Stavropol Region and achievement of Karachaiyan autonomy within the Russian Federation first cropped up. Simultaneously, a

Table 5.4

Some Figures on the Course of Economic Reform in the Republics and Regions
of North Caucasus as of January 1, 1993

	1	2	3	4
Russian Federation	25.3	7.9	35.0	3.75
Republic of North Ossetia	39.7	15.2	77.0	3.21
Daghestan Republic	29.9	17.8	92.0	11.76
Kabardino-Balkaria				
Republic	28.7	13.7	63.0	22.67
Karachai-Cherkessian				
Republic	35.8	29.4	12.0	2.61
Chechen-Ingush Republic	—	8.9	—	3.26
Krasnodar Territory	24.4	13.9	35.0	3.87
Stavropol Territory	33.7	23.3	8.0	5.64
Rostov Region	20.0	10.4	77.0	4.53

Column 1: percent of retail stores with private juridical status versus number still to
be commercialized.
Column 2: proportion of privatized flats versus total still subject to privatization.
Column 3: proportion of collective and state farms which retain their previous status
compared to the total number registered as farmsteads.
Column 4: growth in number of farmsteads as of January 1993, compared to January
1992.

Source: O razvitii ekonomicheskih reform v Rossiiskoi Federatsii (dopolnitelnye dannye) v
1992 godu (Additional Data on Progress of Economic Reform in Russian Federation in
1992) (Moscow: Goskomstat, 1993), pp. 20–21, 48, 92–93, 95–96.

society was formed called "Djamagat" which purported to "support perestroika" (as its founders put it). On October 29, 1989 a mourning procession on "Stalin's persecution of the Karachaiyan people and their
national tragedy" was attended by 30,000 people.

November 1990 saw the convocation of a Karachaiyan Congress of People's Deputies of all levels where a number of decisions regarding the formation of a Karachaiyan Republic were adopted. In its "Declaration of the
Karachaiyev Soviet Socialist Republic as a sovereign State within the
RSFSR," it stressed that it was a *national Karachaiyan People's* state. It
particularly noted that "representatives of all national Karachaiyan groups
are equals."[5] A Draft Constitution was adopted containing the following
postulates (see article 6): "The Karachaiyev Republic is a sovereign state.
It has become a member of the Russian Federation by mutual agreement,
which presumes its right to leave the Federation of its own will."[6] The
liberal character of this document, with its emphasis on human rights, is
noteworthy.

In July 1991 the Karachaiyan people held an "Extraordinary Congress" at which they definitely claimed sovereignty. For instance, the Congress elected a "Provisional Committee on the Restoration of the Karachai's National Statehood." A delegation was chosen to negotiate with the president of the Russian Federation concerning the creation of such a republic.

On October 27, 1991, a Mourning Procession in memory of those who were deported took place in Karachaievsk. November 17 of that year witnessed the launching of an uninterrupted national meeting of Karachai people. It was caused by the forthcoming election of deputies to the Karachai-Cherkessian Soviet Socialist Republic Supreme Soviet scheduled for January 27, 1992. The aim of the elections was to support the existence of a "twin" republic. People at the meeting demanded that the Karachaiyev Republic be included in the Russian confederation, as seen in the appeal that was addressed to the president of Russia and the dispatch of a delegation to negotiate with him on the subject.

In March 1992 the Presidium of the Regional Soviets of Karachai-Cherkessia decided to hold a referendum by secret ballot on the national structure of the republic. The purpose of this referendum was to elicit support for a unified republic. On March 11, 1992, the leadership addressed an "Appeal to the People of Karachai-Cherkessia" in which they condemned the arbitrary proclamation of five republics (Karachai, Cherkessk, Abazinsk, Batalpashinsk, a predominantly Cossak zone, and Zelenchuk-Urup), and also the formation of preparatory organizational committees for the creation of each such separate republic. Their principal objection to the idea was that the very process of forming five such separate states would disrupt economic ties and undermine the economy of the whole area. In a word, the leaders of the republic were appealing to the population to come out in favor of preserving its unity.[7]

This decision to hold a referendum evoked a negative response from a section of the public and administrative personnel (some even cancelled the referendum in their precincts) on the ground that it contradicted the "Law On the Repressed Peoples." Still, the referendum took place, even though a good many Karachaians did not participate in it. Only 75 percent of those entitled to a vote took advantage of the privilege; of these, 51.9 percent voted in favor of unity (or 46.3 percent of all those entitled to vote). The issue received the least support of all in the city of Karachaievsk, where only 17.1 percent of potential voters expressed support for unification. In Zelenchuk and Urup the vote was 24.4 percent and 18.7 percent, respectively for union; in Malokarachayevsk, 49.6 percent. In other words, the referendum showed that the people of Karachai-Cherkessia were by no means of one mind on the question. The most negative stand was taken by the Karachaians themselves, and also the Cossacks.

Speaking of the Cherkess national movement, it remains that we have touched on only one aspect of the broad Adygh national problem. The aim is the amalgamation of all Adygheians—and that includes the Cherkes, Adyghei, Kabardinian, Shapchug, and other groups; another goal is recovery of the territories the Adygheians lost as a result of the Caucasian War.

The Adygh diaspora has done much to promote such organizations as the Adygh National Congress, the International Cherkes Association, the Confederation of Caucasian Peoples. Adygh irredentism as such does not rule out the idea of republican separatism. On October 24, 1991, a Cherkes Congress convened deputies of all levels as well as some Abazinian and Cossack spokesmen and voted for the formation of a Cherkes Republic; it also launched a Committee of National Accord embracing representatives of the Cherkes and Abazinian peoples and appealed to the Cossacks and Nogais to appoint delegates and join in its activities. "Adygh-Hassa" and "Adyglar" are two well-known and popular Cherkes ethnopolitical organizations.

The Cossacks represent another political element in the republic to be seriously reckoned with. Today they have their own political formations and have launched their own movement. A society called "Russ" was established on December 7, 1991, at a constituent congress of Cossacks and Russians, residents of the republic. There is a "Cossack Club" and an organization called "Slavs of Karachai-Cherkessia." The goals of these Cossack formations change from time to time, from that of preserving the unity of the republic to proclaiming their independent Cossack state.

Take the example, for instance, of the Congress of Upper Kuban Cossacks (July 1990) which came out against the inclusion of Cossack territory within the Karachaiyev Republic, and voted for the transfer of all its territory to Stavropol. Then in July 1991 a referendum was held in the Zelenchuk and Urup Districts affirming the desirability of creating a separate Cossack republic there, and that idea was upheld by the majority of the local people. And at another Cossack congress held in August the same year, the creation of a Zelenchuk-Urup Cossack Soviet Socialist Republic within the confines of Russia was likewise proclaimed. In December 1991, Zelenchuk and Urup deputies met in joint session and decided that the Zelenchuk Cossack Territory should be reinstated as the Zelenchuk-Urup Cossack Republic of southern Russia within the jurisdiction of the Russian Federation and a constituent assembly was appointed to legalize its formation. They stipulated that if that demand were rejected, they would support the alternative of the two districts being incorporated in Stavropol.

The Cossack movement has the backing of the administrations and the Cossacks of Krasnodar, but less so of their counterparts in Stavropol.

Although the aims of the Cossack community and the Karachai national movement contradict each other, they manage to maintain fairly good contacts. February 1991 saw the adoption of a "Declaration of the Kislovodsk Cossack district and Kislovodsk Karachai Society 'Alan' to the citizens of Kislovodsk and Republic of Karachai-Cherkessia on juridical, cultural, economic, and ethnic cooperation." The underlying purpose of this joint document was to preserve the stability of the area and prevent the rise of inter-ethnic confrontation.

The chief opponents of the division of the republic are the local nomenclature under their temporary head, V.I. Khubiyev. Indeed, they have not tried to conceal their intention of solving this vexing problem by force, with the backing of certain important representatives of the central Russian authorities. Among the latter was the advocate of preserving a united republic, the former Russian Minister of Justice N. Fyodorov, chairman of the Government Committee of Realization of the Law on Rehabilitation of the Repressed Peoples. Thus, a telegram addressed to President Yeltsin in June 1992 by a number of civic organizations informed him that the chairman of one of the regional Soviets by the name of Saveliev was planning to bring a battalion of the Special Police Force to Cherkessk and supply the heads of all local districts with firearms. Even if that message was untrue, the very fact that it was dispatched indicates that the situation in Karachai-Cherkessia has been very tense and that the possibility of bloodshed cannot be entirely excluded.

Thus, one may speak of the actual dissolution of the Karachai-Cherkessian Republic, and it is by no means clear so far what the future configuration of the area will be. Preservation of a united republic is mostly to the advantage of the local nomenclature, for otherwise they will lose their jobs. At the same time, its dissolution and the subsequent unmanageable processes which follow are bound to lead to serious clashes between the new administrative and governing bodies in Karachai-Cherkessia, above all over concerns about portioning out the land.

It is perfectly apparent that the breakup of the republic will lead to grave material setbacks inasmuch as most of the new formations will have exclusively agricultural economies. That is why, along with the process of political separation, the region must simultaneously base its orientation on strong ties of economic integration. That is only possible if political confrontations are avoided. Let us hope that the process of political integration gathers strength in the region and orients itself on the ethnic bonds linking Karachaians and Balkars, and the Cherkes, Kabardian, and Adyghei peoples and the Cossacks and Russians. Regions populated by these peoples will be united in some form of territorial federative or confederative structure.

The Kabardian-Balkar Republic

Kabardino-Balkaria is an agrarian and industrial republic. Its industries include power production (the Baksan Hydroelectric Station) light, food, machine-building and metalworking industries, including electrotechnical, instrument, and tool plants. It has deposits of wolfram and molybdenum ores. There are also some chemical and woodworking plants. Most of its industries are concentrated in Nalchik, Tyrnauz, and Prokhladnaya. Light industry and food production (meat, butter, cheese, confectionery, and canned goods) account for half the total output of the republic. Livestock breeding and grain growing are its main agricultural occupations. Its cultivated fields and pasturelands occupy 45 percent of its total land.

Kabardinians and Balkarians make up half the population of the republic; their proportion of the total is expected to increase. Of the two peoples, the Kabardinians are considered to have identified themselves more closely with Russian culture than the Balkarians and to be better integrated with Russia's economy.[8] "Divisive" processes are now increasing, similar to those we described in Karachai-Cherkessia.

On November 17, 1991, a Congress of Balkarians proclaimed the existence of a Balkarian Republic within the Russian Federation embracing all the territory the Balkarians occupied on March 8, 1944, when they were forcibly dispersed (that territory corresponds on the whole to their present distribution). A National Council of the Balkarian People was formed with B. Chabdarov as its chairman.

On November 19, 1991, the Kabardinian-Balkarian Supreme Soviet published an "Appeal From the First Congress of the Balkarian People to the KB Supreme Soviet" urging that body to support the decision of the Balkarian People's First Congress to create a Balkarian Republic within the jurisdiction of the RSPSR and to promote the realization of that decision in every way; also, to appoint a special committee to define the mechanism for the implementation of this decision on Balkarian sovereignty.

It must be said that, from the very first, the adoption of a privatization policy in Russia conflicted with the interests of the repressed peoples, including the Balkarians. In their opinion, privatization could start only after their territorial rehabilitation. Therefore, in December 1991 the National Council of the Balkarian Republic issued a draft law "On the Privatization of State and Municipal Enterprises in the Kabardino-Balkarian SSR," which required that all such privatization be halted in the territories occupied by the formerly repressed peoples of the RSFSR until they were fully rehabilitated in the territorial, political, and economic sense, and that the adoption of such a privatization law in Kabardino-Balkaria must be withdrawn from the agenda.

The Balkarian people as a whole officially confirmed their desire to form their own republic within the Russian Federation at the referendum which was held on December 29, 1991, at all inhabited points with the support of the Balkarian urban, township, and village Soviets. They were asked to answer the following question: "Are you in favor of the proclamation of a Balkarian People's Republic as a subject of the RSFSR?"; 84.9 percent of all citizens on the voting list participated in the referendum, and 94.8 percent of these answered the question in the affirmative. That result, as well as its political implementation, did not contradict the Declaration on Kabardino-Balkarian State Sovereignty adopted on January 30, 1991, which stated that "the Kabardian and Balkarian peoples are sovereign subjects of a united republic; they have an inviolable right to self-determination, including the right to leave the republic and each form an independent state." In the opinion of A.L. Kovalenko, a lawyer and legal consultant for the Russian Supreme Soviet, the Balkarian referendum did not infringe on existing legislation and was lawful and juridically tenable.

In February 1992, the Supreme Soviet and president of the Russian Federation received an "Appeal from the National Council of the Balkarian People" which said:

Since March 1990 numerous documents have been signed and dispatched to various authorities. These include: the resolutions adopted at meetings in memory of the victims of arbitrary deportation of the Balkarian population of the Kabardino-Balkarian SSR; a resolution of the Balkarian Peoples' Conference of all levels of Soviets to the Supreme Soviet of the USSR and Congress of Peoples' Deputies of the USSR; information on the results of the discussions on the Draft Declaration on State Sovereignty of the Kabardino-Balkarian SSR held at public meetings and conferences of Balkarians at their places of residence; the decision of the first stage of the First Congress of Balkars held on March 30, 1991. However, all these messages were left unanswered by the Federal authorities in spite of the fact that an understanding had been reached with the Kabardino-Balkarian government. The creation of a separate Balkarian Republic within the Russian Federation is feasible thanks to such factors as the desires of the Balkarians themselves, their compact settlement, the fact that they have not made any other territorial claims; their declaration of independence has received recognition and support from the Supreme Soviet of the Kabardino-Balkarian SSR and all the civic and political organizations of the republic. Approval for the formation of such a Balkarian Republic has been expressed by the Kabardinians, that is, the other sovereign subject of our united republic.

The message stressed the loyalty of the national-political movement of the Balkarian people to the Federal authorities.

In view of the fact that the juridical settlement of the problem of forming a Balkarian Republic in conformity with the constitution of the Russian Federation is exclusively the right of the Congress of Peoples' Deputies of the Russian Federation and that we wish the solution of the problem of the formation of our republic to be based exclusively on the constitution and law, the National Council of the Balkarian People has postponed the decision of its First Congress to hold republican parliamentary elections on March 10, 1992.

On July 6, 1992, the National Council of the Balkarian People addressed another message to the President of Russia resolving:

1. that the work of the Committee of the Balkarian People's National Council on the regulation of its administrative and territorial problems be approved, inasmuch as its conclusions were based on the collection, systematization and scientific analysis of the ethnic holdings and ethnic borders of Balkaria;

2. that it be recognized that the borders between Balkaria and Kabardia were defined on only one occasion between the two peoples in the year 1709; they were decided simply by mutual agreement and common law. Also that it be recognized that the two sides were not asked to participate either in 1863 or in subsequent determinations of the national boundaries of Balkaria and Kabardia;

3. Considering that the Balkarians today form a compact ethno-territorial mass of people living on the territory they occupied before they were forcibly deported on March 8, 1944; and proceeding from articles no. 3 and 6 of the Russian Federal "Law on the Rehabilitation of the Repressed Peoples," let it be decided that a Balkarian Republic may be formed in the territory where they lived and tilled the soil before they were deported on March 8, 1944;

4. that the final demarcation of the borders between the Republic of Balkaria and the Kabardinian Republic be entrusted to the competency of the proper state bodies of the Russian Federation;

5. that the Executive Committee of the National Council of the Balkarian people continue to negotiate with the Executive Committee of the Kabardinian People's Congress on the realization of the decisions of the congresses of the Balkarian and Kabardinian peoples, proceeding always from the Law as the proper basis for determining the territorial boundaries of the two republics.

And events in Kabardinian society developed in much the same manner.

Between January 10 and 12, 1992, a congress of the Kabardinian people took place. It was attended by over 1,500 people including 900 delegates from Karachai-Cherkessia, Adyghei, the Chechen Republic, Krasnodar Territory (Shapchugs), Georgia (Abkhazians), and also some delegates from foreign countries, such as the United States, Holland, Turkey, and others. The Congress was chaired part of the time by the newly elected president of Kabardino-Balkaria V.M. Kokov, who had just taken the oath of office, and by the chairman of the Republic's Council of Ministers, G.M. Cherkesov. It was attended for one day by the chairman of the Russian Federation's Council of Nationalities, R.G. Abdulatipov, then visiting the republic.[9]

After five speeches were delivered at the Congress, the following problems were singled out for discussion:

1. Present problems and tasks of the Kabardinian people; their solution (speaker: A. K. Guchev, a "thamada" (leader) of the Adygh Hassa Society).

2. Political and legal assessment of the consequences of the Caucasian War; the rehabilitation of the Adygh people (speaker: A.S. Elmesov, of the faculty of KB State University).

3. History of Kabardinian-Balkarian relations concerning land ownership (speaker: Assistant Professor Sokurov of the KB Institute of Language and Culture).

4. Attitude of the Congress toward the Confederation of Caucasian Mountain Peoples (speaker U. N. Shanibov, Assistant Prof., KB State University, President of the Caucasian Mountain Peoples' Confederation).

5. Formation of a Republican Guard (speaker, Colonel H. N. Kashirgov, Department Head at the KB State University).

6. Election of the Congress' Directors.

The Congress proclaimed the formation of a Kabardinian Republic within the Russian Federation. It decided to appeal to the Republican Committee on the Rehabilitation of the Repressed Peoples and request its assistance in appointing interested parties to define the boundaries between the two republics. A Cossack spokesman who addressed the Congress requested that the interests of the Cossacks be taken into consideration when defining the status of the Maisky and Prokhladnaya Districts, which he maintained should be made separate subjects of the Russian Federation.

The Congress also approved the formation of a Confederation of Caucasian Mountain Peoples and appealed to the authorities of the republic to establish a Republican Guard. The Congress of the Kabardinian People was proclaimed the highest organ of power and government in the period between congresses, and U.H. Kalmykov, president of the World Cherkessian Association formed in May 1991 in the city of Nalchik at the First World Cherkess (Adygh) Congress, was named its head.

Among the documents adopted at the Congress was a "Decision on the Restoration of the Kabardinian Republic." That meant: restoring a sovereign Kabardinian Republic on the historical territory once occupied by the Kabardinian people; settling territorial and other questions by negotiations between the interested sides in conformity with the dictates of international law; guaranteeing the equality of all its citizens before the law regardless of social status, property, racial or national affiliations, sex, education, language, political or religious convictions. The decision concluded that the Kabardinian People's Congress, Supreme Soviet, and president of the Kabardinian Republic must be regularly informed of the realization of these decisions.

The "Appeal to the People of Kabardino-Balkaria" in particular stressed that "by no means shall the restoration of a sovereign republic pursue narrow nationalistic aims or be directed against any other nationality." Age-old ties of friendship have always linked the Kabardinians with the Balkarians, Russians, Cossacks, and other nationalities.

Kabardinians have always felt friendship for the Russians, and this Congress hereby confirms that friendship. The other peoples and nations inhabiting the territory of this republic shall be guaranteed equal conditions with the Kabardinians to fully realize their ethnic identity, to participate to the utmost in our political, economic and social life. Pending the final regulation of the problem of the national and state structures of the Kabardino-Balkarian SSR, its constitution and laws must be unconditionally observed. The main task of all its inhabitants today is to "help the republic out of the present crisis and achieve social and political stability."

The decision on "The Formation of a Republican Guard" ordered the Supreme Soviet and Presidium of the Kabardino-Balkarian SSR to create a single battalion of guards so as "to secure state sovereignty, legality, public order; the peaceful solution of inter-ethnic problems, protection of the rights and liberties of citizens; prevention of the rise of illegal military formations," and made it incumbent on the Congress of the Kabardinian People to ensure the implementation of this decision.

At the same time, some sentiments that were rather inimical to the Balkarian community were expressed by a few speakers, particularly with reference to the determination of the territorial boundaries of the two peoples. For example, A. Guchev, second "Thamada" of the "Adyg Hassa" Society delivered himself of the following sentiments:

What are the basic principles and stages to be observed in partitioning the republic? Their partitioning must conform to their historical borders. A commission must therefore be set up to define the 1863 borders, and this commission must be composed of specialists or both sides. After the borders have been defined, the Supreme Soviet must confirm . . .

Or:

The settlement of Kabardinian territory by the Balkarians continued for more than 200 years. . . . To define their borders we have to go back to documents defining those 1863 borders that were signed by both sides on the basis of the decision of the Tersk Land Estate Commission. . . . We consider the 1863 borders that were published by the newspaper *Balkarian Forum* to be nothing but a provocation!

In spite of the obvious contradictions between the Kabardinian and Balkarian sides on the border question, the conflict between them has nevertheless been kept within peaceful bounds, with emphasis on negotiation. That is borne out, for instance, by a document formulated by the Kabardinian Executive Committee and submitted to the Balkarian National Council entitled "Principles To Be Faithfully Adhered To in Restoring the Ethnic Boundaries Between Kabardia and Balkaria." This document stipulates:

1. Restoration of the borders must take place with respect for the age-old friendship and good-neighborly relations of the two peoples, their interwoven history, economy, culture, kinship and other ties.
2. The basis for the formation of the two independent republics is their ethnic territorial place of residence.

3. The legal basis is the LAW: the normative acts of the Kabardinian Republic. In the event of disagreement, international legal norms shall be given primacy.

4. All problems relating to the restoration of frontiers and division of property are to be resolved by experts. Their decisions are to be endorsed by the Executive Committees of the Kabardinian People's Congress and Balkarian People's Council set up by the congresses of each side. In the process, the principle of mutual concessions must be honored; each side must refrain from pressuring the other in order to gain advantages for itself.

5. At the same time as the borders are determined, properties that may be jointly utilized such as pastures, timberlands, transportation arteries, national parks, tourist facilities, etc. may be defined, as well as the legal base for their joint utilization.

6. Problems arising in the course of the restitution of the borders must be solved exclusively by political methods. The Congress and Council have rejected one-sided actions which are liable to complicate international relations.

7. Restoration of the borders must be based exclusively on cartographic and his-torical-archive material.

8. Restoring ethnic frontiers does not mean that either Balkarians or Kabardinians are to be forcibly moved to their ethnic homes against their will.

Thus, as you can see, the Balkarian-Kabardinian conflict has had every chance of being regulated legally in the course of negotiations—in view of which it is quite impossible to understand the position of the federal authorities, who are ignoring an objective, progressive process, and who, as a matter of fact, are not even responding to the perfectly reasonable proposals of the national-political movements. Perhaps this state of affairs has come about because of lobbying by the local *nomenclatura* operating in the federal government. The short-sightedness of the center has led to the outbreak of serious conflicts (as in Nalchik in September-October 1992). That was a conflict not between the Balkarian and Kabardinian communities; it broke out as a general public protest against the local authorities.

According to the findings of the Russian Federation's "Committee on the Nationalities," the impetus for that crisis was the stand taken by a bloc of civic organizations bent on making the president of Kabardino-Balkaria, V.M. Kokov, resign and the Supreme Soviet of the republic disband and on replacing them by new leaders. The opposition had the support of the Kabardinian youth, a section of the deputies' corps, and a group of women activists. Its recognized leader was U.K. Kalmykov, whose position was oriented on the principle of peaceful opposition. A prominent underground figure was F.A. Kharaiyev (a deputy to the Russian Federation and the Kabardino-Balkaria Soviets), who as the head of the republic's transport system had formed 100 cooperatives inside his system which yielded their members huge personal incomes. Except for the Kabardinian People's Council and "Adygh Hassa," no other civic or national organizations participated in the conflict. The majority of the population failed to attend the meetings, as predicted by experts of the State National Committee, itself oriented toward preserving the integrity of the republic. There were no more than fifty activists in the movement, although in the daytime and evenings several thousand demonstrators did gather. The slogans were contradictory, but there were very few anti-Russian ones. The arrest of U. Shanibov by a member of the Russian Magistracy aid provoked meetings that lasted many days. The situation was aggravated by the declaration of a crisis situation and posting of additional army units. The public's demands were escalated during the last few days, from defense of U. Shanibov to the demand that the Kabardian-Balkarian government resign.

The Nalchik conflict was solved when the local authorities agreed to make a number of concessions. A meeting took place between republican leaders and public spokesmen. The protocol of their get-together stipulated the following:

1. that it be deemed essential to disband the Supreme Soviet of the Kabardino-Balkarian Republic after adopting an Electoral Law (prior to December 1, 1992).

2. that the central and all levels of precinct electoral committees be renewed and all civic and political movements be represented in these new committees.

3. that the special corps be withdrawn from the House of Soviets right after a meeting was adjourned: that it was necessary in general to evacuate from Kabardino-Balkaria the militarized units brought in from other parts of the Russian Federation and complete their withdrawal as of November 15, 1992; that joint measures be taken to disarm and prohibit the spread of arms among the people of the republic.

4. that persecution of those who participated in the Shanibov affair or the following meetings, shall not be permitted except in the case of those accused of serious crimes.

5. that deputies corps be set up to investigate the circumstances of the September 27, 1992 happenings on the square facing the House of Soviets.

6. that roundtable discussions take place between civic and political spokesmen and the leaders of the Kabardino-Balkarian Republic, and their evaluation of these past events as well as reports on the agreements they reach be published.

7. In order to realize the proposals formulated in the present protocol, a special session of the KBR Supreme Soviet must be convened.

8. The text of this protocol and report on the course of its implementation must be publicized by the mass media.

Judging by the above demands, the meeting may be considered to have been chiefly antinomenclature in intent. It was directed against the local authorities who were obstructing the process of separation of the two republics. But its stand did not perceptibly affect the position of the federal or local authorities. The formation of independent Kabardinian or Balkarian republics was not expedited. In fact, the legal persecution of U. Shanibov continued. The only result of the meeting was the Russian government's traditional response of solving problems by granting material aid.

October 14, 1992 saw the publication of the Russian president's decree "On State Aid for the Social and Economic Development of the Kabardino-Balkarian Republic," which enumerated various measures: on the structural perestroika of the republic's economy; on measures to attract foreign investments; on allocations to help develop the social sphere, and so on. Although this help will certainly not be superfluous, it will not call a halt to the divisive processes we have described or influence the political processes already under way.

Kabardino-Balkaria clearly illustrates the reality of the predominant trend of our times—the creation of national states. We are witnessing a process whereby government rule is being replaced by the leadership of national-political groups. This process is typical of all the North Caucasian republics. It is clear that conflicts are taking place primarily not between ethnic groups, but between the people and the local nomenclature who have been losing their authority (a process which may be said to have reached its apex only in the events of autumn 1991, in Chechen-Ingushetia).

In our view, inter-ethnic clashes are by no means inevitable. They are mostly instigated by the authorities. Unconditional support for the local nomenclature seems to mar federal policy. It appears to be bent on freezing any objective processes that might infringe on the integration of Russia and set the localities against it.

Under these conditions, it is imperative for the Russian government to let these objective processes assume a civilized form. And that is possible only by continual negotiation with the participation of all political elements and a deep understanding of the will of the people.

The Republic of Adyghei

This republic is a young state (subject of the Russian Federation), former autonomy within Krasnodar Territory. Today, this is probably the quietest area in the Northern Caucasus, which is due first of all to the peculiarities of the ethnic structure of its population: the "titular" people makes up here not more than 22 percent of the population while the main ethnic group (68 percent) are Russians, including the Cossacks. The Adygheis are rather well adapted to the Russian culture and the urban way of life, and "overlap" with the Cossacks and the Russian population of the republic.

Adyghei has an agrarian-industrial orientation in its economy. It possesses a developed food-processing industry (about half of all industrial production), gas industry (there are natural gas fields), wood and woodworking, and machine-building industries. The republic also has its own water-power resources (hydroelectric stations on the Belaya River). The major enterprises are in Maikop, Yablonovsky, Gagarinskaya, and Natyrbov. Half of the republic's lands are used in agriculture. The main specializations of agriculture are grain (50 percent of the arable land) and technical (16 percent of the arable land) crops, as well as horned cattle breeding (more than one-third of all arable land is sown to fodder crops).

The core of a possible conflict in the republic is the confrontation between the Adygheis and the Cossacks, since in the 1920s some of the Cossack lands were included in the Adyghei (as well as the Karachai-Cherkessian) Autonomous Regions. At the present time, however, this conflict has a latent form. Nevertheless, there are conditions already now for its progress. Involved here are, on the one hand, the Cossacks' national-cultural revival, the development of Cossack self-government on traditional Cossack lands; on the other, the growth of "Adyghei irredentism," that is, the striving for a political unification of the Adyghei-Abkhazian peoples as well as a possible repatriation to the Northern Caucasus of foreign Adygheis, who number not less than 150,000 in Turkey, Syria, Iraq, and Jordan.

The national-political processes in Adyghei will no doubt be influenced by the Confederation of the Peoples of the Caucasus (CPC), which comprises a clearly expressed "Adyghei bloc" (Kabardinians, Adygheis, Cherkes, Abazinians, and Shapsugs). The bloc is oriented to the creation of a confederative mountaineer state, and the repatriated Adygheis intend in their settlement to join together Kabarda, Cherkessia, Adyghei, and "Shapsugia," now divided by the enclaves of Cossack population. Imbalance will thus be overcome between the Adyghei West and the Veinakh East within the CPC.

To our minds, these plans are hardly feasible because Adygheis' massive repatriation is quite problematical. A political condition for such repatriation could be the secession of Adyghei and the other republics of the region from Russia; this is, however, hardly probable. At the same time, as already mentioned, a serious destabilization of the political situation is not excluded here. As in other cases, the universal means for reducing the possibility of conflict here can be an intensive, permanently operating negotiation process between the different political entities.

Krasnodar and Stavropol Territories

Both territories are subjects of the Russian Federation, although they do not represent national-state units. The territories' administrative bodies take part in the negotiations that have started in the Northern Caucasus (in Pyatigorsk and Kislovodsk) and consequently influence political life in the region.

Krasnodar Territory has enterprises of machine-building and metal-working industries, electric power, wood pulp and paper, chemical and petrochemical industries. Krasnodar, Novorossiisk, Armavir, Tikhoretsk, and Tuapse are well-developed industrial centers. Oil and gas are mined and refined here (the Prikubanskaya Plain fields); other products include cement (Novorossiisk), rock salt and mercury (Tuapse). The food-processing industry uses local farm produce for winemaking, dairy products and meat packing, fruit-and-vegetable and fish canning. The food-processing industry accounts for half of the total industrial production, and the machine-building and metalworking industries for approximately ten percent. It is noteworthy that Krasnodar Territory has an outlet on the Black Sea and the Sea of Azov with important ports (Novorossiisk being the biggest).

Stavropol Territory is more developed industrially: it accounts for about 20 percent of all industrial output of the Northern Caucasus. Nevertheless, here, too, food processing and light industries are in the lead. Heavy industry branches account for approximately one-third of the total industrial production (power industry, machine-building and chemical industries). Stavropol Territory mines oil and gas, copper and complex ores. More than half of the Stavropol Territory agricultural lands are used in grain farming. Industrial crops, vegetables, melons and gourds, rice, and grapes are also grown. More than half of the total agricultural output in Stavropol Territory are products of animal husbandry of all branches (horned and small cattle breeding, pig and poultry farming).

Of the main national-political problems of the region mention should be made of the Cossack movement, the Shapsug people's efforts to obtain autonomy (Krasnodar Territory), frictions between the Russian Cossack population and the migrants from Trans-Caucasia (primarily Armenians, although Russians are responsible for most of the population growth through migration), and the Nogai people's desire for autonomy (Stavropol Territory forms part of the Nogais' area of residence).

Potentially, the gravest situation is to be found in Krasnodar Territory, where conflicts are now ripening due to the following factors: (1) the demand of creating a Shapsug autonomy in the vicinity of Tuapse (it is supported by the Confederation of the Peoples of the Caucasus; the Chechen Republic wants the creation here of an autonomy with an outlet on the Black Sea); (2) projects for a single Cherkessia including the areas of residence of Shapsugs, Adygheis, and Cherkes proper; (3) the proposals of creating an autonomy of the Kuban Cossacks along the Kuban River (it should be mentioned that there is movement for the annexation of the Kuban area in the Ukraine); (4) the Armenians' autonomy in the vicinity of Armavir; (5) the Greeks' autonomy in the vicinity of Gelendzhik; and (6) a German autonomy in the vicinity of Adler.[10]

A major problem for the territory is the inflow of refugees from hot spots, whose number, according to different data, totalled in 1992 from 45,000 to 80,000. The stream of refugees, besides purely ethnic problems (for example, the settlement of Meskhetia Turks here), spells also social hardships by increasing pressure on the local social infrastructure and the labor market. The chances of employment being limited, the refugees are compelled to work primarily in the nonproduction sphere, which serves to form the Armenians' or Meskhetia Turks' negative stereotype (thus 85 percent of the population of the Crimean district of the territory believe that it is Meskhetia Turks who are potentially criminals).[11]

The situation in Krasnodar Territory is made worse by the extremely tough policy of the territorial administration, which is clear from the article cited below[12]:

Russia must guard its integrity and inviolability of its borders. These are threatened by the Congress of the Mountaineer Peoples of the Northern Caucasus intending to create an Islamic confederation of mountaineer peoples; by the Chechen "revolution"; the Shapsug people's congress in Sochi ("Though it is hardly possible to call the witches' sabbath held there a congress . . ."). With the Shapsugs as a cover (they live in two districts adjoining Sochi, where they scarcely make up four percent of the population), there was declared the establishment of a Shapsug state, the seizure of the seaboard from Sochi to Anapa and the creation of a naval base in the vicinity of Blovanka. This "state" was immediately included in the Confederation of Mountaineer Peoples. Chechens threatened to unleash a war throughout the entire territory of Russia. This was announced at a closed conference held by the head of the administration of the Territory, V. Dyakonov. Not to sacrifice Russia's interests, "Russia alone can become the guarantor of international peace." The administration is preparing a number of emergency measures with the participation of the military, the Ministry of Internal Affairs and the Federal Security Agency (former State Security Committee). The measures are to prevent territorial changes in the Territory—on this issue the administration has found a common language with the leaders of the territorial Soviet. An alarming stand has been taken by the upper circles of the Cossack Rada (Council): they are in no hurry to help but cherish the hope of cutting off the Kuban area from Russia. An appeal to the "brethren Cossacks" has been adopted.

Obviously, if the territory's administration will act in the same spirit, it will arrive at very negative results. As we see it, there are no contraindications in Krasnodar Territory for the creation of territorial autonomies of the Shapsugs (within reasonable bounds, of course), the Cossacks, Armenians, Greeks, and Germans. The problems of refugees and migrants must be solved with the most active participation of the respective federal department, financing, in part, the migrants' needs. What is most important, however, is that the local administration should start a dialogue with representatives of the national-political movements. Possibly the territorial administration's participation in the talks already in progress in the Northern Caucasus will help them to benefit by this experience. At the same time, inter-ethnic conflicts in the territory can be successfully resolved only within the general long-term concept of Russia's policy in the Northern Caucasus—and broader—in the Caucasian Region.

The North Ossetian Republic

Northern Ossetia is industrially the most developed republic in the region. Heavy industry products make up two-thirds of the republic's total industrial output; light industry products, over 10 percent. There are enterprises of nonferrous metallurgy, mining industry, engineering industry, electrotechnical, light, and food-processing industries. The power grid of the North Caucasian economic region includes the local hydroelectric stations and thermoelectric plants using their own water and gas resources. The republic mines and processes lead and zinc. The main industrial centers are Vladikavkaz, Beslan, and Adon. Well developed are grain farming and dairy cattle raising, as well as vegetable growing.

According to the 1989 census, Ossetians made up more than half and Russians more than one-fourth of the republic's population, with Ingush, too, constituting an appreciable ethnic group (concentrated mostly in the Prigorodny District). At the present time, however, it is hard to say anything definite about the composition of North Ossetia's population. There can be no doubt that the number of Ossetians has considerably grown (by tens of thousands of persons) through the influx of refugees from South Ossetia; the number of Ingush has radically declined owing to their having been compelled to leave the Prigorodny District (63,500 Ingush refugees live today in Ingushetia);[13] a decrease is shown also in the proportion of the Russian population involved in the migration stream from the North Caucasian region. The republic has thus in the past few years become more mono-national.

Ossetia differs from the other republics of the Northern Caucasus not only in its high socioeconomic development but also in a number of other features. First, the majority of Ossetians are Christians; therefore, their historical relations with the Christian Russia were rather good. There have been no major anti-Russian revolts here; moreover, part of the Ossetians were even included in the Cossack community near Mozdok. Second, the Ossetians more than other peoples in the region are oriented to the urbanistic culture adopted together with the attendant Russian culture and language. Third, the grip of the former "Soviet" officialdom is stronger in Ossetia than in the other republics of the Northern Caucasus. All these circumstances make the situation in Ossetia unique against the North Caucasian background.

The national-political situation in the republic is at the present time extremely unstable owing to the operation of three important factors:

1. The unsolved problem of South Ossetia. The Ossetian-Georgian truce

maintained for six months already (supported by the CIS peacemaking forces) is very fragile. Obviously, the main reason for the still surviving truce is the continuing Georgian-Abkhazian war that makes the Georgian side refrain from scattering its forces. Generally speaking, this problem is beyond the pale of the present work; still, mention should be made of the following. The North Ossetian politicians recognized South Ossetia in March 1993, but this recognition is of no great importance, as neither Ossetia is subject to international law (not an independent state). Consequently, there is still a possibility in the region to avoid the "Karabakh" pattern of events. The possibility can become a reality only in the course of quadrilateral talks between Georgia, South and North Ossetia, and Russia (with possible mediation of other CIS countries or international organizations). The main underlying principles of the talks must be (1) to ensure territorial integrity of Georgia; (2) to guarantee the autonomous status of South Ossetia; (3) to use only political methods of resolution of conflictual situations; and (4) to promote extensive contacts between the two Ossetias (including aid to the South Ossetian side in restoring what has been destroyed). The main task of the talks is to make these principles concrete realities and to guarantee to both Georgia and South Ossetia the implementation of the agreements achieved.

2. The previous item has a bearing on the continuing conflict between Ingushetia and Ossetia over the official possession of the Prigorodny District (refugees from South Ossetia are accommodated there). This point will be considered below in greater detail; here it should be pointed out that official aid to the refugees and, what is most important, providing conditions for their return to their native land will largely facilitate the resolution of this conflictual situation.

3. The revival of the Cossacks' status threatens the territorial integrity of North Ossetia, since a movement is growing in the Russian Cossack Mozdok District for its transfer to Stavropol Territory. Traditionally, Cossack lands exist in the Prigorodny District as well, but this district is territorially separated from Russia proper. As we see it, the solution of this issue is possible through the Cossacks being guaranteed cultural or territorial autonomy in the places of their traditional and compact residence. It is desirable, moreover, to unify the southern Russian Cossack community, which would decide the questions of ethnocultural revival and protection of the Cossack population's rights. Such a union could become a member of the Confederation of the Peoples of the Caucasus, especially as the exclusion of the word "mountaineer" from the name of the organization plainly invites a dialogue between the Cossacks and the "mountaineers."

It is clear enough that if these conflicts are resolved to the detriment of North Ossetia alone, this will bring about an explosive situation aggravated by the "presence of numerous armed groupings with fighting experience in the republic going through the ruin of national ideals and aspirations. The latter can lead to most unforeseeable consequences, including the attempt at severance from Russia".[14]

The general political climate in the republic is determined, of course, by the political position of the republic's administration, especially after the start of the Ingush-Ossetian armed clash. To give an idea of the present authorities in North Ossetia it is enough to mention the fact of the North Ossetian government's support of the August 1991 putsch. Official propaganda in Ossetia extols the ideology of Ossetina-Russian ethnic kinship and religious unity in contrast, moreover, to the other autochthonous peoples of the Caucasus. This propaganda has an obvious political tendency: "Possessing in the Caucasus Ossetia alone, Russia is the master of the Caucasus. By losing Ossetia, Russia not only loses forever access to Transcaucasia but also finds itself threatened by the solid, almost a thousand-kilometer-long hostile front of Moslem with Chechnya at the head."[15] "The Ossetians are a peaceful people and, remembering the good done by Russia, have always been faithful to it."[16] The reader is given to understand that Russian policy in the Caucasus must consist primarily of Ossetia's support.

The republic's authorities, however, judging by their official statements, do not exclude a possibility of joining the anti-Russian bloc in the Northern Caucasus. This is confirmed, in part, by the silence kept by the leaders of the Confederation of the Peoples of the Caucasus regarding the Ingush-Ossetian territorial conflict ("all mountaineers are different tribes of one nation, and to speak of borders between them is blasphemy"—such is the Chechen Republic's official view of this conflict in 1991). It is to be expected, however, that the choice between Russia and the Mountaineer Republic will still be made by the leaders of North Ossetia in favor of the former.

As to the political spectrum of North Ossetia, it is quite diverse, including about thirty public organizations of various trends. Among them are:

- The "Democratic Ossetia" movement. It proved to be an active and truly democratic movement in August 1991, when it opposed the coup d'état. The movement then demanded resignation of the Presidium of the Supreme Soviet, the government and the members of the local State Emergency Committee. The movement does not express a definite view as to where the Prigorodny District belongs, but it is against an immediate redrawing of the borders and insists on a peaceful solution of territorial disputes. In North Ossetia this movement is probably the natural partner of the Russian Democrats and the democratic government.

- "Our Ossetia" (affiliated with the "Democratic Russia" movement formed in 1991). The declared aims of this society include the building of a truly law-governed state, and that with the participation of all national-political units of Ossetia.

- The Progressive-Democratic Party of North Ossetia (formed in 1990), whose programmatic aim is transition from a totalitarian to democratic republic based on general human values. The Party as a whole disapproves the territorial claims of the Ingush Republic. The Party members criticize the policy of Galazov and of the former Communist Party apparatus, as well as the "Adamon Tsadis" organization demanding the unification of the two Ossetias.

• The "Vladikavkaz" society with Terek Cossacks as its members (created in 1990). The purpose of the society is to revive the Cossack culture. At the same time the society is under the influence of the Communist Party leaders, and even sided with the putsch-makers in August 1991.

• "Adamon Tsadis" (People's Union) was formed in 1989. The society is a sort of public disseminator of the ideas of the local administration. It tries to influence all public organizations in the republic. The society advances the idea of uniting North and South Ossetia. In August 1991, the society's leaders publicly gave support to the putsch-makers.

• "Alania Union of National Revival" (formed in 1991) has as its programmatic aim the revival of the Ossetian nation in the South and the North.

• The Mozdok organization of the Democratic Party of Russia expresses the interests of the Russian population of this area (its joining to Stavropol Territory in the first place), and is also engaged in antinomenclature activities.

• There are several societies of Marxist orientation, for instance, "Edinstvo" ("Unity"), ecological ("Kolybel," The Cradle) and other organizations that do not set themselves national-political tasks.

There exist (existed prior to the armed clash in the Prigorodny District) also Ingush national-political organizations, registered, however, not in Ossetia but in Ingushetia. Among them are the following:

• "Voinakh-Bart" supporting the creation in the Prigorodny District of an Ingush autonomy and its inclusion in the future in the Ingushetia struggle against the nomenclature and for the preservation of Russian unity. The society categorically protested against the August putsch. A similar position was adopted by the Organizing Committee for the Restoration of Ingush Autonomy.

• The "Niisko" organization (The Equality, formed in 1989) is oriented not to Ingush autonomy but to the creation of a republic and therefore holding more extremist views.

Among societies of other national minorities mention might be made of the Armenian society "Nairi," the Greek "Prometei," the Azerbaijan "Azeri," and the Jewish "Sholom."

Concluding this section, it should be stressed that the situation in North Ossetia is extremely complicated and unclear. There is a real danger of an explosion, which would be tantamount to the outbreak of a civil war in the Northern Caucasus. The principal problem of the republic—to which territory the Prigorodny District should belong—should be decided after a thorough consideration, relying on written and unwritten (negotiation pro-

cess) law. To our minds, the present administration of the republic will in
the future use its objective position in the region to exert pressure on the
federal authorities. It is necessary, therefore, to now foresee the search of
worthy (as regards their political position and moral qualities) partners in
North Ossetia. An important role can be played by the defense by the
federal authorities of the interests of the South Ossetian peoples.

The Ossetian-Ingush National Conflict: Legal Aspects

The Ossetian-Ingush conflict has its origins in the territorial administrative changes that were taking place in the USSR from 1920 to 1950. There
are also more "distant" causes of the conflict connected with the change
of population in the territory of the present Prigorodny District in the 18th
and 19th centuries.

Prior to 1924, both Ingushetia and North Ossetia were parts of the
Mountaineer Republic. In 1924, the latter ceased to exist. Autonomous
regions were formed within Russia: Ingush, North Ossetian, and some others. The border between Ingushetia and Ossetia was the Terek River, which
divided the city of Vladikavkaz, too, into the Ingush and Ossetian parts,
the latter serving as the administrative centers of the respective republics.
This border, first, marked the residence of the Ingush and Ossetian peoples
and, second, was drawn by mutual consent of the two autonomies' leaders.

From 1934 to 1936 the Ingush and Chechen autonomies were united
and, with the adoption of the new Constitution, there came into being the
Chechen-Ingush Autonomous Soviet Socialist Republic (with the city of
Grozny as capital) and the North Ossetian Autonomous Soviet Socialist
Republic (with the city of Vladikavkaz, former Ordzhonikidze, as capital).

From 1944 to 1957, as the result of deportation of the Ingush and
Chechen peoples, the Chechen-Ingush ASSR was done away with. Ossetia
received the Prigorodny District, which, together with a number of Ossetian
lands proper on the left bank of the Terek River, formed a separate administrative unit in the North Ossetian ASSR. After the rehabilitation of
the Ingush and Chechen peoples in 1957 and the reestablishment of the
Chechen-Ingush ASSR, the Prigorodny District remained within North Ossetia. The Ingushes, who prior to the deportation made up the greater part
of its population, were in their majority deprived of the opportunity to
return to their native places. The ethnic composition of the Prigorodny
District inhabitants in 1992 was for a number of reasons precisely not
known.

In March 1990, the Soviet of Nationalities of the Supreme Soviet of the
SSSR set up a Commission to consider the appeals of the Ingush population
(with A. Belyakov as its chairman). The Commission decided that "the
demands of the Ingush population for the return to the Chechen-Ingush

ASSR of the Prigorodny District within its borders preceding 1944, and of the other territories that were formerly components of the Chechen-Ingush ASSR, are well-grounded and are to be examined by the Supreme Soviet of the RSFSR."[17]

After the declaration of the Chechen Republic in September and October of 1991, Ingushetia, which was not included in it, found itself in an uncertain position: without its own administrative structure, almost without industry, with vague borders dividing it from both Ossetia and Chechnya. Moreover, communication between the mountainous and flat parts of Ingushetia are possible only across the territory of the Prigorodny District. The decision of the Ingush side to remain a component of Russia was probably stimulated by the Law of the Russian Federation of April 26, 1991 "On the Rehabilitation of Repressed Peoples," which meant restoring the repressed peoples' national-state borders as they existed at the moment of deportation (in this case in 1944). One of the authors of the Law, A.I. Kovalenko, rejecting the objection that the Law lacks mechanisms for its realization, writes: "Since the Law of the Russian Federation 'On the Rehabilitation of Repressed Peoples' establishes but the starting principles of legal regulation, mechanisms for their realization must be 'individualized' in respective acts of the state organs'."[18] In other words, the responsibility for the realization of the Law is laid on the organs of executive power.

To carry out the Law there was formed a special commission of the Council of Ministers of Russia, which included working groups from North Ossetia (G.A. Dzhigkayev, A.S. Aboyev, and F. Kh. Gutnov) and from Chechen-Ingushetia (Kh. A. Fargiyev, B.B. Bogatyrev, and T. Kh. Mutaliyev). The commission "proposed fixing a transitory period, envisaging a by-stage realization of territorial rehabilitation, and also forming a conciliatory commission to work out legal and organizational measures to implement the Law in these republics. The commission believes that the first stage should be recognition of the national-territorial borders that existed at the time of adoption of the Decree of the Presidium of the Supreme Soviet of the USSR 'On the Abolition of the Chechen-Ingush Autonomous Soviet Socialist Republic and the Administrative Organization of Its Territories' (i.e., March 7, 1944 with their subsequent by-stage restoration).[19]

The joint sitting of the working groups of North Ossetia and Chechen-Ingushetia on October 1, 1991 revealed a number of contradictions in the Ossetian and Ingush approaches to the problem; nevertheless, the Ossetian side recognized the following:

The issue of borders between Ossetia and Ingushetia can be solved only within the framework of the Law "On the Rehabilitation of Repressed Peoples" and the Decision of the Fourth Congress of Peoples' Deputies "On the Appeal of the Supreme Soviet of the North Ossetian Soviet Socialist Republic to the Fourth Congress of Peoples' Deputies of the RSFSR."[20]

In December 1991, owing to a number of difficulties in the realization of the Law "On the Rehabilitation of Repressed Peoples," the government of the Russian Federation proposed "establishing a transitional period during which the Government of the RSFSR will work out and submit to the Soviet of Nationalities of the Supreme Soviet of the RSFSR draft legislative acts with regard to each of the repressed peoples. The proposed dates of the transitional period are December 1991 to December 1995."[21]

On January 30, 1992, the Presidium of the Supreme Soviet and the Council of Ministers of North Ossetia addressed to the president of Russia a statement containing this:

As far as we know, the Supreme Soviet and the Government of Russia are preparing a document concerning the creation of the Ingush Republic with the inclusion in it of part of the territory of the North Ossetian Soviet Socialist Republic. Its authors, moreover, are guided by the unconstitutional Article 6 of the Law of the RSFSR 'On the Rehabilitation of Repressed Peoples'. In view of this the Presidium of the Supreme Soviet and the Council of Ministers of the North Ossetian SSR deem it necessary to declare that any actions envisaging, contrary to the Constitution of the Russian Federation and the Constitution of North Ossetia, *a forcible change of the borders of our republic will be regarded by us as a gross encroachment on territorial integrity of the sovereign North Ossetian SSR* (emphasis here and elsewhere is the authors').

The contrivers of this unconstitutional action must bear in mind that it *will inevitably lead to a large-scale civil war in the south of Russia,* and all responsibility for the possible tragic consequences will be borne by them.

Expressing our well-grounded concern over the future of the peoples of North Ossetia, the Presidium of the Supreme Soviet and the Government of the North Ossetian SSR request you to give explanations regarding this matter and *reserve the right to take all measures necessary to preserve the territorial integrity of the republic and to guarantee the security of its population.*

On February 5, 1992, the government of the Russian Federation formed commissions to carry into effect the Law "On the Rehabilitation of Repressed Peoples." The commission for the North Ossetian SSR and the Chechen-Ingush Republic was headed first by V.P. Barannikov, and from April 30, 1992 by V.A. Tishkov, chairman of the State Nationalities Committee.

The Law "On the Formation of the Ingush Republic Within the Russian Federation" was adopted by the Supreme Soviet of the Russian Federation only on June 4, 1992. Thus, Ingushetia had no chance to sign the Federative Treaty (even as part of Chechen-Ingushetia). Moreover, the Law of June 1, 1992 did not fix the borders of the Ingush Republic. The latter has therefore remained but a formal, not real political entity, which is inconceivable without borders. At the same time, the Law intended to make the preparation of legal and organizational measures for official demarcation of territories, taking thereby into consideration the interests of the Cossacks and the possibility of extending their self-government within the Ingush Republic, as well as the interests of the national minorities; to decide other questions connected with the creation of the Ingush Republic.

The solution of all disputed issues is effected in accordance with the Constitution and laws of the Russian Federation.

The Decision of the Supreme Soviet of the Russian Federation of June 4, 1992 "On the Procedure of Implementing the Law of the Russian Federation 'On the Creation of the Ingush Republic as a Component of the Russian Federation' " contained the following provision:

5. To establish that the territory of the Ingush Republic is formed by the decision of the Supreme Soviet of the Russian Federation on presentation of the results of the work of the state commission set up by the Government of the Russian Federation.

The state commission, formed by the Government of the Russian Federation, in accordance with the Constitution of the Russian Federation on the basis of co-ordination of interests of all the parties concerned, is to submit proposals before December 31, 1993 as to the defining of the borders of the Ingush Republic and its normal functioning.

By the Law of the Russian Federation of July 3, 1992 "On the Introduction of a Transitional Period in the Official Division of Territories in the Russian Federation" the date of the real constitution of the Ingush Republic, directly defined by the territorial rehabilitation of the Ingush people, was postponed until July 1, 1995.

On September 21, 1992, however, the Presidium of the Supreme Soviet of Russia adopted the Decision "On the Procedure and Dates of Holding Elections to the Supreme Soviet of the Ingush Republic." It contemplated this:

1. Elections of the Supreme Soviet of the Ingush Republic are not to be held before the territory and borders of the Ingush Republic are determined.

2. The Government of the Russian Federation is to instruct the state commission immediately to start work to prepare legal acts defining the borders of the Ingush Republic. The results of the work are to be reported to the Presidium of the Supreme Soviet of the Russian Federation before October 20, 1992.

As we see, the armed clashes between the Ossetians and the Ingushes were preceded by important legislative and administrative work. At the same time, far from being able to halt the development of the conflictual situation, it largely spurred, as it will be shown further, the escalation of tension. On October 20, an armored carrier of a North Ossetian special-purpose militia unit ran over and killed an Ingush schoolgirl. Ingush-Ossetian clashes followed, leading by November 1, 1992 to a large-scale armed conflict. On November 2, 1992, a state of emergency was introduced in the territory of North Ossetia and Ingushetia by the Decree of the President of the Russian Federation.

On December 10, 1992, the Seventh Congress of People's Deputies of Russia approved the Law on the Creation of the Ingush Republic as Part of Russia. Appropriate amendments were made in the Constitution of the Russian Federation: The Ingush and the Chechen Republics were recognized as subjects of the Federation (to repeat, they never signed the Federative Treaty). Note the fact that the Seventh Congress actually recognized the Chechen Republic. However, the details of discussion of the Ingush-Ossetian conflict are unknown because the respective Congress sittings were held in an atmosphere of secrecey.[22]

Let us see how the Ossetian-Ingush conflict caused by the unsettled territorial problem looks from the legal point of view. The main sources of law in this issue are the Constitution of the Russian Federation, the Federative Treaty, and the Law of the Russian Federation "On the Rehabilitation of Repressed Peoples." How far do these documents' standards agree with each other?

Article 70 of the Constitution of the Russian Federation says: "The constitutional and legal status of the republics, territories, regions, autonomous regions and autonomous areas, as well as their division and unification, may be altered only by the expression of the will of the majority of electors living in them, subject to ratification by the Congress of People's Deputies of the Russian Federation." Article 80 contains an even more definite norm: "The territory of a republic in the Russian Federation may not be altered without its consent."

Point 1 of Article III of the Federative Treaty (signed on March 30, 1992) proposes: "The territory and status of a republic forming part of the Russian Federation may not be altered without its consent."[23]

These norms are incompatible with the norms of the Law of the Russian Federation "On the Rehabilitation of Repressed Peoples" in cases when the latter intend territorial alterations of the now existing subjects of the Russian Federation. This applies, in part, to the following provisions of the Law:

Article 3. Rehabilitation of the repressed peoples means the recognition and exercise of their right to the reestablishment of the territorial integrity that existed prior to the unconstitutional policy of forcible recarving the boundaries ...

Article 6. Territorial rehabilitation of the repressed peoples envisages carrying out, on the basis of their will, legal and organizational measures to re-establish the national territorial borders that existed prior to their unconstitutional forcible alternation.

To accomplish territorial rehabilitation a transitional period may be set if necessary. The decision of setting a transitional period and re-establishing national territorial borders is taken by the Supreme Soviet of the RSFSR.

It should be mentioned that the Decision of the Supreme Soviet of the RSFSR of April 26, 1991 "On the Procedure of Implementation of the Law of the RSFSR 'On the Rehabilitation of Repressed Peoples' " directed the Council of Ministers of the RSFSR to submit before the end of 1991 to the Supreme Soviet draft legislative acts providing for "the re-establishment of territorial integrity of the national state entities and the administrative territorial borders that existed prior to their forcible unconstitutional alteration." The Decision was not effected, owing partly to the sluggishness of the Russian machinery of state and partly to the changed situation: the disintegration of the USSR and the conclusion of the Federative Treaty.

The norms of the Constitution and of the Federative Treaty refer to different values: the value of national state sovereignty and the value of restoring justice involved in the elimination of the consequences of deportation. Both the one and the other group of values found their expression in the standards of international law. It is precisely the collision of values and legal norms that most often underlies conflicts among nations. The resolution of such conflicts on legal grounds is extremely difficult.

Obviously, the norms of the Constitution and of the Federative Treaty as its component are "above" the provisions of the law intended to elaborate them.

The Law on Rehabilitation, adopted before the conclusion of the Federative Treaty, at the moment of its adoption already contradicted the above articles of Russia's Constitution. And in this respect it is not important whether it was adopted before or after the conclusion of the Federative Treaty. Its norms could have force after April 30, 1992 only if the Federative Treaty contained a provision according to which the effectuation of its norms were not to clash with the realization of the Law on the Repressed Peoples. Indeed, the Law on Rehabilitation is to correct the unjust and illegal actions taken in the past. But does it mean that the realization of these principles must lead to the violation of the Constitution today?

The Ossetian side's changed position means just this fact—that the sovereignty of North Ossetia acquired as the result of the conclusion of the Federative Treaty has created a firm legal foundation for the preservation of its present borders. (This conclusion was likewise confirmed by the 7th Congress of People's Deputies of Russia, which resolved that transfer of territories could be done only by the two republics' mutual consent.) Moreover, Ossetia changed its position also due to the differing circumstances such as the diminished strength, prestige, and real (including legal) potentialities of the Russian "center" by the spring of 1992 (as compared even with the potentialities the Union "center" possessed in 1991).

Thus, the issue of territorial rehabilitation of the Ingush people (as of the other repressed peoples) has landed in a legal impasse, and how to overcome it is far from being clear. Regrettably, this issue has to this day not been examined by the Constitutional Court. Professional lawyers could probably find a way out of the situation; for instance: to recognize the repressed peoples as victims of racial discrimination and to apply to them the appropriate standards of international law, which is originally "above" national. In this case Article 32 of the Constitution of the Russian Federation will come into force, the article that says: "the generally recognized norms concerning human rights have priority over the laws of the Russian Federation and directly engender rights and duties of the citizens of the Russian Federation."[24]

Let us consider this issue in greater detail. On March 7, 1966, there was adopted the International Convention on Abolition of All Forms of Racial Discrimination (it was ratified by the Presidium of the Supreme Soviet of the USSR on January 22, 1969). The Convention excluded any discrimination or restriction of human rights on racial or national grounds, color of skin, and so on.

The recognition of the Ingushes and other deported peoples as victims of racial discrimination (and this can be done by both the Constitutional Court of the Russian Federation and the European Human Rights Court, which is preferable)[25,26] entails the application of the Convention standards requiring that effective measures be taken against racial discrimination and protection be ensured to each person in case of violation of human rights on racial grounds.

The next possible step of the Constitutional Court is to recognize the norms of the Law "On the Rehabilitation of Repressed Peoples" acting in elaboration of the provisions of the Convention on Abolition of All Forms of Racial Discrimination. This is probably the only chance of obtaining a strict legal foundation for territorial rehabilitation of the repressed peoples. Nevertheless, the gravity of the Ingush-Ossetian territorial conflict is such that formal juridical measures are not nearly enough to localize and end it.

It was mentioned above that the Ossetian-Ingush conflict is a collision of two values: sovereignty and justice. As is clear, the clash of these values is almost insoluble on legal grounds. This spells the necessity of achieving consensus and compromise in a different (not juridical and legal) way; for instance, common-law form. Common law, based on ordinary attitudes, gives preference to justice over sovereignty.

This indicates the need to seek an organizational form of such compromise, which could switch the conflict over from the armed to the peaceful and legal channels. In our opinion, there is at present only one possibility of settling this and other smoldering international conflicts in the region— to start an extensive, permanently functioning negotiation process with the participation of the main political forces of the region. This requires a special institution for prevention and resolution of international conflicts, based, above all, not on juridical, but on common or decisional law.

As we see it, Russia's organs of power (the parliament, government, or president) can initiate the creation of a special organ (it can be named, for instance, the North Caucasian Congress) representing the major—both official and public—political forces of the region. The purpose of the Congress is to find out the most influential views of the concrete issues; to conduct talks intended to reach a compromise in conflictual situations; to exert pressure on the sides in the conflict. The power and influence of such Congress will depend on the influence of its participants. On the other hand, the political movements and official organs that do not take part in the work of this body, owing to their radicalism, will find themselves in political and moral isolation.

Decisions of the North Caucasian Congress, of course, will have rather a moral than juridical force. Its weight will be greater if decisions are adopted through consensus (i.e., will be discussed until they become acceptable to all or almost all participants). It is safe to say that common/ decisional law in the Northern Caucasus is more influential than juridical standards. In any case, the creation and functioning of a North Caucasian Congress can remove tension in the region.

Summing up the above, it is possible to offer the following complex of measures for resolving the Ingush-Ossetian territorial conflict:

1. Continuing state of emergency in Ossetia and Ingushetia, whose zone can gradually be narrowed to the territory of the Prigorodny District. The state of emergency will be used instead of the district's transfer to the direct federal administration, which is hardly envisaged by the acting constitutional norms. The state of emergency must be carried into effect by Russian and not Ossetian units. It presupposes disarmament of the illegal armed detachments.

2. Immediate provision of aid to the refugees from both sides and to the Prigorodny District in eliminating the consequences of the armed conflict. Assistance to the Ingush Republic in the establishment of its state system and in economic development. As politicsal measures, it would be useful to establish relations with the Chechen Republic and to carry on an active policy in South Ossetia and Abkhazia (talks with Georgia concerning the status of the two entities). In the conditions of state of emergency, refugees should be encouraged to return to the Prigorodny District guaranteeing their security.

3. Careful investigation of the fact of armed conflict. The findings of the investigation should be made public and the criminals should be punished.

4. Appeal to the Constitutional Court or the European Human Rights Court with the purpose of recognition of the deported peoples (just as the forcible settlement of citizens on their lands) as victims of racial discrimination. Repeal of all acts on the strength of which the deportation was effected. Bringing the Law "On

the Rehabilitation of Repressed Peoples" in line with the standards of the International Convention on Abolition of all Forms of Racial Discrimination.

5. Creation of a North Caucasian Congress (or a body with a different appellation but similar functions) to discuss extensively the Ingush-Ossetian territorial dispute and other issues. Assistance in drawing new boundaries, if the sides sign an agreement on the transfer of territories.

These items do not, of course, reflect the sequence of some actions or other. The complex of measures should be carried out simultaneously or almost simultaneously.

Further events in the region (December 1992 to February 1993) largely followed the course we predicted. The Kislovodsk meeting of the leaders of the North Caucasian republics and regions on January 16 was obviously held under the motto precisely formulated by S. Shakhrai: "Peace in the Northern Caucasus is peace throughout the Russian Federation."[27] Stress should be laid on the exceptionally accurate approach of the head of the State Nationalities Committee to the region's problems: The Caucasus has self-regulating mechanisms, which should be put in action.[28] So far the North Caucasian Coordinating Council is making only its first steps but they, too, are worthy of attention and approval.

First, the Coordinating Council includes not only officials but also representatives of public movements, which considerably increases its influence. Second, its creation means passing from the use of primarily power methods and secret intrigues to the "collective responsibility" policy. Third, the North Caucasian Coordinating Council appears to have the potentialities of becoming a working organ. Its first sitting already, despite the tangle of serious contradictions in the region, adopted a decision on the beginning of Ingush-Ossetian talks. In other words, the Coordinating Council was wise enough not to deviate to minor issues but to choose the main problem.

Worthy of attention is the changed position of the Confederation of the Peoples of the Caucasus. Its participation in the meeting of the Council may be indicative of the Confederation's tendency to start constructive work. The exclusion from the name of the organization of the word "mountaineer" means invitation to a dialogue with the Russian (Cossack above all) population of the region. These tendencies must be promoted and welcome in every way. It is uncertain, however, whether the symbolic gesture on the part of the Confederation will be duly appreciated by the leaders of the North Caucasian Cossacks. There is danger that in the near future the Cossacks' problem will become the main "irritant" of the situation in the region.

The North Caucasian Coordinating Council's successful work can be hindered, to our minds, by the following factors:

- the inconsistent position of the "center," which may consider the activities of the regional organ dangerous for itself;
- amateurish work of the Council itself. If its decisions are not carried into effect, the Council will cease to have any influence;
- the splitting activities of some of the republic's leaders and heads of public organizations.

As to the Council's participation in the settlement of the Ingush-Ossetian conflict, as we see it, it cannot confine itself to the mere organization of the talks between the sides and mediation (thus in Nagorny Karabakh several mediatory missions turned out a complete fiasco). The North Caucasian Coordinating Council, it seems, should play a more active role, in the elaboration of concrete decisions in particular: Collective decisions have a greater chance of being carried into effect than bilateral agreements. The side refusing to carry out such decisions becomes an outsider with all the ensuing consequences. It is noteworthy that the recent consequence of the Council's activities was the decision of the North Ossetian authorities to disarm the illegal armed units.

It can be added that the creation of the North Caucasian Coordinating Council and its participation in the efforts to normalize Ingush-Ossetian relations in no way cancel our other proposals regarding this matter formulated above. It applies, in part, to the juridical and legal collision over the Law "On the Rehabilitation of Repressed Peoples." Common/decisional law, which will undoubtedly underlie the activities of the North Caucasian Council, cannot nevertheless serve as a long-term foundation for the functioning of a civilized state. It can only be the first step to the achievement of a civil peace.

The Chechen-Ingush Republic: The Armed Conflict in the Chechen Republic

Such a republic can actually no longer be found on a political map of Russia. The 7th Congress of People's Deputies of Russia in practice recognized the division of Chechen-Ingushetia into the Chechen and Ingush Republics. This fact is confirmed in the Constitution of the Russian Federation adopted on December 12, 1993. But the process of division and creation of the new state entities—in the economic sphere above all—has not yet been completed. It applies to a greater extent to Ingushetia, actually deprived as the result of the division of its own industrial production.

The backbone of Chechenia's and Ingushetia's economy is the oil, oil-refining, and petrochemical industries. There also exist here enterprises of the power industry, engineering industry, metalworking, and food-processing industries, and enterprises producing building materials. Chechen-

Ingushetia has four power-and-heating plants included in the North Caucasian power grid. Oil and gas fields are concentrated in the vicinity of Grozny, Malgobek, and Gudermes. Petroleum products are made at enterprises in Grozny, turning out motor fuel, oils (about 90 percent of aviation oil of the Russian Federation) and other petroleum products. Grozny's monopoly on aviation oils production already led in the winter of 1992 to an acute economic conflict between the Chechen Republic and Russia (it should be pointed out that economic sanctions were mutual). However, having no access to international markets today, and even common borders with foreign countries (with the exception of Georgia), the republic will anyhow be compelled to deliver its products to Russia.

Chechen-Ingushetia's industry is concentrated in Grozny, Nazran, Gudermes, Argun, and Chiri-Yurt. Besides the heavy industry enterprises, there have been built in the region also separate enterprises of light industry; for instance, the ones manufacturing knitted fabric (Nazran and Grozny). Agricultural specialization of Chechen-Ingushetia is the production of fruit and vegetables, as well as fine-fleece sheep breeding, and meat and dairy cattle raising. According to our information, this former "twin" republic is one of the socially and economically underdeveloped regions of Russia, with Ingushetia substantially less developed than Chechenia. (According to the 1990 data, the value of the mass of commodities imported to Chechen-Ingushetia exceeded that exported from it by 200 million rubles.) For many decades the inhabitants of the republic specialized in seasonal work in Russia (builders). At present this trade, due primarily to political, but also to economic reasons, is at a low ebb and, consequently, redundant manpower has an even greater pressure on the local labor market.

Chechen-Ingushetia, primarily Chechenia (Gudermes), is a major railway and motor-road junction connecting Russia and Trans-Caucasia (Azerbaijan). Of course, this fact, too, can be used for pressuring Russia. Thus, according to mass media reports, in February of 1993 already the Chechen authorities introduced a permit system on their borders.

Chechen-Ingushetia numbers among the regions with the prevailing autochthonous population. Cossacks, however, constitute an appreciable group as well, living compactly in the Naursky and Shelkovskoi districts (near the middle reaches of the Terek River). It should be mentioned that these districts were transferred to Chechen-Ingushetia from the Stavropol Territory in exchange for the Prigorodny District in 1956. According to the letter of the Law "On the Rehabilitation of Repressed Peoples," if the Prigorodny District is joined to Ingushetia, these two districts along the Terek River are automatically to be included into the Stavropol Territory. This is utterly to the disadvantage of the Chechen Republic, which through its leaders proclaimed the inviolability of Chechenia's borders. This makes clearer why the Chechen Republic did not support Ingushetia during the conflict with North Ossetia.

The Naursky and Shelkovskoi districts have been actively settled by Chechen migrants since 1956. The Russian and local Nogai population are struggling to have the districts joined to the Stavropol Territory. The outflow of Russian population, however, leads to a gradual decline of its proportion. At the present time Russians and Cossacks retain the majority in the Shelkovskoi District but have already lost it in the Naursky District.

Another district of the Cossacks' traditional residence is Sunzhensky, on the border between Ingushetia and Chechenia. It is, as a matter of fact, a disputed district and can be used to exert pressure on Ingushetia by the Chechen Republic. The outflow of Russians from here is especially evident. Their relations with the Ingush and Chechen are of a pronounced conflictual nature. Thus, in April 1990 a clash in the village of Troitskaya between the Cossacks and Ingush resulted in the death of seven Russians and the burning down of many houses. One can forecast for this district (if the political situation remains the same) that its population will change completely in the near future.

Below is a more detailed analysis of the situation in the Chechen Republic:

1. *The development of the conflict in the Chechen Republic before Russian troops were brought there in December 1994.* After the August 1991 putsch, power in the republic was unconstitutionally taken by the Executive Committee of the National Congress of the Chechen People (ECNCCP), the directing organ of the national political movement. The Supreme Soviet of the Chechen-Ingush Republic was dissolved (under the pretext of its support given to the State of Emergency Committee and corruption), and a provisional organ of power, the High Council, was formed. This was followed by the proclamation of the Chechen Republic, which did not include the Ingush part of the territory.

Unfortunately, the policy of the Russian leaders proved inadequate to the situation. The nonrecognition of the unconstitutional coup d'état made by the ECNCCP was combined with the methods of power pressure exerted on the republic. Thus, by the order of A. Rutskoi, then vice-president of Russia, there was created on November 4, 1991 an Operational Headquarters to deal with the critical situation in the Chechen-Ingush Republic. On November 7, by the decree of the president of Russia B. Yeltsin, the state of emergency was declared in the republic. The decision was soon adopted to send troops to Chechen-Ingushetia to disarm the local population and "to restore law and order." These measures achieved the opposite result—the rallying of the entire people against the "Russian aggression" and the quick election of D. Dudayev as president of the republic. Support to the "Chechen revolution" was given by the Confederation of the Mountain Peoples of the Caucasus as well as foreign Chechen-Ingush societies (for instence, the "Vainakh" society in the United States).

The immediate consequence of the Russian leaders' clumsy actions was the incessantly growing confrontation between Russia and Chechenia, attacks on Russian military units in the republic to capture arms (these units were withdrawn in 1992), and a sharp rise in the criminogenic situation in Chechenia. The latter was furthered, in part, by a widespread distribution of weapons among the population undertaken by the release of prisoners from the republic's reformatories. D. Dudayev's attempts to ensure the surrender of the weapons by the population were unsuccessful.

In the spring of 1992, an abortive attempt at a coup d'état was made in the republic.

By the winter of 1992–1993, serious frictions began to be felt between the executive and legislative branches of the republic's administration, brought about by the different views of the fundamentals of the Chechen state system (presidential or parliamentary republic) as well as of Chechen-Russian relations (D. Dudayev and his followers shared a more radical anti-Russian position). A public opinion poll held in February of 1993, however, showed that a considerable part of the population were inclined to the draft of the Constitution offered by D. Dudayev. The polls conducted at that time in the republic convince us that most of the people supported Chechenia's political independence from Russia.

In the spring and early summer of 1993, the country's usual confrontation between the legislative and executive branches of power, occurring in the conditions of an undeveloped division of powers (including the judicial power), assumed in Chechenia the form of the dissolution of parliament by the elements of the presidential apparatus. In their struggle against the opposition, the president and his supporters used armed forces. Data concerning the number of casualties in the armed clashes are contradictory: from seven to fifty. At the same time, the authorities of the Nadterechny District, in opposition to the official Grozny, declared the secession of this territory from the republic.

All these years saw in the republic a "sluggishly proceeding" civil war against the background of an acute economic crisis, a criminalization of society, and an appreciable decline in the political activity of the population.

All attempts to start the negotiation process and to reach agreement came to nothing. Thus, in March of 1992 Russian and Chechen experts met at the Dagomys tourist center in Sochi to begin the negotiations. The meeting yielded no appreciable results since the Chechen side announced that the most important and main question for discussion at the talks should be "The recognition of political independence and state sovereignty of the Chechen Republic." Simultaneously, the Chechen leaders circulated a statement which practically amounted to the possibility of introducing by the republic of its own currency.

Another round of the Russian-Chechen talks was held in Grozny in Janury of 1993. From the Russian side they were attended by Vice-Premier S. Shakhrai, chairman of the State Nationalities Committee (now Ministry for the Affairs of Nationalities and Regional Politics), and R. Abdulatipov, chairman of the Council of Nationalities of the Russian Parliament, and from the Chechen side by a parliamentary delegation. The most important impetus to the negotiations was the conflict in the Prigorodny District (the disputed territory claimed by the decision of the 7th Congress of People's Deputies of Russia), which confirmed the division of Chechenia and Ingushetia (the Congress, however, did not recognize the legality of the presidential election that had taken place in Chechenia). These talks, too, yielded no results.

Until November of 1994, Russian politicians had two dominating conceptions of further development of relations with Chechenia. One of them was expounded in the numerous publications by the vice-premier of the Russian government, S. Shakhrai. Its essence was that the Russian-Chechen dialogue was being obstructed by the illegitimacy of the Dudayev ruling regime. The official authorities of the Chechen Republic had, moreover, compromised themselves by corruption, the armed suppression of the opposition, and the participation in criminal economic activities (petroleum, trade in arms, the creation in Chechenia of a "criminal free economic zone"). Therefore, the Russian side could not further the negotiation process with the officials in Grozny but should seek partners for the talks and support among the more influential opposition forces. This political line is reflected in the numerous official statements of both the government and parliament of the Russian Federation concerning the events in the Chechen Republic.

Another idea was advanced early in the summer of 1994 by a group of politicians close to the president of Russia (S. Filatov and V. Shumeiko, first of all). It presupposed holding immediate talks with Chechenia's official administration at the summit (presidential) level. Judging by the fact that these talks did not take place, the "peace-making initiative" of Filatov-Shumeiko excluded forcible intervention on the part of Russia in Chechenia's affairs. However, after the beginning of combat operations in the Chechen Republic these top-level state officials had become in essence supporters of the use of force.

The "realpolitik" of the Russian Federation in the region since the summer of 1994 has been conducted, to all appearances, not by the parliament or the government of the Russian Federation but by the presidential power structures (the President's Administration, the Security Council, the Presidential Council) and the "power departments" subordinated to them. In September-November 1995 it included the following components: economic, political, and military blockade of the Chechen Republic as well as financial, military, and organizational aid to the opposition.

Another spiral of the intra-Chechen confrontation was in the summer and autumn of 1994. It developed at the time when, after the October events in Moscow, the adoption of the new Constitution and the December 1993 election, the political situation in Russia itself had sharply changed. Thus, mention should be made, as applicable to the subject of the given work, of the greater concentration of administrative powers in the structures of presidential authority, an increased trend toward the country's federalization and the achievement of a certain compromise with the regional (republican) political forces of Chechenia, in opposition to D. Dudayev and supported by the federal authorities, began coordinating their efforts and made the military overthrow of the political regime ruling in Grozny their aim. A number of successful and unsuccessful military operations of the opposition in Grozny, in some of the district centers and other inhabited localities of the republic, as well as the governmental troops' counterattacks, showed that with the existing correlation of forces, with the absence of unity in the ranks of the opposition and of the military support from Russia, it was hardly possible to change the status quo with the help of arms.

In November of 1994 the Chechen opposition made an unsuccessful attempt to storm Grozny (a military coup d'état). During this action, Russian servicemen recruited by the Federal Security Service "to overthrow the Dudayev regime" were taken prisoner. There actually began the settlement of the political crisis in the Chechen Republic with the use of force, sanctioned by the supreme organs of state power of the Russian Federation. After ultimatums, negotiations, and "demonstration of strength" (air raids on Grozny) the war prisoners were released by the Chechen side, but the Russian war machine began gathering speed. Around December 10, 1994, before the expiration of the term of an ultimatum, Russian troops were brought into the Chechen Republic. The peaceful talks were interrupted. Bombings of Grozny and other inhabited localities in the Chechen Republic were resumed. By the end of December, Grozny was surrounded by the Russian army but the armed forces of the Chechen Republic continued their resistance.

Prior to December, the issue of future relations with the Russian Federation included a wide range of views in the Chechen Republic both among the official politicians and in the midst of the opposition: from Chechenia's complete political independence (D. Dudayev, president of the Chechen Republic) to its inclusion in Russia as a subject of the Federation (U. Avturkhanov, head of the Nadterechny District). The more cautious of the opposition and official Chechen politicians proposed preceding the political solution of the question by a series of economic agreements as though "dividing" the competence of the Russian and Chechen authorities. The fundamental question of the political situation before the beginning of the military operations was with whom, in fact, to conduct talks in the republic.

2. *The situation after the arrival of Russian troops in the Chechen Republic.* It can be presumed that the bringing of Russian troops into the Chechen Republic on December 10, 1994 pursued not only the officially declared purposes, namely, the disarmament of the illegal military units and the return of Chechenia to the Russian Federation. It is known that the Russian leaders are the ones who are most to blame for such a high concentration of armaments and military hardware in the republic: An enormous arsenal had been left in this unstable region after the withdrawal of the Russian troops from it; the opposition's armament had primarily the Russian source; the channels of illegal trade in fuel from the territory of Chechenia were not shut off, and the petro-dollars thus obtained were largely used to buy weapons. Moreover, only a few months were left until the expiration of D. Dudayev's term of office as president, and in the conditions of an economic crisis, the declining popularity of the president of Chechenia and the existence of an organized opposition it could be forecast with certainty that the election in the republic would result in the coming to power of less radical political forces.

We believe that the spiralling of a large-scale armed conflict in the territory of Russia was in the interests of the following influential political groups:

- the top officials: the administration and surroundings of the president of Russia (the cancellation or postponement of presidential elections);
- the leaders of the army and of the other "power" structures (growth of the status and influence, increasing budgetary expenditure on "national security," the possibility of uncontrolled trade in arms);
- the leading groups of the "post-Soviet industrial directorate," first of all from the military-industrial complex and so-called fuel-energy complex (growth of their own political weight and increase of the respective shares of the "budgetary pie").

All these political forces had one important interest in common: to preserve in Russia the status quo, to hamper the country's progress from the existing "nomenklatura capitalism" to the normal proprietary and democratic relations, to the law-governed state. This could be done, however, in only one way: under any pretext to introduce in the country an authoritarian regime of government. Two other points should be taken into consideration: the administration's utter disregard of the Russians' public opinion (their being on the whole against the use of Russian troops "to put down the Chechens"), and of constitutional procedures of using armed forces within the country (the state of emergency regime).

The winter and spring of 1995 were marked with the maximal intensity of bloodshed in Chechenia. By the beginning of June, the federal troops, at the price of considerable casualties (not less than 2,000 men) and a heavy loss of life among the peaceful population of Chechenia (according to avail-

able estimates, from 25,000 to 30,000), were able to take under their control the flat lands of the republic and to a considerable extent to suppress
the organized resistance of the Chechen armed units. This, however, had
led not to the end of the war but to its assuming a new phase: the launching
of a guerrilla movement and an increased actual independence of the field
commanders.

In mid-June of 1995 there occurred an event that cardinally changed the
course of the conflict and imparted to it new military-political aspects. It
was the large-scale act of terrorism committed by Sh. Basayev's group in
the city of Budennovsk, Stavropol Territory, with the terrorists capturing
several hundred hostages. Basayev's action had also certain features of a
military operation "deep in the enemy rear." The Basayev group put forward the demand of ending military operations on the territory of the
Chechen Republic and starting peace negotiations. The Russian power
structures were unable either to prevent the act of terrorism or to terminate
it with the minimal number of victims. The terrorists' ultimatum was accepted.

Despite the odious nature of the act of terrorism in Budennovsk, it provided a convenient occasion for an attempt to untangle the "Chechen knot"
in a peaceful way, desirable for Russia's leaders in connection with the
coming parliamentary and presidential elections. Military actions were sus-
pended and the high officials of the law-enforcing organs who headed the
military-police operation in the Chechen Republic were made to resign.
Talks were started under the aegis of the Organization for Security and
Cooperation in Europe, their parties being the federal authorities, Dudayev's supporters, and representatives of the groupings opposed to Dudayev.

The objective common to all the participants in the negotiation process
could be described as the achievement of an acceptable formula for ending
military operations and establishing peace in the Chechen Republic. Precisely such was the desire of the overwhelming majority of the republic's
population, including a substantial part of the fighters of Dudayev's armed
forces. The impression was that for the majority of the republic's inhabitants the fatigue from the war was no lesser factor than the striving for
independence. "We believe no one. We shall recognize no government, if
we see that it is for continuing the war." Such sentiments have now become
dominant among the Chechen.

As it could only be expected, the main stumbling block at the talks was
the question of the future political status of Chechenia. The Chechen side
insisted on the recognition of independence of the Chechen Republic of
Ichkeria. Obviously, an unyielding position regarding the problem of independence was natural for any Chechen politician mindful of the moods
in the republic (according to public polls, independence here is at present
supported by up to 50 percent of the population). It is significant that this
view was shared even by Dudayev's opponents, including the head of the

Government of National Revival of Chechenia, S. Khadzhiyev. There was every ground to believe that the idea of independence would also be dominant at the parliamentary and presidential elections to be held in Chechenia, which, as the Russian leadership declared, could take place in the autumn of 1995.

At the start of the talks the Russian delegation made the achievement of agreement on military matters dependent on a political agreement, but soon this hopeless position was changed. On July 30, the Russian and Chechen sides concluded an agreement on a bloc of military issues envisaging the withdrawal from Chechenia of the main part of the federal troops, the disarmament of the Chechen units through redemption of weapons (except the self-defense units in inhabited localities), and the exchange of war prisoners. The realization of this agreement, however, proceeded with much difficulty.

The situation in Chechenia in the autumn of 1995 could be described as the state of "neither peace nor war." Systematic military actions were terminated but episodic clashes between the "Federals" and Chechen groups continued. There was no political unity among the Chechen leadership: if the chief of staff of the Chechen troops A. Maskhadov expressed his adherence to a peaceful settlement of the conflict on the basis of the July 30 agreement, Dudayev, who did not want Maskhadov's positions to strengthen, made inconsistent, and also bellicose, statements. Simultaneously, the Russian leaders are still influenced by those in their midst who insist on the settlement of the Chechen problem by force.

It can be said, in general, that with but few exeptions (mostly from among the former dissident human rights champions) Russian politicians are against granting to Chechenia the right to self-determination "up to secession," giving preference to the idea of territorial integrity of Russia. At the same time some of the influential politicians and ideologists (N. Gonchar, S. Govorukhin, A. Solzhenitsyn) demanded in one form or another the separation and isolation of Chechenia from Russia in the interests of the Russian State and the people (the deliverance from the economic burden, elimination of the "Chechen" criminality, etc.). These ideas are often combined, even at the official level, with the proposal of returning to Stavropol Territory the three northern districts of the Chechen Republic historically settled by Cossacks. Since discontent with the Chechen war is widespread in society, such position could find a response in many of the Russian voters.

The events in Chechenia have once again demonstrated serious defects in the constitutional and political system of Russia; first of all, a noticeable "bias" toward the executive power. The timid and inconsistent attempts of the lawgivers to check the continuation of the war were practically ignored by the president and the "power" structures subordinated to him. Unsuccessful was the attempt made by the deputies of both chambers of the

Federal Assembly to dispute at the Constitutional Court of the Russian Federation the decrees of the president and the decision of the government on the strength of which military operations were started in Chechenia. In its decision of July 31, the Constitutional Court pronounced these normative acts conforming in principle to the Constitution of the Russian Federation.

The decision of the Constitutional Court of the Russian Federation, passed despite the disagreements among the judges, obviously testified to the judicial system being unbalanced. The "division of labor" between the Constitutional and the general jurisdiction courts is such that the former verifies normative acts as being not in keeping with the "letter" of the Constitution, while the latter examines concrete illegal actions within the framework of the existing laws. Although it is common knowledge that during the military operations in Chechenia there were violations, on a mass scale, of human rights guaranteed by the Constitution of the Russian Federation, the normative acts, for the sake of whose execution these violations were committed, were recognized as constitutional. Thus, the country's supreme authorities dropped out of the common legal field and found themselves, in fact, outside the jurisdiction of the courts.

The talks now still in progress were, of course, an important step forward as compared with the military actions. However, in the autumn of 1995, too, there remained both the threat of the talks being wrecked and the danger of an internal war between the Chechen armed units. To our minds, it would be useful to have in view not so much a comprehensive settlement of the Chechen crisis based on an agreement on Chechenia's political status as the adjustment of relations between the representatives of the Federal center and individual field commanders and the local self-government institutions. The resolution of the principal issue can be achieved only as the result of a long, multilateral negotiation process.

The situation in Chechenia and Ingushetia shows that the federal authorities must pursue a more active policy in the Northern Caucasus (and, broader, their nationalities policy as a whole). This implies, of course, not exerting power pressure on the "rebellious" but devising new political conceptions, carefully analyzing the situation and the positions of the sides, seeking "weak points" in the programs of separatist movements. As regards Chechenia and Ingushetia, such weak points are: (1) the low level of economic development and economic dependence on Russia, (2) border conflicts that are insoluble through unilateral declaration of independence and territorial integrity, (3) the remaining menace of civil war in the Northern Caucasus, and (4) the resulting caution of the world community in recognizing the self-proclaimed independent states. As we see it, given a well-advised policy (including non-use of force and emphasis on negotiation) in the contest with the separatists, time is on the side of Russian unity. Much may now depend on the change of the generation of politicians who staked on, and firmly linked their career with the struggle for political independence from Russia. There is no doubt, too, that the main argument in the struggle against separatism will be the course of economic and political reforms in Russia itself, which can make the country attractive for the national outlying areas. But in any case, the role of Russia as a metropolis has come to an end. It can save its territorial integrity only if it actually effects a radical transformation of its internal structure and really puts in operation the federative mechanisms.

The Cossacks

The North Caucasian Cossacks represent an independent political force in the region, whose influence is incessantly growing. (When this section was being written, the Decree of B. Yeltsin on the creation of Cossack military units to guard Russia's state frontiers was made public. Political consequences of this decision are hard to foresee). The numerical strength of this group of population of the Northern Caucasus today is difficult to name precisely, but it may approximate hundreds of thousands. Cossacks live in compact enclaves in the midst of the native and Russian population. The Cossacks' main groups in the republics and territories of the Northern Caucasus were enumerated above with the exception of the Lower Terek (Grebensk) Cossack community in Daghestan, who will be described below.

By the beginning of the 20th century, Russia had eleven Cossack armies: those of the Don, Kuban, Terek, Astrakhan, Urals, Orenburg, Semirechensk, Siberia, Transbaikal, Amur, and Ussuri. There were also the Krasnoyarsk and Irkuts Cossacks, who formed in 1917 the Yenisei Cossack Army and the Irkutsk Cossack Regiment of the Ministry of Internal Affairs (see Table 5.5).

All Cossack troops and regions were subordinated to the Chief Administration of Cossack Troops, and from 1910, to the Cossack Department of the War Ministry General Staff, headed by the Ataman (Chief) of all Cossack troops (from 1902 this post was held by the heir to the throne). Each army was headed by an appointed ataman and an army headquarters with appointed atamans of departments (district atamans). Cossack village atamans were elected at general meetings. Men above eighteen years of age did military service for twenty years (with their own outfits).

The Cossacks took an active part in the national-territorial reforms in the Northern Caucasus after the revolution. From March to May 1918 there were formed the Don, Kuban–Black Sea, and Terek Soviet Republics within the RSFSR. In 1920, however, the All-Russian Central Executive Committee extended to the Cossack territories the application of all general laws in force in the RSFSR regarding the use of land and its tenure, which

Table 5.5
The Cossack Population and the Cossacks Serving in the Army of 1916
(thousands)

Cossack Armies	Population	Serving in Army
Don	1,495	100.0
Kuban	1,367	90.0
Orenburg	533	27.0
Transbaikal	265	14.5
Terek	255	18.0
Siberia	172	11.5
Urals (in 1917 Yaitsk)	166	11.5
Amur	49	3.5
Semirechensk	45	3.5
Astrakhan	40	2.5
Issuri	34	2.5
Yenisei Cossacks (Irkutsk & Krasnoyarsk)	10	0.6
Yakutsk Regiment	3	0.3
Total	4,434	285.4

meant the end of this estate. In the 1920s, the North Caucasian Cossacks were subjected to repressions (the "dispossession" of Cossacks policy). Only on April 20, 1936 did the Central Executive Committee of the USSR abolish the restrictions that existed on the Cossacks' service in the army (i.e., made the Cossacks' descendants the country's citizens enjoying full rights).[29] In the course of national-territorial changes in the Northern Caucasus, the Cossacks lost the autonomy of their territorial entities. Officially, the Cossacks are included in the category of repressed peoples and, consequently, the action of the Law "On the Rehabilitation of Repressed Peoples" applies to them as well.

First Cossack organizations appeared in the Northern Caucasus in the spring of 1990. At that time they had as their objective to revive the Cossacks' traditions and customs. There are facts to show that the Cossack movement's politicization was the consequence of activities of the communist officials in their struggle against the democratically oriented movements. Thus, the Kuban Cossack Rada (Council) received sponsorial donations from budgetary organizations and even credits amounting to 10 million rubles.[30] As to the source of financing of the Don Cossacks' Union, even the district atamans do not know it. This is known only to the ataman of the Union, formerly secretary of the Communist Party organization of one of the collective farms in the region. Also unknown is the source of financial receipts of the Terek Cossacks' Union.

The Cossacks' policy in Pridnestrovie (the Dniester River area), where they have sent their volunteers, in Abkhazia and now in Serbia shows that the Cossacks in Russia are attaining a certain unity and solidarity and that they act as a national military force. The latter should be stressed especially, for the Cossack leaders want to emphasize precisely the ethnic character of their activity. S. Meshcheryakov, Ataman of the Don Cossacks' Union, said in one of his interviews: "the Cossacks do not defend in Pridnestrovye socialist ideals, they defend the Slavs."[31] Among the views popular among the Cossacks, mention should be made of the ideas of Russia's unity and the share system of land tenure. There are growing demands for the revival of the Cossacks' autonomy on their traditionally used lands. Proposals are being spread for creating separate Cossack republics as Russia's components. Such a decision was adopted, for example, in the autumn of 1991, under the Cossacks' pressure, by the 8th session of the Rostov Regional Soviet of People's Deputies: to transfer power in the region to the Cossacks' Council and, finally, to establish the Don Republic. Interestingly, this decision was approved by all the Cossacks of Russia.[32]

Of course, the Cossacks' movement is not monolithic and consists of a number of currents. Thus, the Don Cossacks are divided into "Whites" and "Reds"; the Kuban Cossack Rada is represented by two trends as well: one part headed by Ataman Gromov wants to create its own state, while others support exclusively a cultural revival.

Let us say a few words on the Cossacks' attitude toward the national-political processes taking place in the Northern Caucasus. It is reflected in the data of the sociological (expert) poll conducted in March 1992 on the subject "Ethno-political situation in the midst of the Cossacks of the Northern Caucasus." The poll was held in North Ossetia and outside it among members of other than native ("nontitular") peoples with a wide coverage of Cossacks (about 50 percent of those polled) and Russians (about 30 percent). A total of 127 persons were polled. Atamans of all Cossack movements in the Northern Caucasus acted as experts. The social composition of those polled approached the social composition of the region's population.

As many as 78.3 percent of the polled were categorically against Russia's political "withdrawal" from the Caucasus, with 91 percent favoring a more active Russian policy in the region. Most of the experts were unanimous in their opinion that the now existing territorial status quo should be preserved; that is, were against starting a territorial redivision of the region (this view was expressed by 68.4 percent of the Cossacks, 71 percent of the Russians, and 56.2 percent of the Ukrainians). As to the Prigorodny District, the Cossacks recall that these are the Cossack lands turned over in the 1950s by the Bolsheviks to the Ingush. A total of 94.3 percent of experts were against satisfying Ingushetia's territorial claims. Most of the participants in the poll, especially Cossacks, believe that the only justified way of solving such problems is by negotiation.

Let us have a more detailed analysis of the position of the Terek Cossacks in Daghestan.[33] The number of Russians living today in Kizlyar is 24,400; in the Kizlyar District, 14,100; in the Tarumovsky district, 7,500. They can be divided into the following groups: the Russian population which migrated here in the 1840s to the 1880s; the people who arrived in the North Caucasian Region in the 1930s and 1940s from different parts of Russia and the former USSR to build large-scale industrial projects; and the Terek (Grebensk) Cossacks who make up the main component of the population of this locality. The Cossacks in Daghestan constitute one of the elements of the Terek Cossack army. It was here, in the lower reaches of the Terek, that the entire Terek Cossack community took its shape in the 16th century. It then began to form its own economic system, traditions, the Terek speech, and self-consciousness.

The authors of a number of publications today are trying to prove the exclusively class nature of the Cossacks' origin. The history of the Cossacks' evolution in the Lower Terek area shows that first the Cossacks became an ethnos (subethnos), which has every reason to be included in the category of native peoples of the North Caucasian Region, and then, owing to historical conditions, it became an estate as well. For two centuries after the emergence of the Cossacks their historico-political partners regarded them as an independent subject of politics and not as an estate unquestioningly obeying the directions of a government. The Cossacks' prosperity in the Lower Terek area was based on agricultural production with a pronounced marketable trend. Its backbone was the individual producer-proprietor oriented in his work both to the regional and all-Russian market. The Cossack communal land tenure and military self-government did not put obstacles in the economic activity of separate persons but supervised the regional use of the available resources.

The Kizlyar (Grebensk) Cossacks specialized in viticulture and fishing. Apart from the thousands of human lives, and material losses amounting in the Terek Cossack army districts to 26 million gold rubles, the main damage done by the civil war and the victory of Soviet power was the abolition of individual commodity production in the lower reaches of the Terek: the Kizlyar vineyards were seized from their owners and the fisheries became the state's monopoly. With the abolition of private ownership of land all forms of rent relations were done away with, eliminating thereby the possibility not only of large-scale but also small commodity production. The economic backbone of the Grebensk Cossacks was broken. It was precisely then that the foundations of the critical situation in which the Kizlyar Cossacks find themselves today were laid.

Along with the repressions to which all the Cossacks were subjected in the 1920s and the 1930s, much damage to the survival of the Terek Cossacks was done by the arbitrary administrative-territorial changes made by the Bolshevik regime: on January 18, 1921, there was declared the autonomous Mountaineer Republics, which included, in part, the lands of the Lower-Terek Cossacks; on November 16, 1922, the All-Russian Central Executive Committee, without finding out the will of the population itself, by its Decree joined a considerable part of the Kizlyar District to Daghestan; on March 13, 1937, because of the formation of the Stavropol Territory, the same area for a period of almost twenty years was again "lost" by Daghestan; on January 9, 1957, the Kizlyar District was returned to Daghestan, again with no attention being paid to the will of the people. The authorities' administrative-territorial orgy ended in the elimination of the territory where the Terek Cossacks developed as a people, as a historically formed subethnos.

No doubt during the years of Soviet power the distinctions between the Cossacks and the other Russian population have become substantially obliterated. This was furthered by Kizlyar becoming in the 1970s to 1980s a powerful center of machine building and metalworking. It is hard to define today the number of hereditary Cossacks. This does not mean, however, that the base for the revival of Cossacks has disappeared once and for all (according to some experts' estimates, the Cossacks' descendants total in this region more than 10,000).

The Cossack gathering held in October 1990 declared the revival of the Kizlyar section of the Terek Cossack community. It included the Cossacks of Kizlyar and of a number of the Lower Terek large and small villages. It should be mentioned that the Cossack leading bodies included a considerable number of the Kizlyar scientists and technicians. The board includes educated people from twenty-five to thirty-six years of age. According to the Rules, the Section's activities are based "on historical principles traditional for the Cossacks' "complete democracy and openness as the foundations of Cossack self-government," "the priority of humane, moral ideals, religious orthodoxy and tolerance," "respect of the national traditions of all peoples, freedom of economic development, spiritual and military-patriotic education." The main objective is "to restore and preserve the Cossacks as a people having all rights to self-expression equally with other peoples."

The Lower Terek Cossacks make an emphasis on agriculture and on the solution of the agrarian question well aware that the real revival of the Kizlyar Cossacks is possible solely with the rebirth of the coutryside in the Lower Terek zone. The formerly prosperous animal-breeding collective farms of the area are now experiencing a deep decline in production. If the process continues, the collapse of the entire collective livestock farming can be expected. Recent years have seen the removal of obstacles to the development of individual forms of farming. The consequence is unrestricted growth of the number of sheep and goats in the private sector. By a spontaneous process the private sector is absorbing not only the fodder intended for the collective farms. There is also a redivision of lands to be used for growing various agricultural crops—first of all grapes, melons, and gourds, and orchards—in favor of the privately owned animal breeding. With the increase of privately owned animals in the villages, widespread damage is done to all plantations and crops through grazing.

Privately-owned, distant-pasture sheep breeding is practiced here (besides the Nogais) primarily by the Avar population, which have appeared in the region in recent decades and their numbers are rapidly growing (while in 1970 4,400 Avars lived in the Kizlyar District, in 1989 they numbered 14,300, and numerically have caught up with the Russians). This demographic and economic "expansion" of the Avars, Darghians, and other mountaineer peoples cannot but worry the local Cossack population. There are no legal codes regulating the economic activities of the peoples having quite different notions of the methods of farming and, consequently, clashing interests (some of them are engaged in intensive agriculture, horticulture, viticulture, and vegetable growing; others, in extensive stock raising and distant-pasture sheep breeding).

All this requires not only preserving the Cossacks as a people, a subethnos in its historically formed territory, but also protecting the economic and cultural sphere of the local population, and not Russians alone. This may be confirmed by the appearance of their own Cossack groups in the Armenian villages along the Terek. If the population groups engaged in their traditional kinds of agriculture are not provided with guaranteed favorable conditions for life and work, the conflictual situation in the region can at once assume tough forms.

With the present growing antagonisms between the major ethnic communities in Daghestan, it is becoming increasingly clear that the only way of preserving the republic's integrity can be its autonomism, the compact ethnic groups receiving their territorial autonomy. In this deep reform of the political system the Lower Terek (Grebensk) Cossacks should be seen as a legitimate subject of the new administrative-territorial model.

The North Caucasian Cossacks are therefore an independent political subject of regional politics and a separate object of attention of the federal authorities. To our minds, their demands can be satisfied and their potentialities realized within the framework of territorial autonomy granted to compact groups of people on their traditional lands. It is desirable, moreover, to orient both the bulk of the Cossack population and the leaders of respective movements to the solution of problems of the sociocultural and economic character. We consider it undesirable to revive the Cossacks precisely as a military estate, for the problem of defense of the southern borders has been replaced for Russia by the problem of preservation of peace and tranquillity in the region, while the Cossacks can serve as an "irritating" factor (and this despite the above-cited sociological data showing the

Cossacks' desire to retain political stability). At the same time, the necessity of encouraging the Cossacks' participation in the development of political self-organization of the region, within the constantly operating negotiation process, should be recognized. The negotiation agenda should include, in part, the issue of the Cossacks' territorial rehabilitation.

The Republic of Daghestan

As was mentioned above, Daghestan is potentially the most dangerous region in the Northern Caucasus as regards international conflict. This is due to a number of factors.

First, this republic is exceptionally multinational, with the state borders of Daghestan crossing the ethnic territory of a number of peoples: Lezghians, Nogais, Azerbaijanians, and Chechens. In 1991, despite the peaceful solution of this problem, tension arose between the Lakhs inhabiting this area and the Chechens-Akkins, one of the deported groups. The multinationality of Daghestan causes constant frictions among the ethnic communities of the republic over a redivision of resources: land and power. As to land, this is one of the most important problems of the mountainous republic. The resettlement of the mountain dwellers "on the flat surface"— the Soviet power's line of nationalities policy in such regions—engendered a permanent conflict between the inhabitants of the plains (Kumyks, Nogais, and the Cossacks) and the inhabitants of the mountains and foothills.

Second, the mountainous Daghestan was in the past one of the major centers of resistance to Russian expansion, which makes itself felt in the attitude toward the Russians to this day. The republic's Russian population is small (about 9 percent), with the influence of Russian culture and generally the degree of "modernization" (Europeanization) of the autochthonous inhabitants of the republic being comparatively trifling. Islam has quite a firm foothold here. There is a powerful Islamic tradition, including the knowledge of the literary Arabic language; the Moslem community "jamaat," as the main element of local socii, is being restored; Islamic parties (for example, the Islamic Democratic Party of Daghestan, the Islamic Revival Party) have been created. To some of the specialists (M. Yu. Roshchin) it appears obvious that Moslem tradition is the foundation of Daghestan's unity and that the future political leaders of the republic are being molded today precisely in this cultural niche.

Third, Daghestan is one of the most socioeconomically backward areas of the Russian Federation. Consequently, ethnic conflicts can be fomented here by social and economic difficulties.

Daghestan's leading industries are electric power production (the republic has several hydroelectric stations of its own) and oil extraction, machine building, building materials, chemical, and food-processing industries. Oil fields are concentrated primarily in the vicinity of Makhach-Kala and Izberbash. Natural gas is also produced. Oil is mostly transported to the oil refineries in Grozny; engineering and metalworking plants are in Makhach-Kala, Izberbash, Derbent, and Kizilyurt. They make metal-cutting machine tools, ship's mechanisms, diesels, and so on. About half of all industrial output is processed food products, primarily wines, fish, and canned food. Agricultural specialization is horticulture and viticulture, and cereal crops. Considerable parts of the lands are irrigated. As regards animal raising, it specializes mostly in small cattle.

In 1922, a sufficiently tense socioeconomic situation remained in Daghestan. Mention should be made of the activities of the republic's administration to protect the needy sections of the population, and also direct economic contacts with other regions of Russia and the CIS countries to provide Daghestan with the more scarce products, on the barter basis in particular. Thus, an agreement was concluded with the Ukraine on the delivery there of canned food, wine, and cognac in exchange for sugar and flour.

Let us examine the main conflictual situations on the territory of the republic. Most acute and conflictual at the present time is the problem of the Kumyk people.

On November 19, 1989, there began the first National Congress of the Kumyk People. It was attended by 375 delegates elected by the conferences of the Kumyk Popular Movement for Perestroika, representing its 22,000 members, and also by some 500 invited from other republics. The Congress discussed the following questions:

• the aims and tasks of the movement;
• approval of the program and the rules of the movement;
• approval of an appeal to the peoples of Daghestan;
• election of the guiding organs of the Kumyk Popular Movement (KPM).

The Congress decided that the main task of the KPM was to attain their own national statehood by creating an autonomous republic. The Congress elected the People's Council of fifty-seven members.[34] Among the programmatic aims of the movement was the following: "The erection of a common Daghestan home of the free, self-governing peoples: abolition of any relations of collateral subordination among the peoples." The "Appeal to All Fraternal Peoples of Daghestan" adopted by the Congress stressed: "We regard as an inalienable right of each people the right to self-determination and national autonomy in forms corresponding to their national status. . . . We have been and remain adherents of the idea of a common Daghestan home."[35]

An independent expert A. Petrov characterizes this movement in the following way (the end of 1991): "Tenglik" ("Equality"; its membership approaches 40,000) opposes Daghestan's separation from Russia and creation in its place of an Islamic Fundamentalist state. It supports the national movements of the Lezghians, Nogais, and the Terek Cossacks. The main problem of the Kumyk movement arises from the resettlement of the mountaineers on the plain where the Kumyks always lived, with the result that the number of the latter on this territory has dwindled to 23 percent. The existing practice of land tenure has deprived the local district Soviets of control over more than half of the arable lands to be used as distant winter pastures by the mountain districts' farms (inhabited by the Avars, Darghians, and Lakhs). The lands of Daghestan have thus been redistributed in favor of the mountain areas. The economic infrastructure created here is administratively subordinated to the mountain areas. The alienated lands are used extensively and often deteriorate.

The crisis was aggravated by the decision of the 3rd Congress of People's Deputies of Daghestan on territorial rehabilitation of the formerly repressed Chechen population of the Aukhov-Novolakh district to create a new national-administrative district for the Lakhs near Makhach-Kala. This decision can result in the Kumyks' ethnic parcellation and actual expropriation of their northern part of the maritime zone. This decision can be used as a precedent in creating new administrative structures for the mountaineers on the Kumyk plain.

The inactivity of the law-protecting organs in the republic leads to unprecedented growth of crime and corruption, to the formation of illegal armed gangs (the Avarian "Imam Shamil Front"). They presumably commit terrorist acts against persons of Kumyk and non-Kumyk nationality supporting the "Tenglik" movement. This is why "Tenglik" demands removing from his post the deputy minister for internal affairs. The unwillingness to react on the part of the republican and federal authorities has compelled "Tenglik" to take actions of civil disobedience, including strikes and picketing, and to block communications. There is a danger that military operations will start in the republic. The Kumyks demand a constitutional reform in Daghestan and the setting up of a commission of the Supreme Soviet of the Russian Federation to clarify the situation on the spot.

The Kumyk public movement sees the way out of the crisis in the following:

- The introduction of a transitional period to carry out a reform of the national-state and administrative system of Daghestan, and also the consensus principle in adopting all decisions. Administratively, the republic is to consist of seven vilayets (the number of the major national communities) and the metropolitan district of "Makhach-Kala."
- The formation on the territory of Daghestan of national sovereign republics as Russia's components. The conclusion of a Treaty on the establishment of a "Daghestan Commonwealth" with appropriate organs of power, with Makhach-Kala receiving the status of a "free city" within the commonwealth.[36]

A serious aggravation of the political situation in Daghestan in connection with the "Tenglik" movement's activities began in October 1991. It was connected with the negative reaction of a number of Democrats and other public groupings in the town of Khasavyurt, supported by the republican committee of the Kumyk "Tenglik" movement, to the forthcoming approval by the republic's Supreme Soviet of M. Abdurazakov (an Avar by nationality) as Deputy Minister for Internal Affairs (Avars hold in the republic the posts of Minister of Justice and Public Prosecutor). At the previous Supreme Soviet session this organ was subjected to serious criticism and was compelled to agree to the high officials' reshuffle. The session of the Supreme Soviet of Daghestan opened on October 22, and the question concerning Abdurazakov's appointment was postponed until the next session.

The Kumyk national movement declared a strike and elected a strike committee, while in the vicinity of Khasavyurt, "Tenglik" movement activists blocked the highways and the Rostov-Baku railway.

The strike committee formulated its main demands in the following way: "1. Resignation of Deputy Minister for Internal Affairs of the Daghestan Soviet Socialist Republic Abdurazakov; 2. Pre-term election of the Supreme Soviet two chambers on a multi-party, democratic basis."[37] A little later these demands were supplemented with the item of "forming a popular-confidence government, including in it representatives of democratic organizations."[38] Support to the strikers was expressed by the leaders of the Darghian society "Maslikhat," the Chechen popular movement "Vainakh," the Social-Democratic Party of Daghestan, the Daghestan branch of the Social-Democratic Party of Russia, the Islamic-Democratic Party of Daghestan, the Islamic Party, and the Darghian popular movement "Tsadesh."

In response the Avars, who arrived from the Khasavyurt District (3,000 to 5,000 people), arranged a meeting in front of the Supreme Soviet building. They demanded restoring order and putting an end to anticonstitutional actions. The organization of the meeting was undertaken by the Avar movement named after Imam Shamil (leader M. Gadzhiev), the "Jamaat" movement, and others. The threat was voiced that if the authorities were not able to maintain order, the Avar movements would themselves use force against the Kumyk public organizations. Thus, in the autumn of 1991 a real danger of an armed clash between the national communities arose in Daghestan. Only after the talks of the republic's administration with representatives of the "Tenglik" movement were the railway and the highways deblocked. Tension, however, remained.

In January 1992 the next session of the Supreme Soviet of Daghestan completed its work. M. Abdurazakov was appointed Minister for Internal Affairs of Daghestan. The session ignored the Kumyk people's demands, and the very possibility of creation of a Kumyk state was denied. From the point of view of the Kumyk national movement, this situation has arisen owing to the Avars' desire to dominate in the republic. As regards the results of the work of the session, the Kumyk side formulated proposals submitted to the organs of power of the Russian Federation:

- to form under the Supreme Soviet of the Russian Federation a permanently functioning commission on Daghestan, including in it representatives of the Kumyk national movement;
- to instruct the commission to make a draft of constitutional reforms in Daghestan to be submitted to the Supreme Soviet of the Russian Federation;
- to cancel the decision of creating the Novolakh district on Kumyk territory.

Simultaneously, a conference of Turkic peoples of the CIS was held in Makhach-Kala at the initiative of the Kumyk popular movement, adopting the following decisions:

- to make Makhach-Kala the center of the Turkic peoples of the Northern Caucasus and the Black Sea coast;
- to create a confederation of Turkic peoples of the Northern Caucasus (Kumyks, Nogais, Balkarians, Karachayevs);
- to support the decisions of the Kumyk people on the recovery of their statehood as Russia's component.

Since neither the federal nor the republican organs of power responded in any way to the Kumyk people's demands, a national, open-ended Kumyks' strike began in January 1992. In their camps near the cities of Khasavyurt and Makhach-Kala, the strikers issue their newspaper, have a functioning radio station and self-defense units.

In 1992, the authorities of Daghestan exerted considerable pressure on the political movement of the Kumyk people. The Presidium of the Supreme Soviet of Daghestan adopted a Decision apropos of the Congress of the Kumyk People scheduled for March 21, stressing the unconstitutional character of "Tenglik's" actions and appraising them as attempts to strain relations among the nations in the republic. The Presidium of the Supreme Soviet of Daghestan warned "Tenglik's" leaders of their personal responsibility for the actions bound to undermine the republic's territorial integrity. In other words, confrontation continues to gain strength in Daghestan. If presidential administration is created in the republic, political conditions will possibly appear for a negotiation process and for easing the confrontation. In any case, R. Abdulatipov, chairman of the Soviet of Nationalities of the Supreme Soviet of the Russian Federation (an Avar by nationality), announced his consent to be a candidate for the post of president of the republic.[39]

It was mentioned above that the federal authorities did not react in any way to the crisis in Daghestan. This is, however, not precisely so. Reaction there was but in a spirit traditional for our country, assuming that a carrot offered to the conflictual region could solve all problems. In January 1992 there was adopted the Decision of the Government of the Russian Federation (No. 40) "On Priority Measures for Practical Restoration of the Legal Rights of the Repressed Peoples of the Daghestan SSR." It contemplated assigning 165 million rubles in 1992 to be invested in the settlement of the Chechens-Akkins in the Aukhovo-Novolakh District, to be used as monetary aid to the repatriates, and for some other measures.

In August 1992, the government of the Russian Federation adopted a Decision (No. 637) "On Socio-Economic Development of the Mountain Areas of the Republic of Daghestan in 1992–1995." According to this document, it is planned to allocate 618 million rubles of capital investments (in 1991 prices) "to give practical aid in the revival of the mountain villages." It should be pointed out that economic aid, however necessary it might be, is unable to solve political problems facing the republic. Therefore, the provision of economic aid can be regarded as an attempt to avoid solving political issues.

Another pronounced conflictual ethnic problem in the republic is the predicament of the Lezghian people divided by the state border between Russia and Azerbaijan. The problem of Lezghians has become more acute since the disintegration of the USSR and the development of conflict in Nagorno-Karabakh (the situation with the Armenians in Karabakh is similar to the Lezghian problem). It should be mentioned, moreover, that the Azerbaijan government is trying to involve in the war in Karabakh the national minorities, including the Lezghians, living on the territory of Azerbaijan. In the spring of 1992, during the escalation of military operations in Karabakh, there were disturbances of the Lezghians in Azerbaijan, who were aware that the future of the Lezghians, too, was being decided in Karabakh.

The Lezghian national movement ("Sadval"; the Lezghian National Council, Chairman N.S. Ramazanov), formulating the main aims of the movement, refers to the following historical facts. From 1809 to 1812, the Lezghian state units voluntarily joined Russia, and in 1813, under the Gulistan Peace Treaty, the Lezghians' entire territory passed to the jurisdiction of Russia. In 1917–1918, with the occupation of Azerbaijan by Turkey, the territories south of the Samur River became part of Azerbaijan. The decree of the All-Russian Central Executive Committee and the resolution of the All-Daghestan Congress of Soviets (1921) on the transfer of the Lezghian lands to Russia were not carried into effect, and they remained within Azerbaijan. The Lezghian national movement therefore sets before itself tasks ranging from granting to the Azerbaijan Lezghians dual (Russian and Azerbaijan) citizenship to creating a single Lezghistan as a component part of Russia. This is necessary, in particular, because, in the opinion of

the Lezghian National Council, forcible assimilation of Lezghians is practiced in Azerbaijan.

The Third National Congress of Lezghians took place on September 28,
1991. The Congress passed a resolution "On the Reestablishment of Statehood of the Lezghian People," which says that "widespread forcible Turk-
ization of the Lezghian People continues in Azerbaijan. . . . The distribution
of the Meskhetia Turks and the Turkic population removed from Armenia
has in the past two years grossly distorted the demographic status of the
Lezghian territories in Azerbaijan. The Congress declares that the only sovereign in the territory of the Republic of Lezghistan is the people of Lezghistan."[40] Thus a republic, with its territory situated within the bounds of
two sovereign states, was self-proclaimed in the autumn of 1991.

The Congress materials were further developed in the "Address of the
Lezghian National Council to the Supreme Soviets of the Russian Federation, Azerbaijan and the Republic of Daghestan," adopted in the spring of
1992, which cited facts of the Azerbaijan Lezghians' national discrimination and demanded the transfer of the entire territory of Lezghistan to the
jurisdiction of Russia.

It cannot be said that the Russian government fully ignores the demands
of the Lezghian people. Thus, in the spring of 1992 the Ministry of Foreign
Affairs of the Russian Federation was making preparations for talks with
Azerbaijan on "the Lezghian issue." Judging by the documents, the Russian
diplomats' position was very cautious and intended such a formulation of
the question as could make it possible to avoid complications in relations
with Azerbaijan. At the same time, Russia's Ministry of Foreign Affairs
intended defending the rights of national minorities throughout the territory of the former USSR. Obviously, such an approach of the federal organs
of Russia could not satisfy all demands of the Lezghians' national movement.

In our opinion, solution of the Lezghian problem is possible under the
following conditions:

- preserving the territorial integrity of both Azerbaijan and Russia;

- granting autonomies to the Lezghians within both states (in this case Daghestan
  and Azerbaijan);

- introducing a system of dual (Azerbaijan and Russian) citizenship on both banks
  of the Samur River;

- setting up a common organ for the administration of both Lezghian autonomies.

This system requires, of course, goodwill both on the part of Russia and
Daghestan and on the part of Azerbaijan. It should be pointed out that the
last item of our proposal has no analogies in world practice and practically

means infringement of the sovereignty of both Russia and Azerbaijan on the territory of Lezghistan.

The Nogais' problems are largely similar to those of the Lezghians, for this people is likewise divided by borders, although within one federative state.

The Nogais of Daghestan demand reestablishing the Achikulak and the Kayasulin autonomous districts; the Nogais of Karachai-Circassia want to recreate (in case of the division of the republic) their autonomous area as part of the Stavropol Territory. The ultimate aim is to achieve Nogai statehood. The ideology of the Nogai national movement includes the theory of a close connection of the Nogais, genetic Polovtsians, with Russia and the Russians; hence the Nogai people's desire to remain a component part of Russia and their demand to defend the interests of the Nogai people in the Northern Caucasus. The idea of Turkic unity is proclaimed simultaneously. Thus, the Nogai national movement has become a member of the confederation of the Turkic peoples of the Northern Caucasus.

In December 1989, there was held the 2nd United Congress of the Nogai People, which adopted the appeals for the unification of the Nogai people and creation of their autonomy, and the repeal of the decrees of the Presidium of the Supreme Soviet of the RSFSR of January 9, 1957, as regards the division of the Nogai people territorially between Daghestan, Chechen-Ingushetia, and the Stavropol Territory. The fact is that before 1957 the Nogai lands were included compactly first into Daghestan, then into the Stavropol Territory, and from 1944, into the Grozny Region. In 1990, the State Planning Committee of the RSFSR was favorably considering the creation of the Nogai people's autonomy, at that time within the boundaries of the USSR.[41] That was not done, however.

The Extraordinary Congress of the Nogai People in November 1990 declared the reestablishment of the Nogai state. The Nogais, moreover, are making efforts to obtain the status of a repressed people on the ground of dismemberment of their territory in the years of Soviet power, and of socioeconomic and cultural discrimination.

The Nogais in the different areas of the Northern Caucasus have their own inter-regional national society "Birlik" (Unity) and their own publication, the newspaper *Nogaistan*. In August 1992, the 4th Congress of the Nogai People took place, confirming its strategical task—to unite the Nogai people in a single national-state entity. The Congress considered questions pertaining to the renewal of the national Nogai village Soviets in the various regions of the Northern Caucasus where Nogais form a compact community. One of the major questions that aroused the Congress participants' interest was the regulation of distant-pasture stock breeding in the Nogai steppe (the above-mentioned problem of using the steppe in the mountaineers' economic system).

We believe that the scheme proposed above for the solution of the Lezghian issue is applicable in the Nogai case as well.

As we see it, the main question for Daghestan at the present time is the following: What is the mechanism for coordinating the interests of the different nationalities in the republic? Answers to this question may differ. Thus, M. Yu. Roshchin, a researcher of the Institute of Oriental Studies, has his own conception based on O. Bauer's views of extraterritorial national autonomy. The essence of the conception of Roshchin consists of the following:

- Daghestan needs the creation of national unions on an extraterritorial basis;
- their election of a national mejlis, which is to control the observance of the rights of the union members to defend their interests before all elected and executive organs, to ensure their full sovereignty in the national-cultural sphere;
- national mejlies carry out elections to the Supreme Mejlis and to the nationalities chamber, seven members from each national union. Each national group in the Supreme Mejlis has the right of veto;
- the Supreme Mejlis elects the highest international arbitration body, whose unanimously adopted decisions have the force of a final verdict. This organ is authorized to settle international issues.

The project resembles the project of the Crimean Tatar people and, to our minds, has a number of defects. First, it does not decide the most important problem in Daghestan, that of land, and, consequently, cannot satisfy the sides participating in the land conflict. Second, it is incapable of helping to distribute real powers between the ethnic communities, that is, in this case, too, the conflict between the ethnic communities will not be removed. Third, the project envisages too many cumbersome procedures and is therefore unworkable. Fourth, this produces no reliable administration that can quickly and professionally respond to arising situations, with the result that the republic will be scarcely governable. Finally, M. Yu. Roshchin's project does not solve the problem of irredentism (the Lezghian and Nogai examples).

To our minds, mechanisms for settling the conflict should be sought in granting to the national communities of the republic, in places of their compact residence, territorial autonomy in various fractional forms (districts, village Soviets, etc.), which would conduct elections to the house of nationalities. Moreover, extraterritorial-cultural autonomy is not excluded either. The main task in such a case is to find an adequate form of dividing powers between the republican and local administrative organs. All this does not exclude but presupposes an organ of the Court of Arbitration type, whose function it is to decide questions connected with international contradictions and conflicts. Finally, only with the help of territorial autonomy is it possible to solve the problems of the peoples divided by administrative and state borders.

Speaking of the situation in Daghestan, stress should be laid on the following aspects. The republic needs an important aid to combat crime (no repressions, however, should be used by the federal authorities against the political and national movements). Objectively, the republic is faced with a confrontation between the people that live in the mountains and in the plains, which is fraught with armed clashes between them. The disintegration of Daghestan is hardly in Russia's interests (the republic's mountaineers will in such a case become active supporters of the Confederation of the Peoples of the Caucasus). However, the elimination of the said confrontation is possible, in our opinion, only on the basis of the model of autonomy outlined above. Efforts should be made to avoid such abrupt political steps as are envisaged by the program of the Kumyk national movement—they can only destabilize the situation in the republic. Daghestan's major problem is the Avar national movement, which has a tendency toward degenerating into a quasi-mafioso grouping.

THE PRESENT SOCIOECONOMIC AND POLITICAL
SITUATION IN YAKUTIA

The Yakuts live compactly in the basins of the Middle Lena, the Lower Aldan and the Vilyui, and the lower reaches of the Olekma. Separate groups of northern Yakuts live along the rivers Olenek, Anabara, Yana, Indigirka, and Kolyma. As many as 95.6 percent of all Yakuts live on the territory of the Republic of Sakha (Yakutia), although their proportion in the population reaches but 33.4 percent. Other nationalities living on this territory are Russians (the largest group), Ukrainians (77,114), Tatars (17,478), and also the peoples included in the category of the minor peoples of the North: Evenks (14,428), Evens (8,668), and Yukaghirs (697).

In the 17th century, the Yakuts had attained, on the whole, a higher level of economic and social development than the surrounding native population. Despite the survivals of the tribal system and the communal land ownership, they had a strongly pronounced stratification as regards property status and estate. The princes (toyons) owned herds of horned cattle and horses totalling thousands. The poor lived, as a rule, by hunting and fishing. There were developed crafts, especially smithery, woodcraft, bone carving, and skin tanning. Capitalist relations and trading began to develop from the mid-19th century with the start of gold mining on the rivers Olekma and Vitim.

The Sakha (Yakut) Republic is at present characterized by a comparatively low level of socioeconomic development, although it leads in per capita national income. The republic's backwardness is due to its one-sided economic orientation, with primarily extractive industry being developed. Yakutia is known as the center of mining of Russian gold (second place in the country) and diamonds (almost 100 percent), as well as tin, antimony, and mica-phlogopite (first place in Russia). Here exist deposits of oil, gas, mercury, rock salt, coal, tungsten, iron, apatites, and so on. In other words, Yakutia is fabulously rich in useful minerals.

The difficulty of using all these resources consists, above all, in the republic's geographical location: the greater part of its territory is situated in the arctic and near-arctic, as well as taiga zones, with productive communications with Yakutia being extremely difficult and expensive. They can be effected by sea along the Northern Sea Route (during the three or four months of navigation, and in the remaining months with the help of icebreakers), by several railway lines, by air, or with the help of pipelines. In any case, Yakutia is now experiencing great difficulties in transportation, which compels the republican authorities (President M. Nikolayev, first of all) continually to appeal to the federal center.[42] The main economic problem of the republic is therefore arranging permanent and uninterrupted communications with the rest of the world. Obviously, Yakutia is unable to solve this problem single-handedly. In this respect it greatly depends both on the aid of the federal authorities and on possible cooperation with foreign partners.

The objective economic situation in the republic, depending on the low level of socioeconomic development and the severe natural and geographic conditions, has predetermined the slow pace and harder consequences of the economic reform started in 1992. The decline in production is greater here, the proportion of unprofitable enterprises is considerably higher, and the fall in retail trade is somewhat more appreciable as well. Money incomes in 1992 were twice higher, however, than consumption expenditures (the figure for Russia is 1.7 times), that is, the population has more unused money. Privatization of housing in the republic was negligible (0.6 percent of flats intended for privatization have been privatized); the growth of privately owned farms likewise somewhat lagged behind. Naturally, such results cannot but put the inhabitants of Yakutia on their guard. Objectively, the general course of reforms requires adaptation to the republic's conditions.

Yakutia was one of the first regions in the former USSR that revealed antagonisms among the nations: student disturbances under nationalistic slogans took place there (in Yakutsk) back in 1987 (scuffles between Russian and Yakut students), practically unnoticed by the Soviet press. Since then, however, such conflicts have not been recorded here, which is due, in our opinion, to two factors.

First, the Russians and Yakuts have had traditionally good-neighborly relations owing to the cultural and religious kinship of the two peoples (Yakuts are Orthodox Christians) and also to the substantial russification of the Yakuts themselves. Moreover, colonization of the region by the Russians was primarily of a peaceful nature, therefore the cultural memory of the Yakut people, too, did not record a hostile attitude to the Russians.

Second, Yakut nationalism (such as exists in the midst of any people) has found a less conflictual and more constructive channel for its manifestation—through the structures of power and the strong presidential administration of M. Nikolayev, Yakut by nationality. Yakut nationalism has thus chosen a constructive form of activity, avoiding direct international clashes.

The ideology of a Yakut national state is based on the exceptional natural wealth of the republic. At the same time, Russia's economy was until recently so organized that the republic practically could not use the main part of the national income produced on its territory. Consequently, investment in the sociocultural infrastructure lagged behind the level of the national wealth created in the republic. This is one of the main reasons for the conflictual situation.

Conflict is contained in the fact that the Yakut Constitution adopted in 1992 actually provides the republic with the rights of a sovereign independent state while formally leaving it within the Russian Federation. Yakutia, however, signed the Federative Treaty without any reservations, thereby paving the way to possible compromises.

As we see it, the present attitude of the national Yakut movement is best of all expressed in the activities of the republic's leader, M. Nikolayev. Among all the efforts made in the republic to develop traditional Yakut culture and to raise the population's cultural level, special stress is laid, nevertheless, on the economic progress and economic aspects of the functioning of the federation, and the "precisely practical, tangible results that we want to achieve by following the course of the Federative Treaty."[43] Thus, in the summer of 1992, the leaders of Yakutia, Tataria, and Bashkiria jointly came out for a one-channel tax collection in the republics. The republic is also developing its international contacts, first of all those connected with the development of its natural resources.

The Russian press sometimes expresses anxiety about the separatist tendencies to be observed in Yakutia. It is hard to say how much the feeling for secession from Russia is spread in the republic itself. The idea of creating an independent Yakut state is founded on the assumption that Yakutia, in exchange for its gold and diamonds, can ensure to its citizens high living standards. These considerations are quite superficial—the republic will not be able to provide itself either with farm products or industrial goods, especially goods of streamlined manufacture, or "intellectual" products. The example of the Persian Gulf countries shows that even the existence of an "unlimited resource" does not lead automatically to the attainment of a high level of socioeconomic development. Serious obstacles to Yakutia's independence are the following factors: the prevalence in the republic of non-Yakut population, the absence of external borders with other countries, poor development of transport communications, and its dependence on Russia for power supply (without the latter's aid Yakutia will not be able to produce oil on its territory).

So Yakutia cannot exist as an independent state. To prevent the tendency toward conflict from growing there, however, the Russian government should agree to a number of concessions and compromises, in the economic sphere above all, and also give important assistance to the republic in developing its natural resources. It should be borne in mind, moreover, that the North is an extremely vulnerable geographical zone from the ecological point of view. In developing this region extensive use should no doubt be made of foreign experience of the "arctic" states (the United States, Canada), including their direct participation in the economic advancement of the region.

NOTES

1. See: A.N. Yamskov (head of a research group), *Sovremennye problemy i veroyatnye napravleniya razvitiya natsionalno-gosudarstvennogo ustroistva Rossiiskoi Federatsii* (The present problems and probable directions of development of the national-state system of the Russian Federation) (Moscow: Institutethnologii i antropologii, 1992), p. 37.

2. Etnopoliticheskie protsessy v Bashkortostane (Informatsionno-analiticheskii obzor) (Ethno-political processes in Bashkortostan /Informational and analytical survey), Moscow, 1992.

3. See: O. Kotov and M. Rogachev, "Pervyi siezd komi naroda: sotsiologicheskii aspekt," *Rubezh* (The First Congress of the Komi People: The sociological aspect, *Alamanac of social research*), no. 1 (1991).

4. "Iz Rossii—s lyubovyu?" (From Russia—With Love?) *Severny Kavkaz*, no. 33 (August 15, 1992), p. 5.

5. See: Gosudarstvennye akty Karacheyevskoi respubliki (Official Documents of the Karachai Republic, Karachayevsk, 1990), p. 8.

6. Ibid., p. 15.

7. *Den respubliki*, March 11, 1992.

8. A.N. Yamskov, *Sovremennye problemy*, pp. 42–44.

9. See: Materialy pervogo Syezda kabardinskogo naroda, sostoyavshegosya 10–12 yanvarya 1992 g (Materials of the First Congress of the Kabardinian People, Held on January 10–12, 1992). *Khasa*, February 11, 1992.

10. See: S. Trostin and V. Gorlova, "Chto kipit v kubanskom kotle?" (What is boiling in the Kuban kettle?), *Rossiya*, May 6–12, 1992.

11. Ibid.

12. "Rossiya ostalas odna i eyo khotyat razvalit! Administratsiya Diakonova govorit 'net'!" (Russia has remained alone, and attempts are being made to disintegrate it! The Dyakonov administration says "no!"), *Kubanskii kuryer*, no. 17, December 3, 1991.

13. "Pachegina N. Respubliko nakonets obrela svoego prezidenta" (The republic has at last acquired its president), *Nezavisimaya gazeta*, March 2, 1993.

14. A.N. Yamskov, *Sovremennye problemy*, p. 42.

15. S. Savostyanov, "Alania—strategicheskii klyuch Rossii k Kavkazu" (Alania. Russia's Strategical Key to the Caucasus), *Glashatai*, Socio-political newspaper of the Prigorodny District SO SSR, May 16, 1992 (reprint from the St. Petersburg newspaper *Golos Rossii*).

16. *Severnaya Osetiya,* November 20, 1992.

17. "Zaklychenic Komissii po obrashcheniyam ingushskogo naseleniya" (rukopis) (The Conclusion of the commission on the applications of the Ingush population, manuscript).

18. A.I. Kovalenko, "Pravovaya ekspertiza dokumentalnykh materialov, otnosyashohikhsya k territorialno-politicheskomu razvitiyu ingushskogo naroda" (rukopis) (Legal examination of documents concerning the territorial-political development of the Ingush People, manuscript).

19. Information of the State Nationalities Committee of Russia of November 21, 1991 "On the Implementation of the Law of the RSFSR 'On the Rehabilitation of Repressed Peoples,' " and of the Decision of the Supreme Soviet of the RSFSR on the Procedure of Carrying It into Effect (signed by L. Prokopyev).

20. "Record of Proceedings of the Sitting of the Working Groups of Northern Ossetia and Chechen-Ingushetia to Discuss the Implementation of the Law of the RSFSR 'On the Rehabilitation of Repressed Peoples' " (manuscript).

21. Document of the Government of the Russian Federation of December 17, 1991, "On Some Questions Connected with the Implementation of the Law of the RSFSR 'On the Rehabilitation of Repressed Peoples,' " forwarded to the Supreme Soviet of the Russian Federation and signed by State Secretary G. Burbulis.

22. The documents concerning this question adopted by the Congress, see in: *Rossiiskaya gazeta,* December 29, 1992. It might be mentioned in passing that the decision of the Congress on the recognition of Chechenia and Ingushetia as subjects of the Russian Federation rests on the question of what sort of federation Russia is—constitutional or contractual.

23. See: Constitution (Fundamental Law) of the Russian Federation—Russia (Moscow, 1992), pp. 19, 84, 236.

24. Ibid., pp. 10–11.

25. See: Mezhdunarodnaya zashchita prav i svobod cheloveka (International Defense of Human Rights and Freedoms), Collected Documents (Moscow, 1990), pp. 125–139.

26. According to the European Convention on the Defense of Human Rights and Basic Freedoms (Second Protocol), the European Court on Human Rights is vested with the authority to make consultative decisions (See Prava cheloveka: Sb mekzhdunarodnykh dokumentov [Human Rights. Collected International Documents]) (Moscow, 1990), pp. 101–103.

27. *Izvestia,* January 19, 1993.

28. Ibid.

29. See: Kazachestvo (The Cossacks) in: *Bolshaya sovetskaya entsiklopedia* (Big Soviet Encyclopedia) (Moscow, 1973), vol. 11, pp. 175–177.

30. *Komsomolets Kubani,* March 12, 1992.

31. *Utro,* March 25, 1992, nos. 40–41.

32. *Terski kazak,* no. 11 (1991).

33. We have used the data of the Kazan regional representatives of the Russian Economic Reforms Center.

34. *Tenglik* (Equality). The publication of the Kumyk popular movement for perestroika, no. 1 (1990).

35. Kumyk popular movement for perestroika. *Tenglik* (n.p., 1990).

36. A. Petrov, "Towards the Question of the Ways of Constitutional Settlement of the Political Crisis in Daghestan" (November 1991, manuscript).

37. *Namus*. Supplement to the newspaper *Tenglik,* October 26, 1991.

38. Ibid., October 29, 1991, no. 2.

39. *Nezavisimaya gazeta,* January 17, 1992.

40. *Sadval* (Unity), nos. 9, 10 (September-October 1991).

41. See: Letter of the State Planning Committee of the RSFSR sent to the Council of Ministers of the RSFSR "On the Unification of the Nogai People and Creation of Its Autonomy" (March 5, 1990. No. Pr-850/15, signed by A.A. Khomyakov, Chairman of the Committee).

42. M. Nikolayev, "Arktika: gosudarstvo i lyudi. O Severnom morskom puti v novykh usloviyakh" (The Arctic: The state and the people. On the Northern Sea route in the new conditions), *Nezavisimaya gazeta,* March 19, 1993.

43. Ibid.

Conclusion

It is a tall task to conclude a book devoted to a problem of such dimensions as "the ethnoses of Russia." Because this country—for its vast territory, for its rich history, and its ethnic diversity—is quite comparable with the rest of the world. The ethnic history of Russia is, moreover, far from its completion. One can well believe that the main events of this history are still ahead. At least precisely, this conclusion can be drawn from the material given in the book.

As it always happens in transitional historical periods, many opposite forces are active in the country and antagonistic tendencies make themselves felt. Therefore, even the study of an enormous amount of material does not make it easy to answer the question: "What will Russia be like in five or ten years; will it preserve its present multinationality and in what form?" The only clue here is the onward march of world history—from the polyethnic empire to the national states and their integration.

When undertaking this work we did not expect, frankly speaking, that the ethnic history of Russia was one of the little explored terrains. This applies not only to the national-political events of recent years, about which, naturally, there is little information and scientific analysis. Most of the problems of the country's ethnic history, both ancient and modern, need a detailed study or at least a new approach. Unfortunately, the most unexplored problem is still the ethnic history of the Russian people, which in our book, too, is given but insignificant attention.

To the best of our knowledge, the present work is the first attempt at this sort of research. So, it provides information based on field studies that can be of interest not just to a narrow circle of specialists.

Selected Bibliography

RUSSIAN

Abayev, V.I. *Osetinski yazyk i folklor* (The Ossetian language and folklore). Moscow-Leningrad: Izdatelstvo AN SSSR, 1949.

Akhiezer, A.S. *Rossiya: kritika istoricheskogo opyta* (Russia: Criticism of historical experience). Moscow: Filosofskoye Obshchestvo, 1991.

Alexeyev, H. "Sovetsky federalism." *Obshchestvennye nauki i sovremennost* (Soviet federalism. *Social sciences and the contemporary time*), no. 1, 1992.

Arutiunov, S.A. "Innovatsii v kulture etnosa i ikh sotsialno-ekonomicheskaya obuslovlennost." *Etnograficheskie issledovania razvitia kultury* (Innovations in the culture of ethnos and their socio-economic causes. *Ethnographic studies of the development of culture*). Moscow: Nauka, 1985.

Arutiunov S.A. *Narody i kultury: razvitie vzaimodeistvie* (Peoples and cultures: Development and interaction). Moscow: Nauka, 1989.

Arutiunov S.A., and N.N. Cheboksarov. "Peredacha informatsii kak mekhanism sushchestvovaniya etnosotsialnykh i biologicheskikh grup chelovechestva." *Rasy i narody* (Transmission of information as a mechanism of the existence of ethno-social and biological groups of mankind. *Races and peoples*). Moscow: Nauka, 1972.

Arutjunian, Ju.V. (Ed.). *Russkiye: ethnosotsioluguicheskie otsherki* (The Russians: ethno-sociological outlines). Moscow: Nauka, 1992.

Arutjunian, Ju.V. (Ed.). *Sotsialnoe i natsionalnoe: ethnosotsiologicheskie issledovaniya po materialam Tatarskoi ASSR* (Social and ethnic: Ethno-sociological research of Tatar autonomy). Moscow: Nauka, 1973.

Arutjunian, Ju.V., and Yu.V. Bromley (Eds.). *Sotsialno-kulturnyi oblik sovetskikh natsyi (Po materialam ethnosotsiologicheskogo issledovaniya)* (Social and cultural portrait of Soviet nationalities). Moscow: Nauka, 1986.

Babakov, V.G. *Krizisnye ethnosy* (Ethnoses in crisis). Moscow: IFRAS (Institute of Philosophy of Russian Academy of Science), 1993.

Bagramov, E.A., A.I. Dorontshenkov, M.M. Morozova, and P.I. Nadolishnii. *Razdelit li Rossiya utshast Soyuza SSR? (Krizis mezhnatsionalnykh otnoshenii i federalnaya natsionalnaya politika)* (Will Russia follow the fate of the USSR?). Moscow: VIK, 1993.

Barg, M.A., and E.B. Cherniak. *Velikie sotsialnye revoliutsii XVII-XVIII vekov v strukture perekhodnoi epokhi ot feodalizma k kapitalizmu* (Great social revolutions of the 17th–18th centuries in the structure of the transitional epoch from feudalism to capitalism). Moscow: Nauka, 1990.

Baziyev, A.T., and M.I. Isaev. *Yazyk i naziya* (Language and nation). Moscow: Nauka, 1973.

Berdyaev, N.A. *Filosofia neravenstva. Pisma k nedrugam po sotsialnoi filosofii* (Philosophy of inequality. Letters to enemies on social philosophy). Paris: IMKA Press, 1970.

Bokarev, E.A. *Kratkiye svedeniya o yazykakh Dagestana* (Brief survey of languages of Daghestan). Makhachkala: Isdatelstvo Dagestanskoi Bazy AN SSSR, 1949.

Bromlei, Yu.V. *Ocherki teorii etnosa* (Studies in the theory of ethnos). Moscow: Nauka, 1983.

Bromley, Yu.V. *Ethnos i ethnografia* (Ethnos and ethnology). Moscow: Nauka, 1973.

Bromley, Yu.V. *Ethnosotsialnye protsessy: teoria, istoria, sovremennost* (Ethnosocial processes: Theory, history and contemporary situation). Moscow: Nauka, 1987.

Bromley, Yu.V. *Natsionalnye protsessy v SSSR: v poiskakh novykh podkhodov* (Nationality processes in the USSR: Searching new approaches). Moscow: Nauka, 1988.

Bromley, Yu.V. (Ed.). *Problemy tipologii v ethnografii* (The problems of typology in ethnology). Moscow: Nauka, 1979.

Bromley, Yu.V. (Ed.). *Sovremennye ethnicheskie protsessy v SSSR* (The contemporary ethnic processes in the USSR). Moscow: Nauka, 1977.

Bromley, Yu.V., and G.E. Markov (Eds.). *Etnographiya. Uchebnik* (Textbook on ethnography). Moscow: Vysshaia Shkola, 1982.

Brook, S.I. *Naseleniye mira. Spravochnik* (Population of the world. Ethnographic sourcebook). Moscow: Nauka, 1981.

Dragomanov, M. *Volny soyuz. Opyt Ukrainskoy politikosotsialnoi programmy* (Free union. The case of the Ukrainian politico-social programme). Geneva, 1884.

Dragunski, D.V., and V.L. Tsymburski. "Genotip evropeiskoi tsivilizatsii" (Genotype of European civilization). *Polis*, no. 1, 1991.

Drobizhev, V.Z., I.D. Kovalchenko, and A.V. Muraviev. *Istoricheskaya geografiya SSSR* (Historical geography of the USSR). Moscow: Vysshaia Shkola, 1973.

Fedotov, G.P. *Sudba i grekhi Rossii. Izbrannye stati po filosofii russkoi istorii i kultury* (The fate and sins of Russia. Selected papers on the philosophy of Russian history and culture). Vols. 1–2. St. Petersburg: Sophia, 1992.

Fomitshev, P.N. *Sotsiologitsheskie teorii natsionalizma: nautshno-analititsheskii obzor* (Sociological theories of nationalism). Moscow: INION AN SSSR, 1991.

Glukharev, L.I. *Evropeiskie soobshchestva: v poiskakh novoi strategii* (European communities: In search of a new strategy). Moscow: Mezhdunazodnie otnoshenija, 1990.

Goncharenko, N.V. *Dialektika progressa kultury* (Dialectics of the progress of culture). Kiev: Nankova Dumka, 1987.

Kalatbari, P. "Demograficheskii perekhod i dinamika narodonaseleniya v razvivayushchikhsya stranakh. Problemy narodonaseleniya." *Sovremennaya demograficheskaia situatsiya v razvivayushchikhsya stranakh* (The demographic transition and the dynamics of population in the developing countries. Problems of population. In *Contemporary demographic situation in the developing countries*). Moscow: Progress, 1982.

Karlov, V.V. *Vvedenie v ethnografiyu narodov SSSR* (Introduction into ethnology of nationalities of the USSR). Moscow: Isdatelstvo Moskovskogo Universiteta, 1990–1992.

Karnovich, E.P. *Rodovye prozvania i tituly v Rossii i sliyanie inovertsev s russkimi* (Family names and titles in Russia and merger of adherents of other creeds with Russians). Moscow: BIMPA, 1991.

Kautsky, K. *Natsionalizm i internatsionalizm* (Nationalism and internationalism). Petrograd: Zhizn i znanie, 1918.

Khudyakov, M. *Ocherki po istorii Kazanskogo khanstva* (Essays on the history of the Kazan Khanate). Moscow: INSAN, 1991.

Koroteeva, V., L. Perepiolkin, and O. Shkaratan. "Ot biurokraticheskogo tsentralisma k ekonomicheskoi integratsii suverennykh respublik" (From bureaucratic centralism to economic integration of sovereign republics). *Communist*, no. 15, 1988.

Kotov O., and M. Rogachev. "Pervyi siezd komi naroda: sotsiologicheskii aspekt." *Rubezh* (The First Congress of the Komi People: The sociological aspect. *Alamanac of social research*), no. 1, 1991.

Kovalenko, A.I. "Pravovaya ekspertiza dokumentalnykh materialov, otnosyashohikhsya k territorialno-politicheskomu razvitiyu ingushskogo naroda" (rukopis) (Legal examination of documents concerning the territorial-political development of the Ingush People). Manuscript.

Kozhanovskii, A.N. *Narody Ispaniy vo vtoroi polovine XX V. (Opyt avtonomizatsiy i natsionalnogo pazvitiya)* (The Spain nationalities in the second part of the 20th century). Moscow: Nauka, 1993.

Kozlov, V.I. *Dinamika tshislennosti narodov: Metodologia issledovaniya i osnovnye faktory* (The dynamics of people's number: Research methodology and main factors). Moscow: Nauka, 1969.

Kriukov, M.V. "Etnicheskie i politicheskie obshohnosti: dialektika vzaimodeistvia." *Etnos v doklassovom i ranneklassovom obshchestve* (Ethnic and political communities: dialectics of inter-actions. *Ethnos in the pre-class and early class societies*). Moscow: Nauka, 1982.

Kukushkin, K.S., and O.I. Christyakov. *Ocherk istorii Sovetskoi Konstitutsii* (Essay on the history of the Soviet constitution). Moscow: Politizdat, 1987.

Kushnir, A.G. *Genezis politiko-administrativnogo ustroistva Sovetskoi Rossii* (Genesis of the politico-administrative structure of Soviet Russia). Moscow: Institut Istozii SSSR, 1991.

Lenin, V.I. *K voprosu o natsionalnostiakh ili ob "avtonomizatsii"* (On the question of nationalities or on the "autonomization"). *Complete Works*. Moscow: Politizdat, 1977, vol. 45.

Lux, L. "Yevraziistvo." *Strana i mir* (Euro-Asianism. *The country and the world*), vol. 55, no. 1, 1990.

Markarian, E.S. "K ekologicheskoi kharakteristike razvitiya etnicheskikh kultur" *Obshohestvo i priroda. Istoricheskie etapy i formy vzaimodeistvia* (On ecological characteristics of the development of ethnic cultures. *Society and nature. Historical stages and forms of inter-action*). Moscow: Nauka, 1981.

Markarian, E.S. *Teoriya kultury i sovremennaya nauka: logiko-metodologichesky analiz* (Theory of culture and contemporary science: Logical and methodological analysis). Moscow: Mysl, 1983.

Mastiugina, T., and V. Stelmakh. "Malye narody Severa i Dalnego Vostoka. Osnovy pravovogo statusa v svete printsipov mezhdunarodnogo prava i zarubezhnogo opyta." *Rossiyskii bulleten po pravam tsheloveka* (Minorities of the North and Far East. *Russian bulletin on human rights*), 1994.

Milov, L.V. "Prirodno-klimatichesky faktor i osobennosti Rossiiskogo istoricheskogo protsessa." *Voprosy istorii* (Natural climatic factors and peculiarities of the Russian historical process. *Problems of history*), nos. 4–5, 1992, p. 53.

Pavlik, Z. "Problemy demograficheskoi revolyutsii." *Brachnost, rozhdaemost, semya za tri veka* (Problems of the demographic revolution. *Marriage, birthrate, family over the three centuries*). Moscow: Statistica, 1979.

Perepiolkin, L.S. "Istoki mezhetnicheskogo konflikta v Tatarii" (The sources of interethnic conflict in Tataria). *Mir Rossii*, vol. I, no. 1, 1992.

Perepiolkin, L.S. "Tshetshenskaya Respublika: sovremennaya sotsialnopolititsheskaya situatsia." *Ethnografitsheskoe obozrenie* (Chechen Republic: Contemporary social and political situation. *Etnological review*), 1994.

Perepiolkin, L.S., and N.E. Rudenskii. "Natsionalnyi vopros i prava narodov v SSSR: opyt sotsialno-polititsheskogo analiza." *Rossiyskii bulleten po pravam tsheloveka* (Nationality question and rights of nationalities of the USSR. *Russian bulletin on human rights*). Moscow, 1991.

Perepiolkin, L.S., and O.I. Shkaratan. "Ekonomitsheskii suverenitet respublik i puti razvitiya narodov: teoretitsheskaya diskussia vokrug voprosov praktitsheskoi zhizni." *Sovetskaya ethnografia* (Economic sovereignty of the republics and the directions of nations development: Theoretical discussions and the questions of practical life. *Soviet ethnology*), 1989.

Petrov, A. "Towards the Question of the Ways of Constitutional Settlement of the Political Crisis in Daghestan" (November 1991). Manuscript.

Petrov, M.K. "Chelovek i kultura v nauchno-tekhnicheskoy revolutsii." *Voprosy filosofii* (Man and culture in the scientific-technological revolution. *Problems of philosophy*), no. 5, 1990.

Petrov, P.N. *Istoria rodov russkogo dvoryanstva* (History of the families of Russian nobility). Moscow: Sovzemennik, 1991.

Pimenov, V.V. *Udmurty: Opyt componentnogo analiza ethnosa* (The Udmurts: Component analysis of ethnos). Leningrad: Nauka, 1977.

Pivovarov, Yu.S. "Nekotorye problemy stanovlenia i razvitia politiko-pravovoi kultury russkogo feodalizma." *Sovremennye zarubezhnye issledovania politiko-pravavoi kultury Rossii.* (Some problems of the emergence and development of the politico-legal culture of Russian feudalism. *Contemporary foreign studies of the politico-legal culture of Russia*). Moscow: INION AN SSR, 1988.

Prazauskas, A.A. *Mezhetnicheskie konflikty v stranakh zarubjejnogo Vostoka* (Inter-ethnic conflicts in the countries of foreign East). Moscow: Nauka, 1991.

Radaev, V., and O. Shkaratan. "Sotsialism ili etakratism?" *Narodny deputat* (Socialism or etacratism? *People's deputy*), no. 10, 1990.

Sagadeev, A.V. *Mirsait Sultan-Galiev i ideologia natsionalno-osvoboditel'nogo dvizhenia* (Mirsait Sultan-Galiev and the ideology of the national-liberation movement). Moscow: INION AN SSSR, 1990.

Shibayev, V.P. *Etnicheskii sostav naseleniya Evropeiskoi chasti Soyuza SSR* (The ethnic composition of the population of the European part of the USSR). Leningrad: Izdatelstvo AN SSSR, 1930.

Shkaratan, O.I. (Ed.). *Ethnosocialnye problemy goroda* (Enhno-social problems of a city). Moscow: Nauka, 1986.

Shkaratan, O.I. (Ed.). *NTR i natsionalnie protsessy* (Scientific revolution and nationality processes). Moscow: Nauka, 1987.

Shkaratan, O.I., and E.N. Gurenko. "Ot etakratizma k stanovleniyu grazhdanskogo obshchestva." *Rabochii class i sovremenny mir* (From etacratism to the development of civic society. *The working class and the contemporary world*), no. 3, 1990.

Sorokin, P.A. "Sotsialnaya mobilnost, eye formy i fluktuatsii." *Problemy sotsialnoi mobilnosti za rubezhom* (Social mobility, its forms and fluctuations. *Problems of social mobility abroad*). Moscow: INION AN SSR, 1974.

Starovoitova, G.V. "Ethnitsheskaya gruppa v sovremennom sovetskom gorode." Sotsiologitsheskie otsherki (Ethnic groups in contemporary Soviet cities. Sociological essay). Leningrad: Nauka, 1987.

Stelmakh, V. *Sibirskoye oblastnichestvo. Iz istorii dvizhenii za regionalnuyu avtonomiyu v tsarskoi Rossii* (Siberian regionalism. From the history of the regional autonomy movements in Tsarist Russia). Stolitsa, 1992.

Sultan-Galiev, M. "Tatary i Oktiabrskaya revoliutsia." *Zhizn natsionalnostei* (Tatars and the October Revolution. *Life of nationalities*), vol. 122, no. 24 (1921).

Susokolov, A.A. *Mezhnatsionalnye braki v SSSR* (Inter-ethnic marriages in the USSR). Moscow: Mysl, 1987.

Susokolov, A.A. *Ustoitshivost ethnosa i contseptsii natsionalnykh shkol Rossii* (Stability of ethnos and a conception of nationality schools in Russia). Moscow: Institute of Nationality Problems of Education, 1994.

Terner, J. *Struktura sociologicheskoi teorii* (The structure of sociological theory). Moscow: Progress, 1985.

Vakhtin, N. *Korennoe naselenie Krainego Severa Rossiyskoi Federatsiy* (Aborigional population of the Russian North). St. Petersburg: Izdatelstvo Evropeïskogo Doma, 1993.

Vishnevsky, A.G. *Vosproizvodstvo nacelenija i obshchestvo. Istoriya, sovremennost, vzglyad v budushchee* (Reproduction of population and society. History, contemporary situation and view in future). Moscow: Finansy i statistika, 1982.

Yamskov, A.N. (Head of a research group). *Sovremennye problemy i veroyatnye napravleniya razvitiya natsionalno-gosudarstvennogo ustroistva Rossiiskoi*

Federatsii (The present problems and probable directions of development of the national-state system of the Russian Federation). Moscow: Instituteth-nologii i antropologii, 1992.

Yeroshkin, N.P. *Istoria gosudarstvennykh uchrezhdenii dorevolutsionnoi Rossii* (History of state institution of the pre-revolutionary Russia). Moscow, 1968.

Yurganov, A.L. "U istokov despotizma." *Istoria otechestva: lyudi, idei, reshenia. Ocherki istorii Rossii IX-nachala XX v.* (At the source of despotism. *History of the fatherland: People, ideas, decisions. Essays on Russia's history of the 19th–early 20th centuries*). Moscow: Politizdat, 1991.

Zhuravskaya, E.G. *Regidonalnaya integratsia v razvivaiushchimsya mire: nemark-sistskie teorii i realnost (na primere ASEAN)* (Regional integration in the developing world: Non-Marxist theories and reality [a case study of ASEAN]). Moscow: Nauka, 1990.

ENGLISH

Brass P. (Ed.). *Ethnic Groups and the State*. London and Sydney: Croom Helm, 1985.

Breakwell, G.M. (Ed.). *Coping with Threatened Identities*. London and New York: Methuen, 1980.

Brown, D. "Ethnic Revival: Perspectives on State and Society." *Third World Quarterly*, vol. 4, no. 11, 1989.

Cohen, R. "Ethnicity: Problem and Focus in Anthropology." *Annual Review of Anthropology*, no. 7, 1978.

Despres, L.A. "Toward a Theory of Ethnic Phenomena." In L. Despres (ed.), *Ethnicity and Resource Competition in Plural Societies*. The Hague and Paris: Mouton, 1975.

Dohrenwend, B., and R.J. Smith. "Toward a Theory of Acculturation." *Southwestern Journal of Anthropology*, vol. 18, 1962.

Gellner, E. *Nations and Nationalism*. Ithaca, N.Y.: Cornell University Press, 1983.

Goelen, R. "Fraternal Interest Groups and Violent Conflict Management: A Socio-Structural Hypothesis." *Zeitschrift fuer Ethnologie*, Bd.115, S.45–55, 1990.

Gottlieb, G. *Nation against State. A New Approach to Ethnic Conflicts and the Decline of Sovereignty*. New York: Council on Foreign Relations Press, 1993.

Griffith, C.T., J.C. Yerbury, and L.F. Weafer. "Canadian Natives: Victims of Socio-Structural Deprivation?" *Human Organization*, vol. 46, no. 3, 1978.

Hechter, M. *Internal Colonialism. The Celtic Fringe in British National Development, 1536–1966*. London: Routledge and Kegan Paul, 1975.

Horowitz, D. *Ethnic Groups in Conflict*. Berkeley: University of California Press, 1985.

Kedourie, E. *Nationalism*. London: Hutchinson, 1961.

Kemilainen, A. *Nationalism: Problems Concerning the Word, the Concept and Classification*. Jyvaskyla: Jyvaskylan Kasratusopillinen Korkegkoulu; Jyvaskylan yeiopistoyhaistys, 1964.

Kohn, H. *The Idea of Nationalism. A Study of Its Origin and Background*. New York: Macmillan Paperbacks, 1961.

Kuper, L., and M.G. Smith. (Eds.). *Pluralism in Africa*. Berkeley and Los Angeles: University of California Press, 1969.

Lapidus, G., V. Zaslavsky, and P. Goldman. (Eds.). *From Union to Commonwealth: Nationalism and Separatism in the Soviet Republics.* New York: Cambridge: University Press, 1992.

Minogue, K.R. *Nationalism.* London: Batsford, 1967.

Moynihan, D.P. *Pandemonium: Ethnicity in International Politics.* New York: Oxford University Press, 1993.

Okamura, J.Y. "Situational Ethnicity." *Ethnic and Racial Studies,* vol. 4, no. 4, 1981.

Otterbein, K.F. "Internal War: A Cross-Cultural Study." *American Anthropologist,* vol. 70, no. 2, 1968.

Riggs, F.W. (Ed.). *Ethnicity. INTERCOCTA Glossary: Concepts and Terms Used in Ethnicity Research.* Washington, D.C. and Paris: ISSC, 1985.

Smith, A. D. *The Ethnic Origins of Nations.* Oxford and New York: Blackwell, 1986.

Smith, A.D. "The Origins of Nations." *Ethnic and Racial Studies,* vol. 12, no. 3, 1989.

Smith, M.G. "Some Problems with Minority Concepts and a Solution." *Ethnic and Racial Studies,* vol. 10, no. 4, 1987, pp. 341–362.

Thompson, R.H. *Theories of Ethnicity.* Westport, Conn.: Greenwood Press, 1989.

Van Amersfoort, H. "Minority as a Sociological Concept." *Ethnic and Racial Studies,* vol. 1, no. 2, 1978.

Van den Berghe, P.L. "Pluralism and Policy: A Theoretical Explanation." In *Pluralism in Africa.* Berkeley and Los Angeles: University of California Press, 1969.

Walker L., and P.C. Stern. (Eds.). "Balancing and Sharing Political Power in Multiethnic Societies." Summary of a Workshop. Washington, D.C.: National Academic Press, 1993.

Index

About the Authors and Editors

LEV PEREPELKIN graduated from the Moscow University. From 1986 to 1993 he was with the Institute of Ethnology and Social Anthropology, Russian Academy of Science. Since 1993 he has been senior fellow at the Institute of Oriental Studies and also senior fellow at the Institute for Economy in Transition, headed by E. Gaidar. He is a scholar of ethnology, ethnosociology, national and political problems of Russia, consultant for the government of Russia, and participated in a number of international conferences. He is the author of more than 70 publications. His main works include *Technical Revolution and National Problems,* and chapters in *Russia's State Program on National and Cultural Policy.*

TATIANA MASTYUGINA graduated from the Moscow University in 1974. Since then she has been with the Institute of Ethnology and Social Anthropology, Russian Academy of Science and since 1993 also with the Institute for Economy in Transition headed by E. Gaidar. She has specialized in the field of ethnography of small peoples of the Far North, consulted the government of Russia on these issues, and has travelled extensively in the region. Her publications include, for instance, several chapters in: *Family Customs of the Peoples of Siberia,* chapters in *Russia's State Program on National and Cultural Policy,* and in *Legal Status of the Small Peoples of the North of Russia.*

VITALY NAUMKIN worked as professor at Moscow University until 1984, and then moved to the Institute of Oriental Studies, Russian Academy of Science, where he was a Deputy Director. Since 1991 he has been the president of the Russian Center for Strategic Research and International Studies. He is the author and editor of numerous works on the history, ethnography and religion of the Middle East, Central Asia, and Russia. His main publications include *The Island of Phoenix, Central Asia: State, Religion and Society* (ed.), and *Central Asia and Transcaucasia: Ethnicity and Conflict* (ed., co-author).

IRINA ZVIAGELSKAIA is Professor and Head of the Sector of Regional Conflicts at the Institute of Oriental Studies, Russian Academy of Science. Since 1991 she has been Vice-President of the Russian Center for Strategic Research and International Studies. She is the author of articles and books on conflicts in the Middle East, post-Soviet territory, including *The US Policy towards Conflicts in the Middle East,* and *Central Asia and Transcaucasia: Ethnicity and Conflict* (co-author).

ISBN 0-313-29315-5

HARDCOVER BAR CODE